NORTHERN

and its subsidiaries

1913 - 1995

'FROM NO PLACE TO SUCCESS'

Keith A. Jenkinson
&
S. A. Staddon

An Autobus Review Publication

Autobus Review Publications Ltd.

Published December 1995

All rights reserved. No part of this book may be reproduced (except for normal review purposes) or utilised or stored in any way or by any means without the prior written consent of Autobus Review Publications Ltd.

ISBN 0 907834 35 3

To keep up to date with the Go-Ahead Group plc we recommend 'Bus Fayre' (published monthly by Autobus Review Publications Ltd.) or membership of The Northern Group Enthusiasts Club.

Printed by Bakes & Lord Ltd., Bradford, West Yorkshire.

Autobus Review Publications Ltd., 42 Coniston Avenue, Queensbury, Bradford BD13 2JD.

Above : Although being operated by Coastline, Roe-bodied Leyland Atlantean 3461 (AUP361W) still carried Go-Ahead Northern fleet names when photographed at Gateshead Metro on the 302 service to North Shields in June 1994. (M.Duffy)

Previous page : Wearing Northern's red & white 'Proud of our Routes' livery, MCW Metrobus 3620 hurries through rural surrounds on its way from Newcastle to Darlington. (K.A.Jenkinson)

FOREWORD

The Northern General Transport Company Limited as a subsidiary of Gateshead & District Tramways was specially created in 1913 to exploit the potential of the then new motor bus. It approaches the 21st century as a subsidiary again but this time of the Go-Ahead Group PLC, the fifth largest bus operating group in the UK. Throughout that time and through the various changes of ownership the company has always been striving to serve its customers as efficiently as possible. It has been at the forefront of technological change whether on the bus or behind the scenes in garages, offices and bus stations.

The co-authors with their painstaking and detailed research have captured some of the spirit of the company and its staff over the years. The book carefully records the minutiae of bus operation in the north-east. It will bring happy memories to many people and will grace any bookshelf; particularly of anyone who has a soft spot for this great company that prides itself on the service it has given and continues to give to the people of Tyneside and County Durham.

Trevor H. Shears,
Director,
The Go-Ahead Group plc.
October 1995

Left to right : Chris Moyes (Commercial Director), Trevor Shears (Finance Director) and Martin Ballinger (Managing Director).

NORTHERN
GO-AHEAD GATESHEAD
Wear BUSES
COASTLINE
VFM mean value for money
Metro BUSES
Voyager
Shaws Coaches
DIAMOND
GYPSY QUEEN COACHES
OK TRAVEL
ARMSTRONGS
LOW FELL COACHES
Brighton & Hove
the OXFORD BUS COMPANY
the Wycombe BUS COMPANY
LONDON CENTRAL

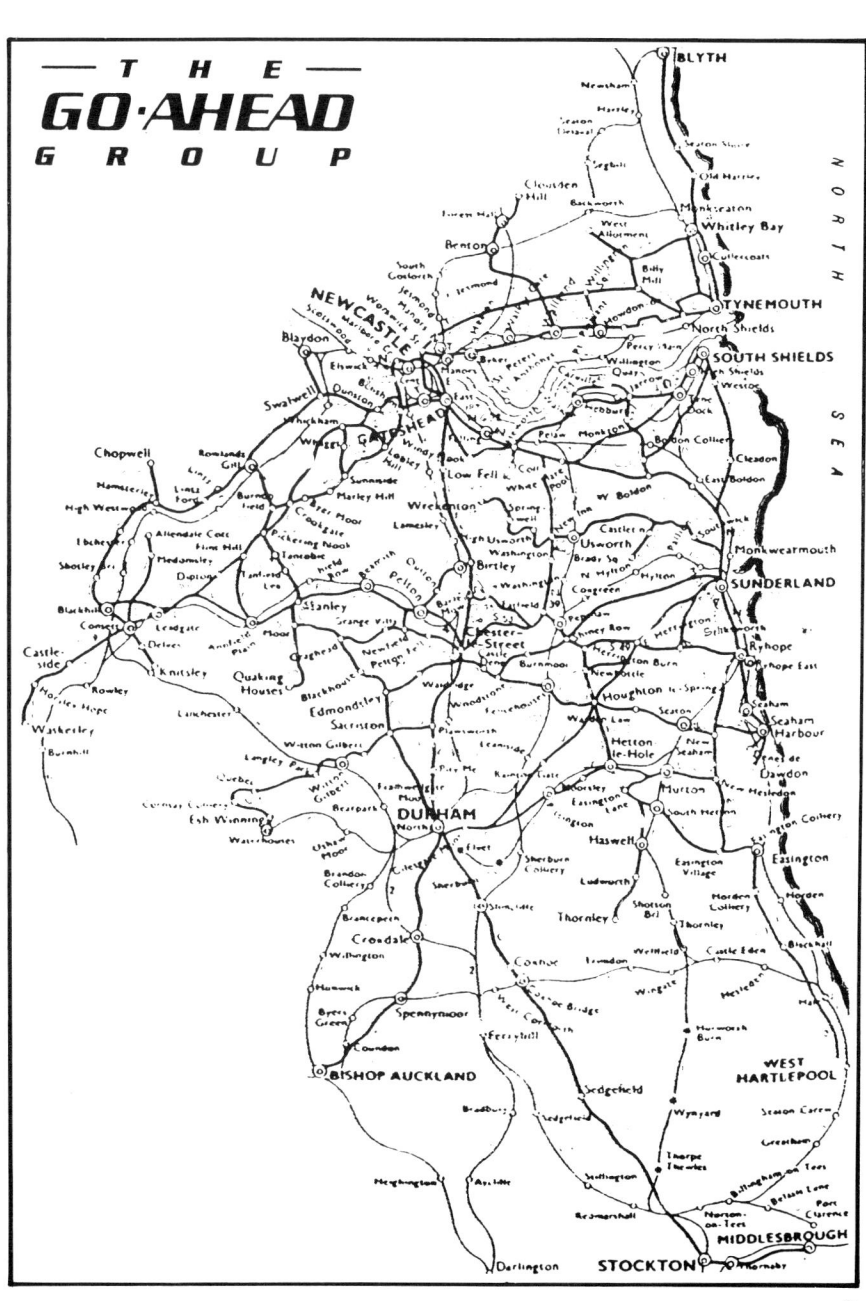

INTRODUCTION

Despite it having been a major bus operator in the north-east for more than eighty years, for some inexplicable reason little has ever been written about the Northern General Transport Company Limited and its various subsidiaries. In order to fill this void, I began researching the company's history almost ten years ago with the intention of placing on record the development of its services and fleet only to find this task to be far more complex than I had at first imagined. Never having lived within Northern's operating territory, my personal knowledge of the company's activities was lacking to a certain extent and had it not been for the generous help of others, this book would undoubtedly never have been completed.

Arthur Staddon, an enthusiast of many years and a resident of the north-east read my original draft and added so much additional information that it almost doubled in size overnight. With his in-depth knowledge particularly of the services operated by the Northern Group, past and present, it was decided to make this book a joint venture and whilst I continued to write the text, he diligently read and re-read each draft, added the events which I had overlooked, and corrected my errors.

Thanks must be extended to Trevor Shears, Finance Director of The Go-Ahead Group PLC for his encouragement and also for making available to us all the minutes books of Northern and its associates from 1913 to the early 'eighties, checking and correcting the draft text and allowing access to the company's superb photographic archives. Without his help, much would have been omitted due to our lack of knowledge of certain past events. Additionally, our thanks must go to The Northern Group Enthusiasts Club for allowing material to be extracted from their excellent bi-monthly news-sheets which have provided an abundance of information particularly in respect of the company's vehicles, and also to the PSV Circle whose new-sheets and other publications have proved invaluable.

Gratitude is also directed to the many photographers without whose work this book would have been difficult to illustrate and particularly to Thomas W.W.Knowles who made his large collection available, thus filling several gaps. It is sad that neither Michael Duffy nor Tom Godfrey, who both provided a wealth of photographic material, survived to see their work in print, and it is hoped that this book will serve as a tribute to their long-standing enthusiasm for buses and coaches in the north-east.

Although Northern has now grown into the Go-Ahead Group and has expanded into other areas of Britain as well as being quoted on the London Stock Exchange, it is in the north-east where it will always be best remembered, an area where industrial and rural surroundings rub shoulders and where quaintly named villages such as No Place, Pity Me, High Handon Hold and Folly are to be found. Despite having experienced competition from other operators ever since its formation over eighty years ago, Northern soon became the driving force and proud of its routes and today, as yesterday, it continues to provide its passengers with the very best in public transport.

If this book gives as much pleasure to those who read it as it has done to those who have compiled it, then the last ten years of hard labour will all have been worth while.

Keith A. Jenkinson,
Queensbury, Bradford.
November 1995

Front cover upper : Now preserved and restored to its original glory is Gateshead & District Tramways car no.10 which was built by its operator on Brill 39E maximum traction trucks in 1928. It is seen here at Beamish Open Air Museum where it is now regularly used in service.
(K.A.Jenkinson)

Front cover lower : Showing off its new dark red & white livery with black window frames as it leaves Stanley bus station in November 1995 enroute to Consett is Northern's Optare Delta-bodied DAF SB220 4740.
(K.A.Jenkinson)

Back cover, left column, top to bottom :

Leaving Wallsend Metro on the 305 service to Newcastle in March 1994 is Coastline's Alexander-bodied Leyland Atlantean 3524 which was one of a number of buses of this type purchased from Tyne & Wear PTE in 1981.
(K.A.Jenkinson)

Gypsy Queen Duple-bodied Volvo B10M 4749 lays over at the Langley Park terminus of the service from Durham in May 1995. (K.A.Jenkinson)

Collecting its passengers at the Newcastle terminus of the Cross-Tyne service is Low Fell Coaches Duple-bodied Bedford YNT 4763 which carries dedicated route lettering along its side panels. (K.A.Jenkinson)

Leaving Stanley bus station at the start of its journey to Durham on the 718 service in November 1995 is Diamond Duple-bodied Dennis Javelin 4797.
(K.A.Jenkinson)

Resting outside its depot at South Shields, VFM Buses ECW-bodied Leyland Atlantean 3555 shows off its then-new livery in the spring of 1994.
(K.A.Jenkinson)

Back cover, right column, top to bottom :

Wear Buses Leyland National 2 4680 looks immaculate as it rests at Washington bus station in November 1995 having just arrived on a short working of the 194 service from Heworth. (K.A.Jenkinson)

Leaving Gateshead Metro in November 1995 is Reeve Burgess-bodied Mercedes Benz 709D 370 which had only recently been transferred to OK Travel from Low Fell Coaches. (K.A.Jenkinson)

One of Go-Ahead Gateshead's ECW-bodied Leyland Olympians, 3739 swings out of Gateshead Metro on its way to Winlaton in October 1995.
(K.A.Jenkinson)

Operating Shaws Coaches 709 service to Newcastle, former Northern Leyland National 2 4700 leaves Gateshead Metro to cross the Tyne in October 1995. (K.A.Jenkinson)

Its destination blind having already been set for its journey to Whitley Bay on the X16 service in March 1994, Metro Taxis Willowbrook-bodied Leyland Leopard 5096 rests in Newcastle before collecting its passengers.
(K.A.Jenkinson)

FOUNDATIONS ARE LAID

Although the Northern General Transport Company Limited was incorporated on 29 November 1913, its foundations were laid many years earlier when the British Electric Traction Group gained a foothold in the north-east in 1897. At first concentrating on street tramways, the B.E.T. later turned its attention to the motor bus as will be seen in the following chapters and became a major operator along both banks of the river Tyne and in County Durham during the twentieth century. Indeed, a letter dated 12 December 1913 to the Chairmen of the various B.E.T. tramways companies in the area stated that 'The Northern General Transport Company Limited has been formed with the object (among others) of carrying out and developing in the Northern Counties transport business in all its branches, including the carriage of passengers and goods by motor vehicles and of acquiring interests in undertakings carrying on such business and especially with a view to consolidating the interests of the shareholders of the Gateshead and District Tramways Co., the Tynemouth and District Electric Traction Co. Ltd. and the Jarrow and District Electric Traction Co. Ltd.' The letter stated that the company operated motor vehicles in conjunction with Gateshead Tramways and the adjoining Jarrow Tramway and that Tynemouth had also decided to acquire vehicles and that as such there was a possible overlap. It continued 'There is moreover a large scope in the Northern Counties for the development of motor traction both for passengers and goods, but such business to be successfully developed requires further expenditure of capital, expert knowledge and special organisation which the Transport Company will be able to provide'.

It can, however, perhaps be said that Northern General's foundations date back to 1883, the year in which the Gateshead & District Tramways Company introduced steam trams over four short routes within that borough (although others might say that the seeds were sown with the passing of the Tynemouth and District Tramways Order in 1879). Gateshead, being a working class area across the river Tyne from Newcastle, was a densely populated area with narrow streets and some steep gradients and, as such, clearly offered opportunities for a tramway system. The Gateshead & District Tramways Act had obtained its Royal Assent on 12 August 1880, with the company's prospectus showing four main and three smaller routes. Unfortunately, a lack of local support in raising the necessary capital, coupled with difficulties in finding a contractor to carry out the construction work, caused the company to be reconstituted and a new board of directors to be appointed. Under its new administration the first rails were eventually laid and during the latter months of 1883 the first trams began operation. These were double deck, open-top, double-bogie cars hauled by tramway locomotives which continued in service until the turn of the century.

Meanwhile, the British Electric Traction Company Limited was registered in London on 26 October 1896 to acquire the business of the British Electric Traction (Pioneer) Co.Ltd. and to develop electric traction in the United Kingdom and elsewhere. From the start, its Managing Director, Emile Garcke, had the ambitious objective of controlling as many of the new and rapidly growing number of urban tramways as possible, and it therefore came as no surprise when he focussed his attentions on the developing north-east. One of his first purchases was completed in November 1897 when the Gateshead company was taken over by the B.E.T., a consequence which set the scene for the electrification of the system. The B.E.T. set about obtaining an Act of Parliament for this purpose in 1899 and after its passage was successfully completed, electrification work commenced in June 1900. At this same time the route network was expanded to provide a total of seven services from Gateshead to the districts of Bensham, Dunston, Heworth, Low Fell, Saltwell Park, Teams and Wrekenton and operation of the 'new' system began progressively on 8 May 1901, with Wrekenton being reached on 2 October 1903 and the Dunston route being completed in November of that year. A total of 45 new electric tramcars was purchased, 20 of which were single deckers whilst the remaining 25 were open-top double deckers and all had bodies built by the Electric Railway & Tramway Carriage Works on Brill trucks powered by two Dick Kerr 25A-type motors. These were joined in 1902 by a further 5 single deckers with Milnes bodywork on Milnes 'Maximum Traction' trucks with 2 Dick Kerr 35A-type motors. During the next three years a start was made on the double-tracking of the tramway system, a task which took until 1924 to complete, and after which the service network was to remain largely unchanged for the duration of its life. A further new single deck tram was added to the fleet in 1907 and on this occasion was 'home-built' by the Gateshead company using Brill 22E-type trucks and 2 Dick Kerr 35A-type motors. In addition, a pair of works trams also made their debut, one of which was a water car.

Seeking to consolidate its position in the north-east even further, the B.E.T. had in September 1899 gained control of another local tramway, this being the North Shields and District Tramways Company. Incorporated under the Tynemouth and District Tramways Order of 1879 as briefly mentioned earlier, this system under the title of Tynemouth and District Tramways Company began operations in 1883 using horse traction. Abandoning its horse trams in favour of steam trams later in that decade, the company after suffering financial failure was, on 21 January 1890, reconstituted as the North Shields and Tynemouth Tramways Company. In 1892 they began two horse bus feeder services from North Shields to Howden and Tynemouth to Cullercoats. These didn't pay, however, and were thus soon discontinued. Upon its acquisition by the B.E.T., its title was changed yet again, becoming the Tynemouth and District Electric Tramway Company Limited, thus reflecting the proposals to electrify the system as soon as was possible. This involved the widening of the tracks from 3ft. gauge to 3ft. 6in. and extending the original route which had operated between North Shields and Tynemouth onwards to Whitley (later renamed Whitley Bay). The new electrically-operated service began on 18 March 1901 and three years later was further extended from Whitley to Whitley Bay Links. The steam trams (5 locomotives and 5 single deck bogie trailer cars) were all withdrawn in 1900, their replacements the following year being 22 new electric cars, all but one of which were open-top double deckers built by the Electric Railway & Tramway Carriage Works or Milnes on Brill 21E or Milnes trucks. Tynemouth & District maintained two depots, the original one at Suez Street, North Shields and another at John Street, Cullercoats and it was at the latter where maintenance and painting etc. was carried out. The tramway system remained basically unchanged for the duration of its life and the only additions made to its fleet were three 1906-vintage open-top double deck bodies purchased from the Burton & Ashby Light Railway (LMSR) in 1927.

Another tramway under British Electric Traction control was the Jarrow and District Electric Tramway Company Ltd. This was the last tramway to commence operations on Tyneside and took six years from its conception before its service began. Following the construction of a steam-powered electric generating station at Jarrow by the B.E.T., an application was made on 18 May 1900 for powers to build light railways in Jarrow and South Shields. Although these were granted on 17 December 1901, it was not until 30 September 1903 that the Jarrow and District Electric Traction Co. Ltd. was formed. This was ostensibly an independent company when originally created, but three months later an agreement was reached with the B.E.T. whereby their 1901 powers were vested in the new company. There then followed years of protracted negotiations with Jarrow Corporation before the necessary land for the new tramway was eventually purchased and it was not until April 1906 that work on its construction could commence. A depot was built in Swinburne Street and the solitary 2.54 mile route from Western Road, Jarrow to the junction of Slake Terrace and Hudson Street, Tyne Dock where it made an end-on connection with a South Shields Corporation Tramways route, eventually opened on 29 November 1906. This was operated by 8 Brush open-top 43-seat double deck cars, two of which were exchanged the following year with Gravesend & Northfleet Tramways for a pair of larger capacity 66-seat cars on Brill trucks. Also joining this small fleet in 1907 was a former Brush demonstrator with 55-seat open-top double deck bodywork which had previously been evaluated by various B.E.T. subsidiaries since its construction in 1902. The only other car to join the Jarrow company made its debut in 1911 in the form of a 55-seat double decker which was hired from Gateshead & District Tramways until its purchase in 1914. Additionally, the B.E.T. had obtained the lease of the South Shields horse tramway in 1899 but lost this in 1906 when South Shields Corporation decided to undertake electrification of their own tramway system.

A far-reaching development which took place in 1909 was the

45, one of Gateshead's 1901 cars is seen at Wrekenton in its original open-top condition. Built by the Electric Railway & Tramway Carriage Works on Brill 21E trucks, it was later rebuilt as a single decker with lengthened body. (R.B.Parr collection)

Gateshead & District Tramway Act of that year which, among other things, gave the company powers to operate motor buses as feeders to the tramway system. Indeed, as early as November 1901, discussions had taken place relating to the running of motor cars over the High Level Bridge and this matter was raised again at a board meeting in September 1906. Due to the high tolls payable on this Tyne crossing, however, these plans never came to fruition and the idea was, at least temporarily, abandoned.

The Gateshead system was an early user of 'simple fares', the cost of making any journey at first being 1d. Not surprisingly, the management was less than happy at this, particularly as the Wrekenton route was around three miles in length, and thus in 1910 the 'fair fare' was introduced on this service. This followed the policy adopted by other B.E.T. subsidiaries and in the case of the Wrekenton route a charge was made of one farthing per stop. Following this move, pay-as-you-enter operation was introduced in 1912 on the Teams route, which was worked on a shuttle basis using one single deck tram, as well as on the Saltwell Park and Bensham service. Although the management was unhappy about 1d fares, the chairman wasn't, as he opposed the introduction of the 'fair fares' system feeling that the doubling of the original halfpenny fare had sufficiently augumented the company's revenue without the need to impose any further increases.

At a board meeting held on 7 May 1912, the possibility of operating motor buses was once again discussed and a month later was agreed in principle. The route selected was from the tramway terminus at Low Fell to Chester-le-Street via Birtley and, after this was inspected by the chairman together with Mr.C.S.Hilton (who was Chairman of the Birmingham & District Power & Traction Co.Ltd. and was to become Chairman of Northern General) and Mr.Shire (the expert) of the British Automobile Traction Company, all agreed that it could be operated at a reasonable cost, presenting a report to the board's September meeting to that effect and giving authority to proceed. It was a year later to the very day, however, before this route was inaugurated with the first bus leaving Chester-le-Street for Low Fell at 2.0pm on 7 May 1913. For this purpose the company purchased eight Straker Squire CO-type buses from the B.A.T.(J2115-22), four of which were fitted with Immisch 32-seat open-top double deck bodies, while the remainder had Birch 28-seat rear entrance single deck bodywork. Mr.Morrison, the Gateshead manager, had recommended Tilling Stevens vehicles as being driveable by tram drivers who would only have to learn steering, but the B.A.T. (or Mr.Hilton) opposed this, wanting instead a completely separate bus undertaking. Moreover, neither Tilling Stevens buses nor Daimlers could be obtained in time and in addition a report was still awaited as to their performance in Birmingham. As Straker Squire were able to offer an earlier delivery date, they thus secured the order and the first two arrived early in April. Prior to their receipt, however, on 1 April 1913 the company had taken delivery of a vehicle of this make fitted with a lorry body (J1194). During June a further Immisch-bodied Straker Squire CO-type double decker (J1205) was received, followed in July by five Daimler CC-type buses (J2336-40). The latter carried Dodson 32-seat open-top double deck bodywork which had originally been mounted on Darracq-Serpollet chassis operated by the Metropolitan Steam Omnibus Company Limited, whilst an additional Straker Squire chassis was also obtained and fitted with a secondhand Birch body. These were used on a number of new services introduced during the summer months. Although as early as October 1912, Chester-le-Street Urban District Council had requested a bus service from Wrekenton to Washington, this did not come to fruition until 30 June 1913, two days after a service had been inaugurated from Chester-le-Street to Waldridge. During the following month, on 12 July, a service was started from Chester-le-Street to Pelton Fell followed a day later by one from Chester-le-Street to Durham, whilst in August, two services were launched from Heworth to Bill Quay on the 7th, and to Jarrow on the 14th. Also a service from Chester-le-Street to Sacriston and Edmondsley was started on the 29th, on which same day on the Chester-le-Street to Pelton Fell route was extended to Craghead and the Chester-le-Street to Waldridge service withdrawn. Owing to unsatisfactory results caused by the dreadful condition of the road between Heworth and Hebburn, the Heworth - Bill Quay and Jarrow services were comparatively short lived, however, and both ceased operation on 9 November 1913. It is interesting to note that despite the B.E.T. already owning Jarrow & District Electric Traction Co. who operated a tramway from Jarrow to South Shields, there were difficulties in constructing a tramway between Jarrow and Heworth due to the road between these two places being crossed by a number of rope-hauled wagonways, hence the reason that a bus service was ultimately provided by Gateshead & District who had earlier considered a tramway extension to Hebburn.

More Daimler buses of the CC-type were purchased later in the year - 5 each in August and September, 2 in October and 1 in November to enable the introduction of more routes following the success of the original services and all these were fitted with Dodson

*Seen when new in May 1913 is Gateshead Tramways Motor Service's Immisch-bodied Straker Squire CO-type double decker J2116. After enjoying only a brief life in the north-east, the chassis of this bus was resold to its makers (Straker Squire) in September 1914, its body being sold three months later to Newcastle Corporation.
(K.A.Jenkinson collection)*

J2122, one of Gateshead Tramways Motor Service's original Immisch-bodied Straker Squire CO-type double deckers new in May 1913, is seen undergoing a primitive type of tilt test outside Chester-le-Street depot. Along with the company's other Straker Squire buses, J2122 was impressed by the War Department in September 1914 fitted with lorry bodywork. (Go-Ahead Northern)

double deck bodies obtained from the London General Omnibus Co. The new services commenced from Dunston to Scotswood on 17 September and from Chester-le-Street to Fence Houses (where they connected with Sunderland District trams) on 6 October, although the former enjoyed but a brief life, being withdrawn on 29 May 1914.

Having by now built up a fleet of 27 motorbuses and a lorry and several services based on Chester-le-Street, towards the end of 1913 it was found neccesary to construct an extension to the bus gagage and workshops which Gateshead & District had built in 1912 on a plot of land it had purchased in Picktree Lane, Chester-le-Street.

Two of Gateshead Tramways Motor Services Birch-bodied Straker Squires, J2119 & J2120 pose for the camera when new in May 1913. After little more than a year in service, both buses were impressed by the War Department in September 1914, their bodies first being removed and replaced with lorry bodywork. (Go-Ahead Northern)

Dodson-bodied Daimler CC-type double decker J2503 is seen here shortly after entering service with Gateshead Tramways Motor Service in October 1913. Parked in the entrance of Chester-le-Street depot, its destination board reads 'To Chester-le-Street & Durham', a comparatively long route in those early days. Its chassis number CC297 can clearly be seen painted on its chassis frame forward of the rear axle. (T.Godfrey collection)

THE BIRTH OF NORTHERN GENERAL

Following the policy of the British Electric Traction Co. where it had various tramway interests in a particular area in which it was also developing motor bus services, an umbrella holding company was created to co-ordinate its various interests and thus, as has been mentioned earlier, a new company was registered for this purpose on 29 November 1913 under the title of Northern General Transport Company Limited, although it appears that the names 'North Eastern Traction Co.Ltd.' and 'Northern Counties Transport Co.Ltd.' had also been considered. Shareholders in the three existing B.E.T. companies in the north-east (Gateshead & District; Jarrow & District and Tynemouth & District) were offered shares in the new company on an exchange basis and on 1 January 1914 the whole of the Gateshead & District motor bus fleet was purchased by the new Northern General company. Although retaining their operating independence, the three tramways companies were now effectively became subsidiaries of Northern despite retaining their individual titles. Prior to these events taking place, Gateshead & District had ordered more new buses, although in the event they did not making their debut until January 1914 under the ownership of the newly created Northern General company. These comprised 8 Brush-bodied Daimler CD-type 30-seat single deckers and 3 Central-bodied Daimler CD-type open-top double deckers, although five of the single deckers and two of the double deckers were delivered direct to Kidderminster & District Electric Light and Traction Co.Ltd. to whom they were loaned until July when they eventually arrived at Chester-le-Street. All these were painted in Northern's recently-introduced new livery of bright red and white with the fleet name 'Northern', this replacing the previous sombre unrelieved-red colour scheme adorned with their operator's full title. It is of further interest to note that whilst the single deckers were equipped with 4-speed gearboxes, the double deckers only had 3-speed units.

The new company quickly began to seek further expansion of its popular motor bus services and during 1914 opened several new routes. Amongst these was one from Chester-le-Street to Stanley and Annfield Plain which started on 9 May and was extended to Consett on 6 June, one from Consett to Newcastle via Dipton which commenced on 1 August, from Stanley to Newcastle on 25 August and South Moor to Newcastle on 5 September. Another new service, that between Heworth and Sunderland which began on 10 October 1914, was abandoned on 20 November of that same year due to unsatisfactory receipts whilst a further new route was considered from Scotswood to Blaydon, Prudhoe and Mickley on 10 September but was, in the event, never started. Commencing on 30 May 1914, in Tynemouth territory was a circuitous service from North Shields to Whitley Bay via Preston Village, Backworth, and which was extended to Seaton Delaval and Earsdon on 11 July. Subsequent changes resulted in Preston Village no longer being served after 12 June and similarly the operation to Backworth ceasing on 1 August, leaving the route to Seaton Delaval to continue until 21 September when it too was withdrawn. Expansion was also envisaged north of the Tyne including the Blyth and Ashington area, but the outbreak of World War I prevented the fruition of these plans.

Having spread its sphere of operation away from Chester-le-Street, it was now found necessary to obtain additional garage premises closer to its new areas of operation and to this end Northern purchased a disused roller skating rink at Stanley in February 1914 which, after conversion, opened as a bus garage in August. In North Shields, the Suez Street tram depot was used to house the buses operated on the Whitley Bay service whilst those on the Heworth and Sunderland service and possibly the other routes from Heworth used the Jarrow tram sheds as their base. A further consequence of the expanded route network was the need for additional buses, and to this end a further 15 new Daimlers were placed into service between April and September 1914. One of these was a CD-type chassis which was given the Immisch double deck body - and its registration number J2121 - removed from a former Gateshead & District Straker Squire whilst the remaining 14 were Daimler B-types, 1 with Birch and 10 with Brush open-top 32-seat double deck bodies and 2 Birch and 1 Brush-bodied 30-seat single deckers. Most, if not all, these Daimler chassis had been purchased under the Government's war-subsidy scheme which meant that in the case of hostilities they were liable to be requisitioned. Fortunately however, only four of the Daimlers suffered this fate along with eight of the ten Straker Squires (one of which was a lorry) which had by then already succumbed to some body swapping (complete with their registration numbers), the latter departing in September 1914 and the former two months later, all being driven to Aldershot by Northern drivers! Prior to leaving Gateshead, however, all the Daimlers were first fitted with lorry bodies by Northern on behalf of the War Department, their bus bodies then being placed in store for up to three years before being sold to Newcastle, Sheffield and Todmorden Corporations and Gravesend Tramways. Indeed, it had been intended to sell one of the Strakers to Barrow Corporation had the War Department not stepped in first! A further Straker Squire chassis was built by Northern from its stock of spare parts for this model and after its assembly was completed, this too was delivered to the military authorities. Also leaving the fleet in September 1914 were the other two Straker Squires, the chassis of which were resold to their manufacturer and fourteen of the Daimler CC-type double deckers (of which only 7 were fitted with bodies) which were at first hired to Aldershot & District and were then in September 1915 sold to the British Automobile Traction Co. of Camden Town, London who rebodied and re-registered them before placing them in service in the capital. Thus, by December 1914, mainly as a result of the hostilities, Northern's fleet had been reduced from 54 to 26 buses. With no immediate sight of peace on the horizon, the company had to suspend its plans for further route expansion and indeed additionally had to curtail some of its present activities. Despite being faced with shortages of manpower, fuel and vehicles, Northern was called upon to provide transport for the occupants of a large new housing colony set up for Belgian refugees in Birtley on the Low Fell - Chester-le-Street route (in the area today known as Elizabethville), whilst another unusual operation by June 1915, was for six vehicles

This scene at Low Fell in 1914 shows one of Northern's Brush-bodied Daimler B-type double deckers (J2683) enroute to Durham in company with Gateshead Tramways 55. Both vehicles were new in 1913, the tram surviving until 1947, the motor bus until 1921 when it was sold to Aylesbury Motor Bus Co. J2683 had, during its life with Northern, been rebodied as a single decker in April 1921 only to be refitted with double deck bodywork some three months later. (T.Godfrey collection)

Daimler B-type D43 (J3066) was new in July 1914 and was fitted with a Birch 30-seat rear-entrance body which featured a rear platform. In October 1917, it was given a lorry body which was later rebuilt as a lorry-bus and later regained a rear-entrance single deck bus body before being withdrawn in 1921 after which its chassis was scrapped and its body transferred to another Daimler chassis. The poster carried in its rearmost nearside window appears to be advertising Northern's 'Day Trips to the Seaside'. (Go-Ahead Northern)

which had been hireed by the military authorities as lorries at Lambton Military Camp. After being used for this purpose for eleven hours per day on five days each week they were returned to the company each weekend for use on ordinary services on Saturdays and Sundays.

No new deliveries took place during 1915, except for one body and five 2-ton Burford chassis received from B.A.T., the latter - which were never fitted with bodies - being resold to South Wales Transport on 15 April at a total profit of £10, and it was not until January of the following year that the fleet size was able to be increased when the first of seven diminutive GMC model 15 buses purchased to combat competition on the Low Fell to Chester-le-Street and the Washington routes began to arrive. Of these, four had Birch 10-seat front entrance bodies whilst the remaining two which had 14-seat rear entrance bodywork by this same coachbuilder were surprisingly refitted with new Tilling 12-seat charabanc bodies before their entry into service, their original bodies being considered unsatisfactory. The seventh chassis was immediately resold to Gateshead Tramways and in its place another was purchased for use as a van. Northern lost more of its vehicles when ten new Daimler chassis were impressed by the military authorities whilst still on their manufacturer's premises and although these never took their place in the fleet, it was decided to still take delivery of six of the single deck bodies ordered for them and to use these to replace some of the company's older double deck bodies. These bodies were received in 1915 (1), 1916 (4) and 1917 (1). Meanwhile, a contract was obtained for the carriage of mail between Newcastle and Sunderland and between Sunderland and Haswell from 1 April to 5 December 1915 and so successful was this new venture that a new contract was signed in February 1916. A surprise acquisition in July 1915 was that of the parcels business of Shipley & Farell of Newcastle. After coming under Northern's control, this operation which relied on horses and carts was, for a time, expanded but was ultimately discontinued on 28 February 1918.

Seen during World War I is 1914 Brush-bodied Daimler CD-type J2542 which was fitted with a wooden frame on its roof in which a gas-bag was accommodated. Its chassis number CD609, which also initially served as its fleet number, can be seen painted on the chassis frame. Allocated number D10 in the company's new 1919 fleet numbering scheme, it remained in service until 1923 when its chassis was dismantled and the parts thereof used in the construction of 'Big Bertha' D281. (T.Godfrey collection)

During the war years, the only services to be maintained to any extent were those from Chester-le-Street to Low Fell, Durham, Fence Houses and Stanley, from Stanley to Newcastle and from Dipton to Newcastle, whilst that from Durham to Chester-le-Street became a through service to Low Fell in 1915. The services from Stanley to Consett and from Dipton to Consett were closed in February 1915

Although new in November 1913, Daimler CD-type J2550, which was originally fitted with a Central 32-seat open-top double deck bus body, did not enter service with Northern until March 1914 having in the meantime been on loan to Kidderminster & District Electric Light & Traction Co.Ltd. In July 1915 it was fitted with the lorry body with which it is pictured here, but in July 1917 it reverted to passenger-carrying duties when it was given a Brush open-top double deck body. After further body changes, it continued in service until 1929 by which time it was a 26-seat single decker! (Go-Ahead Northern)

The only new vehicles to join the Northern fleet in 1916 were seven diminutive GMCs, one of which was J3661. Originally fitted with 14-seat Birch bodywork, this was removed and replaced with a 12-seat Tilling charabanc body (illustrated here) before its entry into service in April 1916. It was withdrawn in 1918. (Go-Ahead Northern)

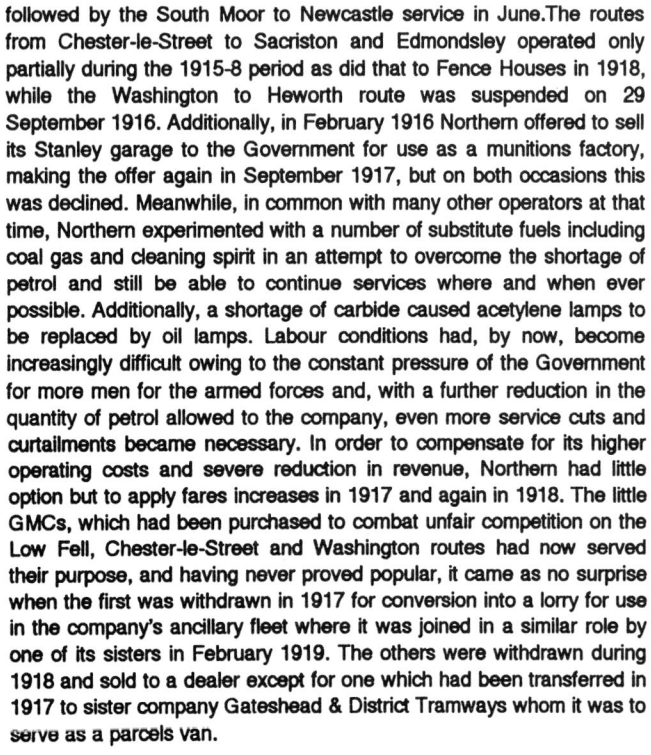

One of seven GMC Model 15 buses purchased by Northern General in 1916, J3665 was fitted with a 10-seat Birch body fitted with perimeter seating. Given fleet number GMC5, this particular vehicle gave less than two years service before being withdrawn and sold in 1918. Note its unusual solid rubber tyres with a deep, circular tread. (Go-Ahead Northern)

followed by the South Moor to Newcastle service in June. The routes from Chester-le-Street to Sacriston and Edmondsley operated only partially during the 1915-8 period as did that to Fence Houses in 1918, while the Washington to Heworth route was suspended on 29 September 1916. Additionally, in February 1916 Northern offered to sell its Stanley garage to the Government for use as a munitions factory, making the offer again in September 1917, but on both occasions this was declined. Meanwhile, in common with many other operators at that time, Northern experimented with a number of substitute fuels including coal gas and cleaning spirit in an attempt to overcome the shortage of petrol and still be able to continue services where and when ever possible. Additionally, a shortage of carbide caused acetylene lamps to be replaced by oil lamps. Labour conditions had, by now, become increasingly difficult owing to the constant pressure of the Government for more men for the armed forces and, with a further reduction in the quantity of petrol allowed to the company, even more service cuts and curtailments became necessary. In order to compensate for its higher operating costs and severe reduction in revenue, Northern had little option but to apply fares increases in 1917 and again in 1918. The little GMCs, which had been purchased to combat unfair competition on the Low Fell, Chester-le-Street and Washington routes had now served their purpose, and having never proved popular, it came as no surprise when the first was withdrawn in 1917 for conversion into a lorry for use in the company's ancillary fleet where it was joined in a similar role by one of its sisters in February 1919. The others were withdrawn during 1918 and sold to a dealer except for one which had been transferred in 1917 to sister company Gateshead & District Tramways whom it was to serve as a parcels van.

Although the war finally ended in 1918, it was not until the following year that Northern was able to start to forge ahead with its expansion programme. Orders were placed for 40 Leylands, - 20 in May 1919 and 20 in October, although the latter were cancelled in May 1920 and indeed, only 6 of the first 20 were placed in service with the other 14 being resold without being registered (these would have been J4609-22). Additionally, owing to the late delivery of the Leyland chassis, 40 AECs were ordered, although only 5 of these were delivered, following which arrangements were quickly made for the disposal of the remaining 35 before they left their manufacturer's premises. A further 10 AECs had also been ordered with the provision that if the Leylands arrived on time these too could be (and were) cancelled after which a decision was taken to concentrate on the Daimler Y-type which in turn led to the disposal of all the Leylands. In June 1919, the board resolved to increase the services on the present routes (requiring 20 buses), to reopen several old routes (needing 15 buses) and to commence new routes (requiring 19 buses). The new buses, which had chassis of four different makes and bodywork by four different coachbuilders, began to arrive in March with deliveries continuing throughout the year and by November no fewer than 21 had been received. Many of these chassis had been acquired from the War Department via the British Automobile Traction Co. or AEC of Walthamstow and five still carried the box van or lorry bodies carried during their use in military roles, entering service with Northern as lorry buses. Making up the 21 vehicles were 4 Daimler B-types. 2 Daimler CDs, 4 Daimler Ys, 5 AEC YC-types, 5 Leyland Ns and a solitary Crossley Tender. All except one of the Daimler Bs and the Crossley were fitted with rear entrance single deck bodies built by Birch, Brown

One of five Birch-bodied AEC YC-type buses purchased new by Northern in 1919, J3076 is seen here in all-red livery with its driver and conductress posing for the photographer. Withdrawn in 1922, it was later converted into a lorry for use by Gateshead & District Tramways. (T.Godfrey collection)

D60 (J2120) was a Daimler Y-type, the chassis of which was purchased from the War Department in 1920 and fitted with a new 34-seat Dodson body. Its re-issued registration number had previously been carried by one of Gateshead Tramways Motor Service's Straker Squire single deckers, a photograph of which is shown earlier. Here D60 is seen in September 1923 after being given a new Brush body which it retained until its withdrawal from service in 1930. (Go-Ahead Northern)

or Brush/Glendower, the Crossley having a Tilling 12-seat charabanc body removed from one of the GMCs and the remaining Daimler B being mounted with Brush 32-seat open-top double deck bodywork. Meanwhile, prior to the arrival of these new additions to the fleet, a number of the company's earlier vehicles had exchanged bodies or had received lorry bodywork only to be refitted with new open-top double deck bus bodies in 1917/8. With these new buses it was possible to reopen the routes which had been suspended during the war. Heworth and Washington, Stanley and Newcastle via Annfield Plain and Dipton resumed in October 1919, Sacriston to Edmondsley in May 1920 and Stanley and Consett, Heworth and Jarrow and Dunston and Scotswood in October 1920 being extended from Dunston to Newcastle (Bewick Street).

Prior to 1919, the buses were referred to by their chassis numbers which were painted on the chassis frame whilst bodies had their own numbers, but in that year a new fleet numbering system was devised in which chassis identification letters were employed. Thus, the AECs were given 'bonnet numbers' prefixed AEC, the Crossley was prefixed C, Daimlers D, GMC's GMC and Leylands L. Body numbers were retained, however, as it was the practise to insure chassis and bodies seperately - a policy which was continued until recent years! The introduction of this new system appears to coincide with a great deal of rebodying and was applied somewhat piecemeal. Further new buses began to materialise in 1920, a year during which 43 arrived, almost all being Daimlers originating from the War Department either by direct purchase or via other sources. Two of these (D2, a Y-type in 1919 and D11, a CD-type in 1920) were built at Chester-le-Street from spare parts and, as a result of this, surprisingly were not given a chassis number. The bodies - all single deck or charabanc - were built by a variety of coachbuilders including Dodson, Birch, Brush, Carrosserie and Latymer or by Northern General itself. Included in their number were 4 Crossley tenders, some of which were used as ancillary

Acquired in 1920, Dodson-bodied Daimler Y-type D54 began life as a lorry in service with the War Department from whom it was purchased via B.A.T. Ltd. Its re-issued registration number J1205 was originally carried by one of Gatehead Tramways Motors 1913-vintage Straker Squire double deckers which was impressed by the War Department in 1914. (T.Godfrey collection)

One of four ex.War Department Crossley Tenders purchased by Northern in 1920, C5 (CN1597) was the first vehicle in the fleet to carry a two-letter registration number. Its 14-seat body was built by Northern in its own workshops and was replaced later by a body built by Ransomes. It remained in service until 1926 when it was sold to a local operator in Blyth who continued to use it in daily service for a further seven years. (T.Godfrey Collection)

11

New in February 1920, Daimler Y-type D24 (J4902) was originally fitted with lorry-bus bodywork. Fitted with a 30-seat rear entrance Birch body in March 1921 it is seen here in the early 'twenties operating the Consett to Chester-le-Street service. It was ultimately withdrawn in 1926. (K.A.Jenkinson collection)

vehicles rather than in a passenger-carrying role, and a solitary Leyland N-type. The Crossleys were all eventually fitted with bus bodies in 1922/3, although the first two so treated were at first temporarily given charabanc bodies. Meanwhile, as had now become customary, a great deal of body exchanging took place within the fleet often involving vehicles only a couple of years old and, in some cases, rebodied buses were soon afterwards re-chassised ending up like the hammer which was given two new heads and a new shaft!

A new development which took place by June 1920 was an agreement reached between Northern and United Automobile Services Ltd., both of whom had a presence in County Durham working services from the north and south respectively. In order that there should be no conflict in future years between the two companies, it was determined that a demarcation line should be set up in central Durham and to this end a line was drawn westwards through Easington and Durham City, the area to the north of which was to be Northern territory and to the south of which would be United's domain and it was agreed that neither company would cross this without the consent of the other. United gave six months notice to cancel this in September 1933 with Northern noting its termination on 6 May 1934. Thereafter, a gentleman's agreement appears to have been applied which was to remain in force for no less than forty-five years, although its existence was to cause some problems with Eastern Express, General County and others in the 'thirties and, as will be seen later, again in 1950.

1921, as far as the fleet was concerned, witnessed another large intake of ex.War Department Daimler chassis totalling 29 in all. Two of these entered service as lorry buses whilst the remainder were given new rear entrance single deck bodies built by Glendower, Dodson or Brush/Glendower before entering service between January and August. On this occasion however, rather than dramatically increasing the fleet size, these new arrivals were used to replace older vehicles including the six Leyland N-types which were disposed of due to being regarded as 'non-standard' and 12 of the older Daimlers of which 5 went to Tynemouth & District Electric Tramways to whom a sixth passed in 1922. Indeed, 1921 proved to be memorable in more ways than one as it was during this year that Northern General opened its new garage and workshops at Bensham in the western part of Gateshead. This enabled the former workshop at Chester-le-Street to be vacated and the space to be used as an extension to the bus operating depot. Early in the year Northern agreed to pay Gateshead Corporation £500 for the sole rights of operation on the Gateshead to Low Fell route, after which

One of five AEC YC-type buses purchased by Northern in 1919 fitted with Birch 30-seat rear entrance bodies, J3077 was given a new Dodson front entrance body in 1925 as seen here but only survived for a further two years before being withdrawn and sold. (K.A.Jenkinson collection)

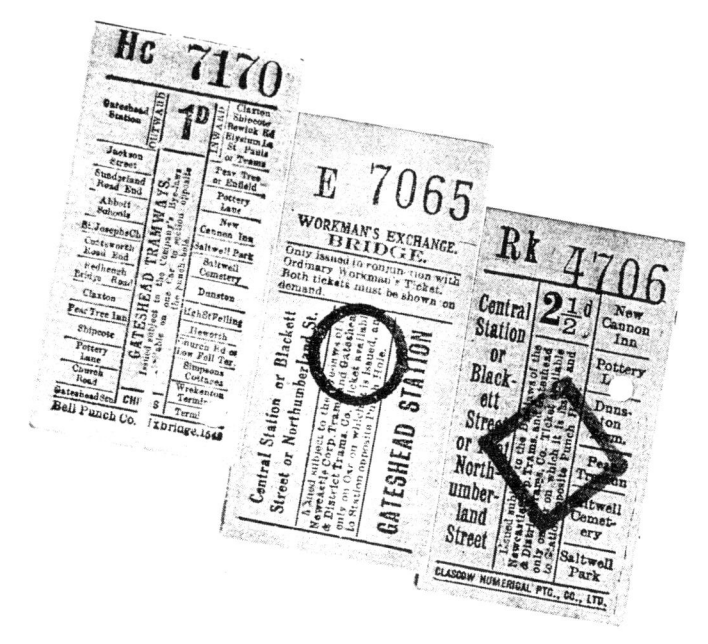

The Daimler CB-type chassis of D111 (CN1563) was one of eleven purchased by Northern in 1922 which had begun life with the War Department. Given a new 20-seat Ransomes body it is seen here working the Sunderland-Durham service in 1929 shortly before it was withdrawn and sold. (Go-Ahead Northern)

Built in 1921 by Gateshead & District on Brill 22E trucks, front exit car no.13 is pictured here in its open cab form, vestibules not being added until 1926.

the Corporation decided they had no right to do this. Later, during the summer, Northern launched its first day excursions to the coast and other places using the Crossley and Daimler charabancs, and as these proved popular from the start, they encouraged Northern to expand in this leisure market during the following years. Much rebodying again took place within the fleet and to alleviate a shortage of buses, five of the Daimler charabancs were fitted with conventional bus bodies. Only one of these ultimately regained its charabanc body, the other four of these, after remaining in storage throughout the winter, then being fitted to new chassis.

During 1921, as mentioned previously, Tynemouth & District received its first motor buses, these being 5 Daimler B-types which had been rebodied using new Dodson bodies and 3 with secondhand bodies purchased from Thames Valley Traction Co. Acquired from the Northern General fleet, they were for use on a service from North Shields to Blyth via Whitley Bay which started on 20 July in retaliation to a route operated by United Automobile Services from Blyth which competed with Tynemouth & District's trams. Their move marked the start of a long line of inter-fleet transfers between Northern and its subsidiaries which was to continue for more than seventy years and involve many different types of vehicles. Meanwhile, Gateshead & Dsitrict Tramways purchased three 1899 vintage open-top double deck tramcar bodies from Liverpool Corporation in February 1921. After being given Brill trucks, these were placed in service in their new home towards the end of 1922 and three years later were rebuilt with closed tops after which they remained in service until 1950! Meanwhile, Gateshead & District was making a start on modernising its tramway fleet and during the next eight years place no fewer than 25 new single deck and 7 new double deck trams in service. All but 7 of the single deckers which, together with the double deckers were fitted with Brush bodywork, were given bodies built in Gateshead's own workshops and all had Brill trucks of varying types and were powered by Dick Kerr motors. Although 9 of the earlier single and double deckers were withdrawn as the new trams arrived, the remaining double deckers were fitted with top covers in 1924/5. Additionally, 8 secondhand double deck bodies were purchased from Sheffield Corporation for fitting to existing trucks.

Returning to the Northern General fleet, although it was now four years since the war had ended, the Slough Trading Company who were the main suppliers of ex.War Department vehicles were still able to provide surplus chassis from this source from stock. It therefore

Standing outside Newcastle Infirmary on 26 July 1923 at the start of the annual trip of Scott & Innes are one-year-old Daimler CB-type D104 (J9340) which had the Latymer charabanc body transferred from D34, and almost new 39-seat Brush-bodied Daimler Y-types D122 (PT1078), D121 (PT1077) and D117 (PT892), the chassis of all of which had begun life with the War Department. In total, four charabancs and seven omnibuses were used on this particular outing on which 330 passengers were to be transported. (Go-Ahead Northern)

came as no surprise when Northern purchased 11 more Daimler CB and Y-types from this dealer in 1922 together with a solitary Crossley X-type. Two of the Daimler CBs were actually gained from Tynemouth & District by whom they had been ordered but never operated whilst another of the chassis of this type was immediately dismantled for spares rather than being bodied for service. On this occasion, the CBs were fitted with new 20-seat front entrance bus bodies built by Ransomes who also provided the 14-seat body for the Crossley X - which incidentally did not enter service until 1923 - whilst the 4 Y-types were given the Latymer charabanc bodywork removed from the Daimlers during the previous year.

Northern's services, which had up to this time generally not started much earlier than 8.00am each day but had run through to around midnight, now began to operate much earlier, commencing about 5.00am, and several of the original routes had been extended or diverted to serve new areas. Although journeys on route 3 still ran from Chester-le-Street to Craghead via Pelton Fell and Grange Villa, there was now a service 3A which ran via Hett Hills on Saturdays and holidays only in 1921. In May 1921 a new Chester-le-Street to Sunderland service had begun, as had one from Sunderland to South Shields while on 18 December 1920 a new service had been introduced linking Durham to Sunderland via Newbottle and Houghton-le-Spring. Also opened in September 1921 were routes from Consett to Castleside and to Medomsley whilst for a short time a Sunday service was run on the North Eastern Railway's Annfield Plain to Durham service until the railway company decided to run it themselves. In February 1922 a West Stanley - Dipton - Tantobie service was started, the early results of which were not very encouraging. Despite re-establishing many of its former services and opening several new routes, the prolonged coal strike of 1921/2 seriously affected Northern's trading results which suffered a further setback during the winter of 1922/3 due to a deepening trade depression and increased competition from the growing number of small independent operators. In 1923 the first poor children's outing to the seaside by road was organised in Chester-le-Street and the long convoy of buses employed attracted thousands of spectators. These outings proved deservedly popular from that date and became an annual event in all 'Northern' areas throughout the inter-war years.

Nine more secondhand ex.War Department Daimler Y-type chassis were purchased, some of which came via the Slough Trading Company, at the start of 1923, and including two which had previously operated with charabanc bodywork for Samuelson Transport Co. Ltd. of London until the failure of that company. These were all fitted with front entrance Brush bodies seating 34 passengers plus a further 5 on tip-up seats. More surprising, however, was the appearance in September and October of what appeared to be 4 "new" single deckers. These were, in fact, not so, but had been rebuilt from some of Northern's older Daimler CD-type buses and indeed one of them had been constructed by the company entirely from spare parts. During the rebuilding, new pressed steel chassis frames lengthened to 16ft. wheelbase were fitted using many of the spares already in stock, and after being equipped with new Brush 38-seat front entrance bodies (of which 6 of the seats were of the tip-up type) they were given new registration numbers prior to re-entering service as "new" vehicles. As a result of their high seating capacity these buses which were officially classed as being of NGT manufacture were quickly nicknamed "Big Berthas" by their crews.

YEARS OF CONTINUING EXPANSION

On 22 November 1923, Northern was approached by Issac E.Walton & Co. Ltd. of Gateshead - who traded as Crescent Bus Company - with a proposal for the sale of their garage and omnibus business to the B.E.T. company. Agreement was reached and the purchase was concluded on 1 January 1924. Walton, who had entered the field of passenger vehicle operation in 1919, was also in business as a dealer having gained the Leyland franchise immediately after World War I. His first vehicle was a secondhand GMC 15-seat waggonette and this was quickly joined by other makes and models until a fleet of some 19 buses and charabancs had been amassed. When taken over on the first day of 1924, Walton was operating 14 Daimlers, 4 AECs and a solitary Crossley, all of which passed to Northern along with Crescent's service from Gateshead to Durham. In addition to the above, a further 2 Daimler chassis were owned, one of which had an incomplete body, and these too were purchased by Northern who, as is noted later, completed one and rebuilt the other as an NGT vehicle. Also included in the deal was a plot of leasehold land in Wellington Street, Gateshead on which Northern built a new bus station later in the year. Walton, however, retained his other business interests which continued into the 'thirties. A further operator to approach Northern with an offer of sale was the Invincible Motor Omnibus Co. of Seaham Harbour, although this was not persued until two years later.

During 1924 no fewer than 40 Daimler Y-type chassis and 3 AEC YC-types were rebuilt at Northern's Bensham workshops in a similar fashion to those of the previous year before being fitted with new Brush or Ransomes 38-seat bodies. Although a few of these used the chassis from Northern's vehicles, the majority had been purchased specifically for this purpose from Slough Trading Co. and were former War Department vehicles. The rebuilding of these chassis by Northern marked the start of a programme which, although not continuous, did not end until 1952, and prior to the above, 3 more Daimler Y-type chassis were acquired from Slough Trading Co. Rather than rebuild and extend these, they were instead fitted with bodies removed from a pair of Northern's withdrawn Daimlers and an AEC.

The most unusual purchase of 1924, however, was a BMMO chassis which incorporated a number of Tilling Stevens parts. Built in the Birmingham & Midland Motor Omnibus Co's own workshops at Birmingham, this was the first large bus delivered new to Northern equipped with pneumatic tyres, although Northern had at the end of 1923 begun to similarly equip some of its older large buses. Probably purchased to eveluate its performance against Northern's own rebuilds, it was immediately hailed as a success and, as such, cemented a relationship between the two companies which was to last for more than a decade. This led Northern to consider placing an order for 20 BMMO front entrance double deck bodies and 20 Leyland chassis, but, owing to their high cost and doubtful delivery dates, this was cancelled and replaced with an order for 20 more Y-type Daimlers with new single deck Brush bodywork. By now, in addition to operating excursions during the summer months of each year, Northern had also entered the field of extended holiday tours, the first of which was a 7-day tour to Scotland. Like the excursions, the extended tours quickly

During 1923 six more double deck tramcars were added to the Gateshead fleet, these being built by Brush and having a front entrance and enclosed cabs and balconies. Seating 70 passengers and mounted on Brill 21E trucks, they spent the whole of their lives on the Wrekenton route upon which 66 is seen at Haymarket, Newcastle in 1938.

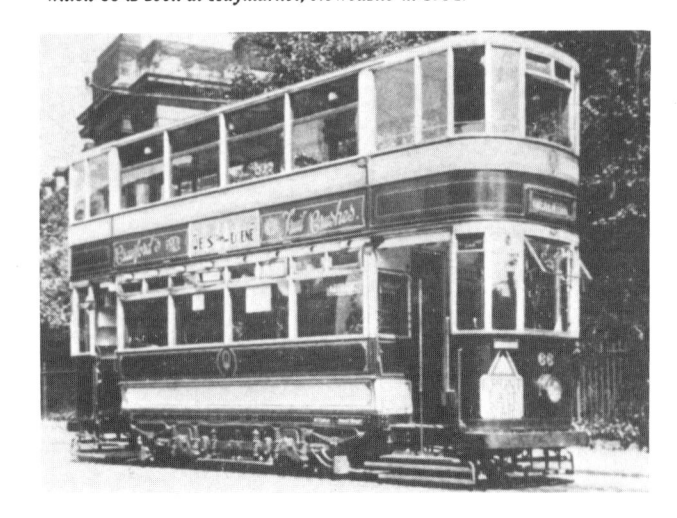

Rebuilt by Northern in 1924 from an earlier Daimler Y-type chassis, the origins of which have never been traced, D192 (CN2117) was given a Ransomes 38-seat front entrance body which incorporated partial covers to the rear wheels. Seen here on a private hire duty, it gave eleven years service before being withdrawn and sold. (Go-Ahead Northern)

1925 witnessed the arrival of the first BMMO buses in the fleet when fifty normal control SOS S-type single deckers were delivered. Amongst these was 31-seat Brush/BMMO-bodied 209 (PT4852) which was to give the company thirteen years service. (Go-Ahead Northern)

gained popularity and soon were running to a number of different locations. Meanwhile, as more new stage carriage services began, including one which started on 25 October from Wrekenton to Washington which had been considered some twelve years earlier when the Low Fell and Chester-le-Street service started, so the need for additional depots became increasingly apparent and thus on 29 April 1924 a new garage was opened in Sunderland followed a year later by one in Consett whilst those at Chester-le-Street and Bensham were both enlarged.

An unusual item recorded in the company's minutes during 1924 related to tickets and stated that stocks were currently held of 3,742,490 obsolete and 2,317 damaged tickets. These, it was agreed, should be destroyed. Three years later, 9,735,885 obsolete tickets were destroyed following the adoption of numbered stages!

1925 witnessed the rebuilding and lengthening by Northern of yet more Daimler Y-types which were then fitted with new 36-seat bodies by Brush, Vickers and Ransomes which were later altered to 31-seat following the removal of the tip up seats across the aisle. Of the 17 buses concerned, one used a chassis purchased from Slough Trading Co. whilst the origins of the remaining 16 which were older Northern vehicles have never been traced. More significant however, was the arrival of 50 BMMO/Brush-bodied BMMO SOS S-type 31-seat buses (which oddly were recorded by Northern and licensed as Tilling Stevens), these being the first truly new chassis to be purchased by Northern since 1920. Of these, 30 had been ordered in 1924 and 20 in 1925. Representing an enormous order for that time, they presaged the withdrawal of a great many of the older Daimler vehicles and provided a much higher standard of comfort for passengers. Built to the design of L.G.Wyndham Shire, BMMO's chief engineer, it was said that their "SOS" chassis designation stood for "Shire's Own Specification", although this has never been resolved. As mentioned previously, a start had also been made on the conversion of the fleet from solid rubber to pneumatic tyres (apart from the smaller vehicles such as the Crossleys which had been thus fitted from new), and this continued until 1927 when the task was completed. Meanwhile, Tynemouth & District Electric Traction Co. supplemented its original depots at North Shields and Cullercoats with new premises at Percy Main, between Wallsend and North Shields, in 1925 and from this date this new garage became home to Tynemouth's growing motor bus fleet. This increased in size during the year with the addition of 5 Daimler CB-type single deckers hired from Northern General whilst by this time the original B-type Daimler double deckers had been rebuilt to Y-type single deckers. Tynemouth & District had also started a North Shields to Wallsend service on 16 February 1923 which was extended to Whitley Bay on 29 May 1928.

Before leaving 1925, mention must be made of another independent operator taken over by Northern on 1 April. This was Hall Brothers of Seaham Harbour who ran under the title of "Invincible Motor Omnibus Company" and had first approached Northern towards the end of 1923. The Hall brothers had started their business at Birtley in 1919 with a vehicle which was used as a bus on weekdays and as a

Rebuilt by Northern General in 1925 from an earlier Daimler Y-type chassis, D286 (CN2761) was fitted with a new Brush 31-seat body and gave nine years service before being withdrawn and sold in 1934. (Go-Ahead Northern)

A massive convoy of Northern vehicles climb Byermoor Bank whilst undertaking a private hire duty in 1928. Heading the line are 1924 NGT/Daimler Y-type rebuild D162 (CN1987) followed by 220 & 239 (PT4904 & PT6243), a pair of 1925 Brush-bodied BMMO SOS S-types. According to the numbers on each vehicle and taking into account the vehicles just coming into sight at the top of the hill in the distance, this private hire must have employed more than 42 vehicles!
(Go-Ahead Northern)

mobile fish & chip shop at weekends by use of interchangable bodywork. Soon afterwards they opened routes from Sunderland to Seaham Harbour and from Seaham Harbour to Dawdon and Murton and by 1925 had built up a fleet of 11 buses and charabancs. All of these were Daimlers, some of which were fitted with lorry/bus bodies, and amongst the 11 were two dismantled chassis which were later rebuilt by Northern and fitted with 32-seat Vickers bodies. Although Hall's two garages and a workshop were not included in the deal, they were leased for around two years.

Northern's first General Manager, R.W.Cramp resigned in March 1926 and then became General Manager of Tynemouth & District, although he was retained by Northern as a consultant until 31 March 1928. He was succeeded by John Petrie who joined the company as Acting General Manager on 9 January 1926 and assumed the full title on 31 March. During the first few months in his new position, he saw the infamous General Strike take place in May followed by a miners dispute lasting from May to November, but once these unfortunate incidents had passed and life had returned to normal, he set forth to assist the company in its future development. As far as the fleet was concerned, the year brought a further 10 BMMO SOS S-type single deckers together with another 29 Daimler rebuilds. Of the latter, 24 were Y-types which were reclassifies LY with the remainder being CBs which became LCBs, all of which were given new 31-seat front entrance bodies by Brush or Ransomes before officially replacing older vehicles. Tynemouth & District was also included in the fleet modernisation programme and received its first ever brand new buses. These were 6 BMMO S-type single deckers and, as additional vehicles rather than replacements, their arrival further increased the size of Tynemouth's bus fleet. A further development took place in March 1926 when approval was given to advertising being carried on the back of buses.

Following the development of services in the area south of Sunderland after the take-over of Hall Brothers, Northern in May 1924 had given consideration to the building of a bus garage in the Hetton-le-Hole area, and on 28 August 1926 opened this at Murton to provide accommodation for the increasing number of buses employed in that area, some of which had been used on a service operated in competition with Sunderland & District between Hetton-le-Hole and Sunderland since 18 September 1924. Seeking to limit this competition, Northern in March 1925 had entered into negotiations with Sunderland & District Electric Tramways Co.Ltd., a company which had suffered mixed fortunes during the previous few years, but these came to nought and on 5 June both companies introduced services between Houghton-le-Spring and Chester-le-Street via Fence Houses. Following this, a working agreement was drawn up in November but was never signed! These events led to a period of great uncertainty as far as the Sunderland District Trnsport Co. Ltd. was concerned, starting on 27 January 1926 when it stated its unwillingness to enter into a working agreement with Northern but being prepared to sell to the company. On the 24th of the following month Northern made an offer to purchase and on 9 March Sunderland District accepted this subject to modification to consent by debenture holders. On 31 March the contract to purchase Sunderland District was sealed but was conditional on it being ratified within three months by the debenture holders and on completion of the purchase, Sunderland District's Manager was to be appointed Assistant General Manager of the Northern company. This is the point of the negotiations at which an

One of six two-year old Davidson-bodied BMMO SOS S-type charabancs purchased by Northern from Midland Red in 1927, 336 (HA2438) along with its sisters was sold in 1931 to Wakefield's Motors. Returning to Northern General in 1933 when it was renumbered 587, its chassis was then rebuilt and lengthened and fitted with a new Short Bros. 36-seat body which it retained until its final withdrawal in 1955.
(Go-Ahead Northern)

369 (UP682) was a BMMO SOS QLC-type new to Northern in 1928. Fitted with Short Bros all-weather charabanc bodywork it was transferred to Wakefield's Motors in 1933 for whom it ran for around five years before being withdrawn and scrapped. (Go-Ahead Northern)

Making its debut in 1928, 424 (BR6765) was one of a number of new BMMO SOS-QL-type buses placed in service during that year. Its Brush-body seated 37 passengers and was fitted with advertising boards above its side windows. After giving 22-years service, 424 was withdrawn early in 1950 and sold for scrap. (T.Godfrey collection)

unexpected occurrence took place. On 18 June, on the application of a debenture holder, Sir Harry Peat was appointed receiver for Sunderland District, this being followed on 22 July by a draft agreement to sell being drawn up by him. Less than a month later, however, on 7 August, the receiver broke off negotiations and the matter remained unresolved until the late spring of 1927. Resuming their attempt to purchase the Sunderland District undertaking, a new offer was made to the receiver on 30 April 1927 but when this was placed before a meeting of the debenture holders they resolved instead to sell the whole of the assets to a new company to be formed. Thus the negotiations with Northern came to an abrupt end and were not resumed until 1929 as will be seen later.

Until 1927, all Northern's fleet had been of the "normal control" type of vehicle, but in March of that year a totally new design made its appearance in which the driver was positioned alongside, rather than behind, the engine. This new type of bus, of which 25 were delivered, was of BMMO manufacture and designated the SOS Q-type by its makers (despite once again being licensed as Tilling Stevens) was fitted with Brush single deck bodywork with seating for 37 passengers. When compared with the rest of the fleet these buses looked extremely modern and 11 of were also supplied to Tynemouth & District, thus increasing its fleet size yet again. Turning to the secondhand market, Northern purchased from Midland Red 6 of its SOS S-type vehicles fitted with charabanc bodywork during the early summer of 1927, these having only seen two years service with their original owner.

Northern's service network was meanwhile continuing to grow steadily and during the 1926-8 period serveral new routes were inaugurated. Amongst these was one from Gateshead to Monkswearmouth via the Boldons which began on 8 June 1926 and in effect resumed the 1914 service, and on 11 November 1926 one from

One of ten Hall Lewis-bodied ADC 416Ds purchased new by Northern in May 1928, D379 (BR6499) gave the company nine years service before being withdrawn and sold. Its second life was with a travelling showman based at Newcastle and in this role it survived until 1960 when it was finally scrapped. Seen here towards the end of its Northern days, it had a roof-mounted advertising board on each side of its body. (Go-Ahead Northern)

Resting in the doorway of Northern's Westgate Road, Newcastle premises and, according to the board placed between them, available for hire, are Brush-bodied BMMO SOS QL-type 347 (UP560) and Short Bros.-bodied BMMO SOS QLC-type 367 (UP680), both of which were new in 1928. (Go-Ahead Northern)

Consett to Chopwell started on 11 November 1926 together with a service from Consett to Newcastle via Dipton whilst on 18 August 1927 the established Gateshead - Hebburn - Jarrow - Monkton service, which had commenced on 27 November 1924, was extended to Monkwearmouth. This was supplemented by a new service from Gateshead to South Shields via Jarrow which, instead of running via Argyll Street operated via Albert Road. More unusual, however, was a service started on 8 October 1927 from Felling to Pottery Lane, Gateshead via Windy Nook, this being operated by Northern for the Gateshead & District Tramways Company! Yet another new route was that from Gateshead to South Shields via White Mare Pool, which was launched on 12 March 1928 and ran jointly with Castles Motor Services' Newcastle to South Shields service. Additionally, following the success of its bus station at Gateshead, Northern had purchased the freehold on a site in Durham City where it proposed to build a bus station, and also purchased the freehold on its Sunderland premises. Without doubt, however, 1928 was "the" year for expansion with new routes springing up all over Northern's operating territory. There was Stanley to Quaking Houses; the linking of the established Durham to Sunderland and Sunderland to South Shields service into a through route and, in January the inauguration of a service from Sunderland to West Hartlepool along with several services which as a result of the opening of the new Tyne Bridge, were extended to Worswick Street, Newcastle where Northern had built and partly opened a new bus station on 10 October but which was not completed until July 1929! The bus station was designed for entry via Pilgrim Street but Newcastle Council refused permission for this right turn. In consequence, buses had, and have, to start on an upward gradient and, in the days of conductors, chocks were placed behind the wheels whilst the buses were stationary. Additionally two limited stop services were started jointly with United Automobile Services Ltd. from Newcastle to Bishop Auckland via Durham and Spennymoor and from Newcastle to Middlesbrough via Stockton-on-Tees, both of which only ran until 1929. 1928 was also the year in which the company introduced its first long distance service, this commencing on 1 May with one journey each day in each direction from Newcastle to Liverpool via Leeds and Manchester. Operated at first as a 'daily tour', as will be seen later, this quickly proved to be an extremely successful venture. In addition, a new omnibus station had been completed at Westgate Road, Newcastle in September 1927. This was in part of the Cross House site (Cross House having earlier been destroyed by fire) close to Westgate Road and Fenkle Street and was leased for 21 years. Initially it was used as a motor garage, offices and booking hall in connection with the company's business as charabanc and omnibus proprietors but in 1933 was leased out to Gaumont Ideal Ltd.

Following the decision of Sunderland Corporation to replace its tramway service to the docks by a bus service and the unavailability of the replacement vehicles by the required date, Northern was contracted to run this service together with one from Humbledon to Sea Lane, one from Sunderland to Whitburn and a further service from Castletown to Sunderland which ran from outside the Borough boundary with the profits arising in the Borough being shared (although in the event none were made!). This arrangement continued until 1929 when operation of the Docks and Humbledon to Sea Lane services passed back to the Corporation and the Whitburn service was discontinued. Similarly, during the following year, Northern hired buses to Jarrow & District Traction Co. as is documented later. As far as the fleet was concerned,

1928 witnessed the largest intake of vehicles in any single year since the company's foundation. No fewer than 85 new buses and coaches were bought by Northern plus a further 11 for Tynemouth & District - and there were secondhand examples in addition to these. All the new arrivals were single deckers with Northern receiving 65 BMMO SOS QLs fitted with Brush or Ransomes 37-seat bodywork, 10 BMMO SOS QLC-type charabancs with Short Bros. 30-seat bodies and 10 ADC 416Ds with Hall Lewis 36-seat bus bodywork and Tynemouth & District gaining 5 Brush-bodied BMMO SOS QLs and 6 ADC 416A buses with Hall Lewis bodies. In addition, although consideration was given to the modernisation of 63 of the Northern rebuilds and 25 Daimler Y-type buses, in the event it was instead decided to only refurbish 25 of the rebuilds. Indeed, the arrival of such a large number of new vehicles allowed many of the older examples to be withdrawn from service in addition to considerably increasing the overall size of the fleet. The two secondhand buses taken into stock, if they can be correctly described in this manner, were both BMMO SOS QC-type 32-seat charabancs. Acquired from Midland Red, it is doubtful if either ever ran for their original owner as they were only a week old when they arrived at Bensham.

During 1928, several members of the General County Omnibus Co. consortium, who had since 1926 competed against Northern between Newcastle, Chester-le-Street and Durham, offered to sell their interests, but as their asking prices were regarded as being exorbitant, discussions were never seriously started. Meanwhile, it was proposed to form a new private company to purchase the omnibus business of Emmerson Bros. of Throckley who ran from Newcastle to Hexham and Carlisle and terms were agreed in October. During the following month, however, these negotiations were broken off by Emmersons who then began discussions with the LNER. Later, in October 1929, when Northern and the LNER were negotiating a working agreement, Northern was again hopeful that it might acquire Emmersons, but a month later it was reported that the LNER had reached the conclusion that Emmersons should instead pass to United. Before the year ended, Northern did, however, succeed in acquiring a further business when, on 24 October 1928, that of Hallett's Bus Service of Pelton Lane Ends was purchased. Hallett's route from Murton to Durham and three buses - a Robson-bodied 14-seat Chevrolet R-type, a Young-bodied 14-seat Reo and a Young-bodied 12-seat Thornycroft A2 - were included in the deal, although the buses, being non-standard as far as their new owner was concerned, were all withdrawn and sold at the start of 1929.

1929 proved to be a year of mixed fortunes. February saw the arrival of yet another new type of bus when the first of 40 BMMO SOS M-type single deckers arrived (referred to as 'Madam' and which, ironically, were the first to be licensed by Northern as BMMOs). These had a dropped frame chassis which enabled their Ransomes 34-seat bodies to be constructed to a lower and more modern design, and by September all had entered service to allow several older members of the fleet to be withdrawn. The temporary increase in the size of the fleet proved to be invaluable during the summer months when the vast North East Coast Exhibition held on Newcastle Town Moor from May to October generated a massive increase in the company's traffic. Soon after the arrival of the first of this new generation of omnibus, the business of G.R.Hunter of Hebburn-on-Tyne was acquired (on 25 February) together with 3 buses - a pair of two year-old Durland-Mason bodied 26-seat Gilford 166OT and a 28-seat Albion PKA26. Hunter

The first buses to be purchased by Northern with a dropped-frame chassis were BMMO SOS M-types which made their debut in 1929. One of these, which were nicknamed 'Madam', Ransomes-bodied 438 (BR7027) is seen here when new and like all Northern's single deckers at that time, it carried its destination details on a board on the front bulkhead rather than being fitted with roller blind destination equipment. (Go-Ahead Northern)

was a comparatively new operator who had only entered the passenger vehicle business some two years earlier when he had started a service from Jarrow to Newcastle. Subsequently, Tynemouth & District, who in 1928 had started operations to Newcastle jointly with Newcastle Corporation, found itself short of buses due to increased demands and to ease this situation, Northern transferred two of its 1927 BMMO QLs to this subsidiary.

Meanwhile, Jarrow & District Traction Co. Ltd. was struggling for survival against competition from a variety of sources. At the start of its operations it had been granted through running powers by South Shields Corporation to the Pier Head in that town, but, following a disagreement on revenue sharing, this facility was withdrawn on 17 June 1911 and was not reinstated until 14 July 1922. From this date the route was served throughout by both undertakings as opposed to the original operation by one company only, but only lasted in this form for five years. After yet another disagreement resulting from Northern's bus operation over the tram route, South Shields Corporation on 17 July 1927 once again withdrew its permission for the Jarrow company to run through to Pier Head, thus leaving it in a very uncertain position. With the track and overhead needing extensive repair and renewal and the rolling stock being outdated, massive capital expenditure was needed if the system was to continue. Added to this, Northern's buses were more comfortable and faster than the trams and, as a result, the number of passengers carried by Jarrow & District was falling almost weekly. After much heart-searching, it was reluctantly decided that the tramway system must close, and this it did on 30 June 1929. On the following day, buses hired from Northern General took over from the trams and these continued to maintain the service until July 1930 when Jarrow & District's licence was officially transferred to Northern. This was not the end of the company, however, due to it continuing to own property, and it was not until after this had been sold that it was finally put into liquidation on 27 October 1948. After the closure of the tramway, the depot in Swinburne Street was then used as a bus depot for a short time before being closed in 1930 after which it served as a store for Northern's surplus vehicles etc. before eventually being demolished in 1946.

Returning to 1929, Northern opened a new depot in South Shields on 21 November of that year, an occasion for which a BMMO XL-type was hired from Midland Red, while on the service front a new route was introduced from Consett to Newcastle via Blackhill and Burnopfield and Tynemouth, Wakefields and Newcastle Corporation began a joint service on 1 July from Tynemouth to Newcastle via North Shields and the new Coast Road. Additionally, the Newcastle to Consett route via Shotley Bridge and Hamsterley was extended from Consett to Knitsley whilst the joint service with United from Newcastle to Middlesbrough, introduced in May 1928, was discontinued on 14 February and on 1 April Northern took over South Shields Corporation's service from that town to Boldon Colliery. The most striking development, however, concerned the service from Newcastle to Liverpool via Manchester. So popular had this become, that it was decided to convert it to a 'Limited Stop' operation and run it every two hours jointly with West Yorkshire Road Car Co.Ltd., Yorkshire (Woollen District) Electric Tramways Ltd. and North Western Road Car Co.Ltd. These companies, together with Northern, formed themselves into the "Limited Stop Pool" under the banner of which the increased frequency commenced on 15 May. Meanwhile, the new omnibus station at Durham, part of which was leased to United, was opened in March.

THE RAILWAYS GAIN AN INTEREST

On 28 December 1929, the London & North Eastern Railway Company acquired a shareholding in the Northern General company and entered into a working agreement with the object of co-ordinating rail and road passenger services in the district. This resulted in the L.N.E.R's services (Durham to Shotley Bridge via Lanchester and Consett, and Durham to Sacriston), both of which were in Northern's operating area, being transferred to the company from 14 January 1930 upon which same date 6 of the railway company's Hall Lewis-bodied Thornycroft single deckers were purchased by Northern. In addition to running buses in its own right, the L.N.E.R. had purchased on 25 March 1929 a controlling interest in an operating company on North Tyneside which traded under the title of Wakefield's Motors Ltd. and was associated with Eastern Express Motors Ltd. with whom it shared two of its directors, and on that same date this was transferred to Northern General. Wakefield's Motors Ltd. had been registered on 30 September 1927 and ran from Tynemouth to Newcastle via the Coast Road, subsequently adding a second service to Newcastle from North Shields. In December 1928, expansion had been achieved with the acquisition of the 8-vehicle business of Archer Brothers Ltd. of Tynemouth (although only 3 of the vehicles involved in the deal were retained) and the taking over of Mr.Wakefield's charabanc and touring business (founded in 1919) and in February 1929 acquired the one bus business of H.Dunn. Later that year, on 31 October, Northern purchased all the shares in Wakefields not held by the LNER and also the company's depot in Albion Road, North Shields, following this by the purchase of 6 AEC Reliance which Wakefields had on hire from Thompson McKay and 2 Daimler buses hired from their makers all of which were immediately hired back to the North Shields company. Thus by this time Wakefields was operating a fleet of some 20 buses and coaches. The services maintained by the company operated between Wallsend, North Shields and Whitley Bay, between Tynemouth and Newcastle and between Whitley Bay and Newcastle and in addition to these, excursions were operated to a wide range of destinations. Though being placed under the control of Tynemouth & District from January 1932 Wakefield's retained its separate identity and its fleet name continued to be displayed on all the vehicles allocated to it.

In addition to the passing of the 1930 Road Traffic Act which for the first time introduced nationwide controls on the licencing of bus and coach services instead of leaving them in the hands of local authorities, the year proved to be extremely eventful as far as Northern General was concerned. As well as gaining control of Wakefield's, the company

One of the Thornycroft single deckers operated by General County prior to the company's passage to Northern General, this example was never operated by the latter company. (Go-Ahead Northern)

Northern's bus station at Wellington Street, Gateshead was modelled on railway station lines.

further strengthened its position by taking over a number of other operators within its area. One of these was General County Omnibus Company Limited of Birtley, County Durham which rather than being "an independent", was a consortium made up mainly of owner drivers, some of whom had originally traded as North Durham Motor Users Association. The man behind this venture was Mr.J.A.Kay, an ironmonger since 1910 who had later added some petrol pumps at the rear of his premises in Durham Road, Birtley. Once a year Mr.Kay had organised a trip to the seaside for the poor people of Birtley, calling upon all the local independent bus owners for assistance in doing so. Resulting from this, a consortium was soon formed from the fifteen to twenty operators concerned, with Mr.Kay supplying the petrol, oil and tickets etc. Although operating successfully under the title of "General", some confusion subsequently arose when a similar association, Durham & District General Motor Services Ltd. also began to use the "General" name. This situation was ultimately resolved, however, when Mr.Kay's consortium began calling itself "General County" following the registration of the company as General County Omnibus Co. Ltd. on 21 February 1927. Eric Pattinson, whose brother was a member of the rival Durham & District association, had surprisingly joined General County when he took delivery of a new Thornycroft 14-seat bus whilst at this same time the original route from Newcastle to Chester-le-Street was extended southwards to Durham City. As a result of it not being licenced to ply for hire in Gateshead or Newcastle, however, no passengers could be picked up after leaving Low Fell on northbound journeys or set down before this point when travelling southwards. Despite this, so popular did this service become that within a few months a second Thornycroft was purchased, on this occasion with seating for 20 passengers. By now the growth of the consortium's fleet presented a need for premises in which it could all be housed and to this end, Pattinson together with a Mr.Moffat who was an engineer with the General County associates, together took over a garage at Low Fell belonging to a Mr.Whittle who had recently become bankrupt. A company under the title of Pattinson & Moffat was formed to run this new garage which, in addition to carrying out commercial repairs and selling petrol, also gained the Renault agency. As the fleet of the General County consortium continued to grow, it was not long before a number of new services were being pioneered, one of which was an extension westward of the original route south of Plawsworth, running via Sacriston, Langley Park and Esh Winning to Waterhouses. Later, the Newcastle to Durham service was extended to Sedgefield and Stockton-on-Tees, eventually continuing in 1930 to Middlesbrough after passing to Northern. Following a disagreement, however, Pattinson left General County in 1928 and moved to Sunderland to set up a new

The first brand new buses purchased by Tynemouth & District were 6 Brush-bodied 31-seat BMMO S-type single deckers, one of which (FT1385) is seen here working the Whitley Bay - Blyth service. New in 1926, it gave nine years service before being withdrawn in 1935. (K.A.Jenkinson collection)

*Numerically the last of six Hall Lewis-bodied ADC 416As purchased new by Tynemouth & District in 1928, FT1824 is pictured before its entry into service.
(K.A.Jenkinson collection)*

Seen in this snowy winter scene operating one of Northern's remote rural services is a 1927 vintage Brush-bodied BMMO SOS Q-type buses.   (K.A.Jenkinson collection)

business under the name of Underwood and during the next twelve months J.A.Kay purchased all the shares and buses of the various constituent members of the General County concern. Despite the company continuing to flourish, Mr.Kay accepted an offer from Northern in January for the whole of his shareholding and 36 buses, all of which were immediately resold to a newly constituted General County Omnibus Company which was to be operated as a subsidiary of Northern General. The bulk of these were 20-seaters which were soon replaced by larger buses hired from Northern. One problem, however, was that General County operated to Stockton and thus crossed the Northern/United dividing line at Durham as well as the Esh Winning and Waterhouses section also being over the boundary and thus it was proposed that although these services would be continued, United would receive the receipts but would pay the working expenses plus 2d per mile for interest and depreciation. United refused to accept this proposal, however, but eventually agreed to purchase part of General County together with 11 buses, although this was not completed until September 1931. Meanwhile, around April 1930, General County purchased seven omnibus licences and two buses from various independent operators in Stanley and Chester-le-Street who collectively traded as Durham & District General Motor Services Ltd. Although all the General County services were operated by Northern from 1 March 1933, the company continued to exist as a subsidiary until May 1936 when it was liquidated.

In October 1929, the question of purchasing a share in Eastern Express Motors Ltd. of West Hartlepool was discussed but was adjourned for further information to be furnished as to its then ownership. Before this matter could be considered further, however, it was learned that the company had been sold to United on 1 January 1930 and this prompted Northern to immediately complain to the Darlington-based operator that this was in breach of their territorial agreement and asking them to withdraw the Eastern Express services which ran north of the dividing line. In March the chairmen of the two companies met and reached an agreement whereby on 11 April Northern purchased 23 Eastern Express buses plus a garage at Hetton-le-Hole which was not used for long and was leased to a firm of corn merchants in 1932. Northern then paid £500 per annum for the next five years to the directors, Messrs Brook and Hodge for not operating road passengers transport in their area during that period. Also in 1930 United agreed to discontinue its Newcastle - Keswick service and in return Northern would not carry local passengers between Newcastle and Hexham on their service. Northern consented to United continuing its Newcastle to High Spen route whilst agreement was reached between the two companies regarding United's London services which also crossed the boundary. All the buses taken over with Eastern Express were ADC 416s, AEC 426s and AEC Reliances, the oldest of which was little more than two years of age and some of these survived in service until as late as 1948. In addition, the

A display mounted at Northern's new South Shields depot in 1929 to mark its opening showed a selection of the company's vehicles dating from 1924. From left to right are a 1924 unidentified NGT-rebuilt Daimler Y-type, 1925 BMMO S-type 241 (PT6245), 1929-rebuilt NGT-Daimler Y-type D150 (CN1883), 1927 BMMO SOS Q-type 318 (CN2867), 1928 BMMO SOS QL-type 402 (UP1728), 1929 BMMO SOS M-type 466 (CN4059) and HA4988, a BMMO SOS RR-type single decker which was borrowed from Midland Red for the occasion.   (K.A.Jenkinson collection)

One of Eastern Express Motors Dodson-bodied AEC Reliances, EF4264 joined the Northern General fleet on 1 January 1930 and was given fleet number 501. It is seen here a few days before its transfer of ownership operating a service to Sunderland.   (T.Godfrey collection)

One of two Hall Lewis-bodied Daimler CF6s ordered by the London & North Eastern Railway and allocated to Wakefields Motors in April 1929, both this bus and its sister were transferred to the Northern General fleet in January 1930. Numbered 503 & 504 they survived only until 1934 when they were withdrawn and sold to a Newcastle dealer. (Daimler)

Several AEC Reliances were acquired by Northern with the business of Eastern Express Motors Ltd in 1930, one of which, Dodson-bodied 509 (EF4243), is seen here enroute to Consett after gaining Northern fleet names on its original operator's livery. This bus enjoyed a long life with its new owner and was not withdrawn until 1948. (T.Godfrey collection)

acquisition of Eastern Express' services from West Hartlepool to Sunderland and Newcastle and from Easington Lane to Chester-le-Street and Newcastle gave Northern a second access to West Hartlepool.

Following the acquisition of shares in the Northern General company by the London & North Eastern Railway, as has been stated earlier the latter's road passenger transport interests were transferred to Northern and although these greatly strengthened the company's position in County Durham, this was not sufficient to deter it from seeking further expansion. This led on 15 March to the acquisition of 7 vehicles from Stobie & Curry (Castle Motor Services Ltd.) of Forest Hall, Newcastle who operated the service from Newcastle to South Shields via White Mare Pool jointly with Northern. Of these, all but 2 were Gilfords of the 166SD and 166OT types, the odd men out being Albion PMA28s which were immediately despatched on hire to General County to whom they were ultimately sold and who later in the year also added some of the recently-acquired Eastern Express buses to its fleet. As part of the deal, Oscar Curry was appointed Manager of Wakefields Motors Ltd.

The final acquisition of 1930 came on 1 June when 10 buses (a

Painted in an unrelieved red livery, 480 (CN4247) was a BMMO SOS SRR-type fitted with Short Bros. 30-seat coach bodywork with outward-hinged front door. In addition to having a roller blind destination indicator incorporated into its front roof dome, it also had a hinged destination board mounted on its roof and route boards above its side windows which gave details of the Newcastle to Liverpool service for which it had been purchased. (Go-Ahead Northern)

One of the buses acquired with the business of Stobie & Currie (Castle Motor Services) was 1929 Albion PMB28 520 (VK41). Seen here after being fitted with a new body by Short Bros. in 1932, it was transferred to Northern's subsidiary General County in 1934, returning to the parent fleet two years later when it was renumbered 731. (K.A.Jenkinson collection)

35-seat Vulcan, an elderly Daimler CKA, 7 Leyland PLSC1s and a Leyland PLSC3) were purchased by Northern from Atkinson & Browell (A.B.C) of Consett following an agreement reached on 27 March. Edward Atkinson and George Browell had, together with a third partner, Davidson, (who had left the company by 1930), entered the bus industry almost immediately after the first world war operating a service from Consett to Newcastle via Blackhill, Dipton and Sunniside and in addition, they were dealers and haulage contractors, having held the Guy and Vulcan franshises for a time during the mid 'twenties. Replacing Davidson in the partnership was Albert Browell.

As far as new vehicles were concerned, 1930 was a somewhat quiet year with only 11 single deckers being taken into stock. Of these, 10 were coach-bodied BMMO SRR-type 30-seaters which, ordered as 'improved XL-type', were bought for the Newcastle to Liverpool service whilst the eleventh was a BMMO IM4-type 34-seat bus, the chassis of which had been rebuilt by BMMO from an MM-type in 1929. Additionally, 28 BMMO COD-type 34-seat buses were ordered and then reduced to 21 before being ultimately cancelled whilst the order for the 'improved XL-type' had originally called for 12 such vehicles. By far the most outstanding additions to the fleet, however, - albeit temporary -were a pair of demonstrators borrowed from their manufacturers for evaluation purposes. Both were double deckers, one a highbridge all-Leyland TD1, the other a lowbridge Short Bros-bodied AEC Regent, and, making their debut in August, they were the first double deckers to be operated for almost ten years since the demise of the old open-top Daimlers. Although registered by Northern, both buses were ultimately returned to their owners, the AEC departing in December 1930 followed by the Leyland in April 1931 after their "in-service" trials were completed. Sunderland District also evaluated a Leyland TD1. On the operational front, Northern began to use Marlborough Crescent bus station in Newcastle from 21 August.

CONSOLIDATION IN SUNDERLAND

If 1930 had been an eventful year, then what can be said of 1931? The first day of this new year saw the acquisition of Sunderland District Omnibus Company Limited, a large and important undertaking with widespread operations in north-east Durham. The foundations of this company had been laid back in 1899 when the United Kingdom Tramways, Light Railways and Electrical Syndicate Ltd. applied to various councils on Wearside for permission to construct and operate a tramway from Houghton-le-Spring to the Sunderland town boundary at Grangetown with branches to Easington, Fence Houses and Penshaw Station. Authorisation for the majority of the application was given in 1900 but due to financial difficulties, the company was unable to proceed. Consequently, a new company was formed under the title of Sunderland and District Electric Tramways Limited and construction commenced in January 1904. The first service from Houghton-le-Spring to Grangetown via The Herringtons, Silksworth and Ryhope, together with the branches to Fence Houses and Penshaw Station opened on 10 June 1905 followed by the branch to Hetton Station on 20 October 1905 and that to Easington Lane in August 1906. The final part of the latter to Easington was never built, however, and neither was that from New Silksworth to Sunderland and thus the final route mileage was just over 14.25 miles, the most of which was single track with passing loops. At first the new company had its own electric power station but this was closed in 1908 after which the power supply was gained from the Durham Collieries Power Company whose premises were next to Sunderland District's depot and headquarters at Philadelphia. The company began its operations with a fleet of 30 double deck tramcars, half of which had open tops, and these were joined in 1908 by a further 3 double deck balcony cars. Of the original fleet, the 15 covered-top Arbel cars which were of French origin were far from successful, and despite 4 of them being extensively rebuilt in 1909, all were withdrawn in 1913 and were then dismantled for scrap. Their replacements were 15 Brush double deck balcony cars which in 1920 were joined by a further 8 of this same make and type.

Being undercapitalised from the start, it was inevitable that sooner or later the company would encounter financial difficulties and this it did in 1913, with the assistance of the disasterous Arbel trams, causing a Reciever/Manager to be appointed. Had it not been for the intervention of World War I which gave the company a reprieve, Sunderland and District Electric Tramways Ltd. would no doubt have gone into bankruptcy. After managing to survive, the company realised that the only way forward was to replace its tramway with motor buses and thus in May 1924 closed its Herrington Burn to Penshaw branch, introducing buses between these two points during the following month and extending the route to Washington. A further conversion was undertaken in June 1924 when buses replaced the trams on the Houghton-le-Spring to Easington Lane route which was then extended to Sunderland via the main Durham road - on a collision course with Northern! For this purpose, 24 new buses were purchased, all but 2 of which were AECs 202s and 403s with United or Strachan & Brown 24 or 32-seat bodywork. The remaining pair were 30-seat dual door Bristol 4-tonners with Bristol bodywork.

Following the successful introduction of motor omnibuses, and, as a result of the urgent need for the renewal of the permanent way, a

Sunderland District Transport placed 24 Bristol 4-ton single deckers in service during 1924, all of which were fitted with Ransomes 26-seat dual-door bodies. One of these buses, 20 (PT4718) is pictured with its crew in Borough Road, Sunderland whilst working the New Silksworth service. (K.Richardson)

Wearing Sunderland District's original livery of mid-blue lower panels, dark blue waistband and white roof and window surrounds is one of the company's 1925 United-bodied AEC 403-type buses seen here working the Easington Lane service.
(S.A.Staddon collection)

decision was taken on 6 October 1924 to completely abandon the tramway as soon as possible and replace it with buses. In view of this, the name of the company was changed to Sunderland District Transport Company Limited in February 1925 soon after another tram route had succumbed to the might of the motor bus. This was the Fence Houses branch on which the last tram operated in January. The demise of the rest of the system was swift, with the Grangetown to Herrington Burn route being converted in March and the final day of operation over the remaining routes being 12 July 1925. In order to accomplish this programme, the bus fleet had of course to be greatly expanded and in 1925 no fewer than 34 new single deckers arrived. 24 of these were 4-ton Bristols whilst the balance were AEC 403s, all of which had dual-door bodywork by United or Ransomes.

The financial burden attached to such a large fleet transformation again put the company into difficulties and once again a Receiver/Manager was appointed following talks held with Northern in April 1926 and a further offer being made in May 1927 as previously mentioned. This resulted in the company being re-formed yet again on 18 June 1927 when the Sunderland District Omnibus Company Limited was registered. The first new buses to be purchased by the reconstituted company were 20 Leyland PLSC3s which arrived in 1927 and these were joined the following year by another 6 of this same type. Meanwhile, in that year the company purchased a site in Houghton-le-Spring upon which it was intended to erect a new garage, but upon finding that tenders for its construction were too high, it was instead decided to extend the Philadelphia premises and the land at Houghton was ultimately resold. Having turned down the approaches by Northern, Sunderland District set about seeking expansion and during 1928 purchased two small independent operators, the first of which was Millward of New Washington who ran 3 Guy 26-seat buses over a route from Washington to Gateshead which after its was extended back to Herrington Burn. Soon afterwards, in September, the business of T.Longhorn & Sons of Walkergate, Newcastle-upon-Tyne whose service from Newcastle to West Hartlepool together with 3 Gilford 28-seat buses was acquired in August and at the same time negotiations were entered into for the purchase of Eastern Express Motors Ltd. but were quickly aborted after finding the price asked was beyond their reach. By now having a need for an additional operational base to supplement that at Philadelphia, the company opened a small depot in Crow Street, Sunderland, which it leased from Vaux Brewery (whose chairman was also chairman of Sunderland District!). Following discussions with Northern early in 1929 an approach was made to the LNER with the suggestion that they should acquire an interest in the company, but after examining the books it was reported in May that they were not proceeding with these negotiations. In June 1929, by which time the company's services had been extended to Durham and Chester-le-Street from Houghton-le-Spring and Fence Houses respectively, a service had been introduced from South Shields to Sunderland which had also been extended to Durham from 1 December 1928. After this date working arrangements were made by Sunderland District and Northern for their competitive routes upon which the interavailability of return tickets was introduced. This co-ordination brought Sunderland District into Worswick Street, Newcastle and Northern's Durham bus stations for the first time.

1929 saw the fleet grow yet further with the arrival of 6 new Leyland Tiger TS1 buses fitted with Leyland bodywork, these being joined in 1930 by a further 4 together with 6 Leyland LT2s and 3 Park Royal-bodied Karrier Chaser Six 32-seaters. The latter, however, being 27ft. 5in. in length, were not permitted to run in Gateshead. During the following year the company had thoughts of running a service from Sunderland to South Shields via the Coast Road but were refused a licence for this. With some determination to fulfil their plans, they then attempted to purchase Economic (Anderson & Wilson) of Whitburn who already operated this service, but, as they were not eager to sell, the talks came to nothing. In May of that year, Smiths Safeway started operations between West Hartlepool and Newcastle, and, fearing this new competitor, Sunderland District almost immediately entered into agreements with both Northern and United for the interavailability of tickets between West Hartlepool and Sunderland. In October, it was reported that Safeway, who it was understood was in financial difficulties, was to be taken over by a Mr.Edmond of Middlesbrough and that it was possible that United were backing him in order to gain a further foothold in this area. This caused some concern as it was feared that if this were true, it might affect the territorial agreement between Sunderland District and United. Meanwhile, negotiations were again started in September 1930 for the sale of Sunderland District to Northern General, these being eventually concluded during the closing months of the year with the date of transfer being agreed as 22 January 1931. Northern was unable to purchase the whole of the share capital of the company, but the 99% it gained was sufficient to give it full control, the remaining shares ultimately being acquired under Section 155 of the Companies Act 1929. However, rather than bring its new acquisition completely under its own umbrella by complete integration, Northern decided to retain it as a subsidiary similar to Tynemouth and Wakefields, and as a result its headquarters remained at Philadelphia. The Sunderland District board of directors resigned on 6 February 1931 when they were replaced by Northern nominees. Northern's vehicle-buying policy was soon implemented however, when, in addition to 6 Leyland LT2s already on order by Sunderland District to replace the last of its Bristols, the company received 4 new BMMO IM6-type single deckers. Northern itself also took delivery of 10 buses of this type together with 10 of the 4-cylinder engined BMMO IM4s. With these vehicles, route number indicators were introduced to the Northern fleet for the first time, these being mounted on the front bulkhead below the canopy.

A further acquisition made during 1931 was that of G.W.Hetherington & Co. Ltd. (who traded as A1 Bus Service) of Coundon who operated 13 buses and two services from Bishop Auckland to Newcastle and to Sunderland crossing the United-Northern boundary. In this instance, the whole of the issued share capital was actually purchased on 17 September 1931 by Mr.J.A.Kay (General & County Omnibus Co. Ltd.) for and on behalf of Northern to whom all the shares were immediately passed. Hetherington then sold 5 buses to United Automobile Services on 30 November while Northern bought 3 (a pair 0f 20-seat Graham-Dodges and a 26-seat AJS Pilot) in November with Sunderland District purchasing a Leyland TS2 in January 1932, the remainder being disposed of to other operators. Following this, G.W.Hetherington & Co. Ltd. went into liquidation in

A general view of Northern's garage and offices at Chester-le-Street which had original been opened in 1913 by Gateshead Tramways showing its extension which was necessary to enable it to accommodate more vehicles.

February 1932, and, until its routes could be re-apportioned (that from Sunderland to Bishop Auckland to Northern, Sunderland District and United and that from Newcastle to Bishop Auckland to United and General County) they were worked by General County. Additionally, in March 1932 Northern purchased the goodwill and omnibus business of Mr.George Flynn who ran between Hebburn and Jarrow, although on this occasion no vehicles were involved.

Prior to the above, the tramway operated by Tynemouth & District which had continued with little change since its inception was by now reaching the stage where large capital expenditure was required if it was to continue. Although it had been well maintained throughout its history, the track and overhead were both starting to cause concern and rather than invest hugh sums in their renewal, it was decided to abandon the tramway and substitute buses over its length. The first stage of the conversion took place on 12 April 1930 when the company began a 10 minute bus service over the whole of the tram route and reduced the tram service to a 15 minute headway. On 18 July 1931 the original single deck buses on the route were replaced by double deckers and the trams were finally withdrawn after the end of service on Tuesday 4 August. In order to bolster the fleet until new buses were delivered, a number of vehicles had to be borrowed from both Northern and Wakefield's on a temporary basis. The first of the new double deckers purchased by Tynemouth were Short Bros-highbridge bodied AEC Regents, 2 of which arrived in 1931 with the remaining 10 following early in 1932 plus 4 for Wakefields for which AEC accepted the 6 1928 ADCs in part exchange. These were the first double deckers to be purchased by the Northern Group since the old 32-seat open-toppers of World War I vintage, and with their petrol engines they provided passengers with an extremely quiet and smooth ride. In addition to operating over its former tram route, Tynemouth also maintained services from Whitley Bay to Blyth (started in August 1922 and operated jointly with United with whom a territorial agreement had been signed and which had by 1928 been extended to Gateshead), from Willington Square to Clousden Hill via Wallsend and from Whitley Bay, Tynemouth and North Shields via the Coast Road to Newcastle.

Having concluded its evaluation of the two double deck demonstrators, Northern had decided that the AEC Regent was the best suited to its needs and placed an order for delivery in the summer of 1932. The first seven of these new double deckers used the old Regent chassis of 25ft. length and were fitted with Brush 52-seat rear entrance highbridge bodies whilst the eighth had the later-type 26ft. long Regent chassis which enabled a 60-seat body to be fitted. This too was built by Brush and was of rear entrance highbridge layout. A further double decker acquired by Northern in 1932 was a former AEC Regent demonstrator with Short Bros bodywork which had started life in December 1929. Sunderland District also received its first double deckers with the arrival of 10 Brush-bodied AEC Regents which were placed in service on 1 August 1932 on the Sunderland to Easington Lane and Sunderland to Silksworth services and which caused the front doorway to Philadelphia depot to be heightened to allow them passage. Towards the end of the year, in October, an unusual double decker was hired by Northern from Midland Red to whom it had been delivered new but had never operated. Of that company's own manufacture to its REDD design and fitted with a Short Bros 52-seat highbridge body it was ultimately purchased by Northern in October 1933 and remained unique as being the only BMMO-built double decker in the north-east.

The first new double deckers to be purchased by Northern since the First World War period were eight Brush-bodied highbridge AEC Regents which made their debut in 1932. One of these, 564 (CN5242) is seen before its entry into service in July of that year.   (Go-Ahead Northern)

Starting life in the Northern fleet in 1932, Brush-bodied AEC Regent CN5242 was that same year transferred to Tynemouth & District who numbered it T50. In 1941 it was transferred to Tyneside Tramways and in 1951 returned to Northern whom it continued to serve until its withdrawal in June 1956. (Go-Ahead Northern)

The last of the eight new double deckers delivered in 1932 differed in its appearance from the other seven by being of 26ft (instead of 25ft.) length and carrying a prototype body built by Brush which featured an attractively-sloped front. After receiving an AEC oil engine in 1939 in place of its original petrol unit and a new NCB highbridge body in 1943, it remained in service until 1950. (Go-Ahead Northern)

New to Archer Brothers, North Shields and later operated by Wakefield's Motors, Leyland PLSC3 570 (FT1740) was acquired by Northern General in 1932. Before entering service with its new owner, its chassis was rebuilt and lengthened and was then fitted with a new 38-seat Short Bros. body, on which the panel forward of the rear nearside wheel arch was cut upwards to allow the stowage of the spare wheel. (Go-Ahead Northern)

During 1932, as a result of the general slump which was affecting all the industries within Northern's operating area including the coal trade, Northern decided that it ought to do something to help the miners, who were after all, amongst the company's best customers. Coupled with a sudden petrol price rise of 3d a gallon on 14 September of that year, which Northern estimated would increase their operating costs by some £21,000 per annum, the company immediately set about finding a way in which this additional burden could be reduced and at the same time might help the miners. The outcome was that it was decided to try running a bus on coal gas carried under pressure in bottles supplied by the Newcastle and Gateshead Gas Company - itself an extremely enterprising undertaking - and to this end, one of Northern's rebuilt CB-type Daimlers was chosen for this experiment. Its conversion in October 1932 included the fitting of two gas storage cylinders which were attached to the chassis frame behind the rear axle, and which containing sufficient gas to operate the bus for 30 miles. One of the problems immediately associated with this form of operation was to arrange for the rapid recharging of the cylinders, it taking around five minutes to transfer gas from storage bottles to the cylinders on the bus. After suffering further problems associated with

573 (CN5506), a 1933 AEC Regent originally fitted with Short Bros. front entrance lowbridge bodywork was rebodied by NCB to MoS specification in 1943 as seen here in this post-war view. Withdrawn from service in 1952 it was scrapped by Northern in March of the following year. (T.Godfrey collection)

The first of Northern's own-designed SE6 single deckers was 586 (CN5674) which made its debut in July 1933 fitted with a Short Bros. 45-seat front entrance body. Of three-axle configuration, the SE6 had its Hercules petrol engine mounted on the offside of its chassis immediately behind the front axle as can be seen in this photograph. Withdrawn from service in 1942, it ended its life as a static caravan in Northumberland.
(Go-Ahead Northern)

the Daimler engine, the cylinders were, in May 1933, transferred to one of Northern's 1928 BMMO SOS QL-type buses and whilst this performed marginally better, it was still much slower than a conventional petrol-engined bus. It was, however, the economics of the scheme that finally killed it off; the cost of electricity for compressing the gas being much higher than the cost of the gas itself. As the very meagre benefit the miner might expect to receive from the use of coal gas in this manner could not materially improve his lot, and there was no economy as far as Northern was concerned, the scheme was abandoned. Whilst both the gas company and Northern took all the credit they could for the scheme by placing notices in the buses concerned so that all could see that the bus was running on coal gas to help the miners, passengers were never told that they were sitting over cylinders containing gas at 3,000lb per sq.in!

Meanwhile, the now customary inter fleet transfers continued with a Leyland PLSC3, an ADC 416 and a trio of AEC 426s joining Northern from Wakefield's, who received in their place 4 new Short Bros-bodied AEC Regent double deckers. The ADC was immediately despatched on loan to General County where it remained until that company's demise four years later whilst additionally, Northern purchased a Thornycroft charabanc from Wakefields which it immediately converted into a lorry.

Several service changes were made during the early 'thirties and new routes were opened up from Stanley to Chopwell in 1930 and Seaham Harbour to Carr's Estate (now known as Deneside) and Consett to Delves in 1931. In the event, however, the Chopwell service was to be short-lived and in 1931 it was cut back to Rowlands Gill. During the following year, the Consett to Newcastle service became jointly operated with Venture & Reed, although the latter entered Newcastle via Scotswood Road whereas Northern ran via Swalwell and Dunston. Venture & Reed were strongly opposed to this move which had been forced upon them by the Traffic Commissioner and which lost them one bus per hour! Later, in 1932, Sunderland Corporation joined in the running of the service from that town to Castletown which was at that same time extended to North Hylton Road Ends. Northern and its subsidiaries by now had a network of services covering almost the whole of North and South Tyneside and a large part of County Durham and serving numerous different types of connurbation. From the shipyards on both banks of the Tyne and on Wearside to the coal mining areas of County Durham, and from the open countryside to the steel works of Consett as well as in towns and cities such as Newcastle-upon-Tyne, Gateshead, North Shields, Tynemouth, South Shields, Sunderland and Durham, the buses of Northern and its subsidiaries were a common sight. With so much industry within its operating area, workers services already played a major role in the company's economy just as they were to continue to do for the next forty or more years.

In many ways 1933 proved to be a comparatively quiet year and, as far as further expansion was concerned, witnessed no acquisitions of independent operators. All but one of the new single deckers purchased came, predictably, from the BMMO factory at Birmingham with 2 IM6s being allocated to Wakefields (who sold them to Northern in the same year, replacing them with 2 new IM4s) and 10 of this same type entering service with Northern itself, two of which were immediately loaned to its General County subsidiary to whom they were ultimately sold in 1934/5. The new double deckers broke with the previous year's tradition however, by having bodywork featuring a front entrance and front staircase. The 3 Brush-bodied AEC Regents for Sunderland District were built to highbridge layout whereas, more unusually, the 3 Regents delivered to Northern were of lowbridge configuration with bodywork by Short Bros, these displacing 3 of the earlier Regents which then passed to Tynemouth. Northern's new trio were to remain unique in the fleet as all subsequent double deck purchases were of highbridge layout. Inter fleet transfers saw 6 BMMO S-type charabancs join Northern from the Wakefield's fleet, 2 of which were immediately rebodied with Short Bros B36F bodies which, combined with their normal control chassis layout gave them a decidedly odd appearance whilst in exchange, Wakefield's gained 4 overhauled BMMO QLC-type charabancs from Northern. Without doubt, however, the most unusual - and revolutionary - bus to make its appearance during 1933 was a high-capacity 6-wheel single decker constructed in Northern's own workshops at Bensham and intended for use on routes upon which low bridges precluded the use of double deckers. This had been designed by Northern's chief engineer, Major G.W.Hayter in conjunction with AEC and had its engine mounted at the side of its chassis aft of the front axle. Powered by an American-built Hercules petrol engine, its three-axle layout and new engine position

The three Burlingham-bodied Commer Centaur coaches purchased by Northern in 1934 are seen here when new. From left to right are 624, 626 & 625 (CN6105/7/6), all of which had all-weather canvas roofs.
(Go-Ahead Northern)

With the Northern name prominently displayed on its radiator header tank, 1934 Short Bros-bodied BMMO SOS ON-type 617 (CN6023) typifies vehicles of this make with their narrow cab which did not protrude above the radiator and thus gave a somewhat unbalanced effect. Seen here in pre-war days, 617 was commandeered by the War Departmrnt in July 1940 but was returned to the company in January 1943 when it was renumbered 1044. Given an AEC oil engine and a new Pickering body in 1947, it remained in service until 1954. (K.A.Jenkinson collection)

The first AEC Regals to be purchased by Northern were six Short Bros-bodied examples which took their place in the fleet in 1934. Numerically the last of these, 603 (CN5918) seen here when new remained in service until 1955 after having received a new Pickering body in 1949. (Go-Ahead Northern)

enabled maximum seating to be incorporated into its Short Bros. body which accommodated 45 seated passengers. Designated the SE6, the front axle of this new chassis was directly below the driver's cab and thus the entrance door had to be placed behind the front wheel arch. It is interesting to note that on 25 November 1933 it was recorded in Northern's minutes "that the Associated Equipment Co. Ltd. had accepted the offer of Northern to take a licence (under their Q-type chassis patents and designs) to construct and use the company's SE6-type omnibuses at a royalty of one guinea per vehicle and to affix a plate to each chassis stating that it was constructed under licence from that company". Major Hayter was a brilliant and forward thinking engineer who, during his time at Bensham had been responsible for numerous experiments including automatic chassis lubrication and the use of coal gas as an alternative fuel. During his designing of the new SE6 chassis, he had given consideration to mounting the engine behind the rear axle - a position which was to become extremely popular some thirty years later - and as will soon be seen, he was an early advocate of moving the passenger entrance door to a position alongside the driver in the interests of safety.

In February 1933, due to the increased price of petrol, the Traffic Commissioners approved a fare increase of 0.5d on every 10d on ordinary fares above 10d. Although Northern had not purchased any further stage carriage operators during 1933, it did however acquire an interest in various limited stop services. The first of these came on 21 March when West Yorkshire Road Car Co.Ltd. on behalf of itself, Northern, East Yorkshire Motor Services Ltd., North Western Road Car Co.Ltd., Yorkshire (Woollen District) Electric Tramways Ltd. and Yorkshire Traction Co.Ltd. purchased the share capital of Fawdon Bus Co. Ltd., a company incorporated on 23 September 1927 who now ran a service from Newcastle to Coventry. Retained as a separate company, although owning no vehicles, Fawdon's registered office was moved to that of Northern at Queen Street, Bensham and thereafter its operations were maintained by the four companies by whom it was now owned. Following this, United Automobile Services Ltd. who, on 11 April, had purchased the business of the Northallerton-based Leeds & Newcastle Omnibus Co., agreed on 25 October to sell to members of the "Northern Pool" (i.e. Northern General Transport Co.Ltd., West Yorkshire Road Car Co.Ltd., North Western Road Car Co.Ltd. and Yorkshire (Woollen District) Electric Tramways Ltd.) such part of this as was concerned with the operation of the service between Leeds and Newcastle. This resulted in Northern, along with others, taking up this offer on 22 November and soon afterwards providing vehicles for operation on this joint limited stop route. Prior to this, in June 1933, Northern together with West Yorkshire, North Western, Lancashire United and Yorkshire (Woollen District) purchased Tyne & Mersey Motor Services Ltd., a company which operated two limited stop services between Newcastle and Liverpool and Redcar and Liverpool, thus expanding their own operations between these two cities, and the Newcastle to Liverpool service was licensed by Northern on 26 July of that year. A further purchase on 27 June 1933 was that of the business of John Maugham of Craghead. In addition to his service from Craghead to Stanley, two vehicles - a Chevrolet LQ and a Willys Overland - both of which were 14-seaters, were included in the deal. On 25 November, Tynemouth & District made two purchases, both of which were joint with United. One of these was the business of A.Howe of Blyth while the other was T.Allen & Sons Ltd. whose service was from Blyth to Whitley Bay.

A notable service starting in July 1933 was that from Newcastle to

One of a trio of 14-seat Burlingham-bodied Commer Centaur coaches purchased new in the summer of 1934, 625 (CN6106) is pictured on the Dornie Ferry in September of that year whilst undertaking an extended holiday tour to the Scottish Highlands. Judging by its open sun roof, the weather must have been at its summer's best!
(Go-Ahead Northern)

Darlington which was worked jointly with United - and is still so to this day. A service from Chester-le-Street to Sunderland via Fatfield jointly operated by Northern & Sunderland District also began replacing a Sunderland District only service and at the same time Sunderland District started running on the Sunderland - Chester-le-Street - Consett route. On the property side, Tynemouth sold the old Suez Street tram depot in September. Unlike 1933 which had been a year of relative calm, 1934 proved to be one of great activity and consolidation, opening with the acquisition of the Ennis & Reed Ltd. of Crook on 28 January. This company, who operated a service from Crook to Newcastle, was purchased jointly with United Automobile Services Ltd. who took all the 13 vehicles involved and a garage at Helmington Row but operated the service jointly with Northern. Following this, on 23 March, a trio of tiny independents who, like Maugham were all members of 'Diamond', sold their interests to Northern, these being T.Harrison and James Long, both of South Moor, and J.G.Robinson of West Stanley. One vehicle was gained from each comprising a Bedford WLB, a Commer Centaur and a Willys-Overland respectively, all of which were destined to give their new owner a further two years service while the route taken over from these operators from Stanley to Quaking Houses was continued by Northern without any significant change. Still seeking to eliminate competition, Northern made a successful bid on 3 August for the operations and fleet of R.M.Prinn of Sunniside, with the transaction being concluded on 4 October. Trading under the title of "Direct", taken as a result of his service between West Stanley and Newcastle running via a new, direct road which had been

The livery applied to Short Bros-bodied NGT SE6 coach 653 (CN6612) when new in 1935 incorporated a cream waistrail which was down-swept at the rear. Posed here with its sun roof fully opened, this coach along with its sisters was rebuilt by Duple in 1937 and again in 1939. (Go-Ahead Northern)

One of six luxurious 28-seat Short Bros-bodied NGT SE6s built in 1935 for use on Northern's extended holiday tours, 655 (CN6614) is seen at Milton Street, Nottingham enroute to the Isle of Wight during its first week in service in July. Painted in a red & black livery, it looks most majestic with its sun roof fully opened. Rebuilt by Duple in 1937, it was rebuilt again two years later when it was also given a fixed roof. (G.H.F.Atkins)

built in the 1920s, Prinn contributed 9 buses and coaches to Northern's growing fleet, these being a pair of Thornycrofts, 6 Leylands and a Maudslay ML6A. Of these, 1 of the Leylands, a TS4, was immediately disposed of to Sunderland District whilst the others joined the main company fleet. Upon its acquisition, Prinn's service was joined onto Northern's existing service 3 from Chester-le-Street to Stanley.

The next acquisition of 1934 came in December when White & Nixon of Chester-le-Street and Sacriston was purchased. This company was a consortium of three operators - T.D.Laing of Langley Park; J.White of Chester-le-Street and T.Hutchinson of Sacriston who between them ran a service from Esh Winning to South Shields via Chester-le-Street whilst White also ran one from Chester-le-Street to Houghton-le-Spring via Great Lumley and Leamside with a mixed fleet of some 15 buses and coaches. Amongst these were Bedford WTBs; Leyland KP3s; a Leyland PLSC1 and a PLSC3; 4 Gilfords; a Reo Pullman and a Dennis EV. Three of the Bedfords were withdrawn almost immediately (January 1935) together with 2 more before the end of the year and indeed authorisation was given for only 9 of the acquired vehicles to be reconditioned and repainted for longer term service.

Before December ended, Northern signed an agreement (on the 20th of that month) for the purchase of the business and vehicles of T.Cowley of Birtley who traded as Cowley & Bracegirdle. Cowley operated a service from Kibbleworth to Low Fell and upon the completion of this purchase on 4 March 1935, Northern extended this to Newcastle. Towards the end of the year, the company made a donation of £750 to Gateshead & District Tramways Co. in respect of traffic lost by that company to Northern's newly-acquired and extended service. Meanwhile, neither Cowley's 20-seat Bedford or 14-seat Chevrolet which were included in the deal were taken into stock by their new owner. Meanwhile, during 1934 Northern's Stanley garage was extended, though the design had to be modified due to mining subsidence which was to be a problem there for many years.

New buses joining the fleet included the last of BMMO manufacture to be purchased new, these being 24 SOS ON-type single deckers with Short Bros. front entrance bodywork. These were split between Northern, Sunderland District and Wakefields who received 12, 10 and 2 respectively. Northern also took delivery of 6 oil-engined AEC Regals with Short Bros. 36-seat bus bodies and, more surprisingly, a trio of diminutive 14-seat Burlingham-bodied Commer Centaur coaches. The arrival of the AEC's was of major significance as it heralded the start of a new era as far as the fleet was concerned, breaking away from the tradition of the previous nine years when single deck standardisation had been of BMMO manufacture. Completing the year's intake of new vehicles were 5 more 'home-built' Short Bros-bodied three-axle SE6s with seating for 44 passengers (three axles were required to meet the length regulations at that time, although only one was powered). These were of a much improved appearance than the prototype, having had the front axle set back to allow the entrance door to be positioned at the extreme front alongside the driver. As can be seen, no further double deckers were included in the year's deliveries and indeed, Northern appeared to not be particularly enhanced with this type of

Pictured near Marlborough Crescent bus station, Newcastle on its way to Blaydon on route 9 in the early 'fifties is 657, a 1935 Short Bros-bodied NGT SE6 which has gained sliding ventilators to its side windows in place of the original half-drop type. Withdrawn in the summer of 1954, 657 was then scrapped by Northern in September of that year. (J.Wyndham)

bus, and placed its entire double deck fleet on its sales list during 1934. As there seems to have been no takers for these, however, they all remained in service, although it was not until 1938 that they were joined by more of their type! Meanwhile, the Tynemouth & District Electric Traction Company, which no longer operated trams or was involved with electric traction, was renamed Tynemouth & District Transport Company Limited on 19 March 1934. Continuing its 'joint working' with Wakefield's Motors Limited, the headquarters of the reconstituted company remained at Norham Terrace, Percy Main.

During 1934, although several services were modified to take into account the needs of the travelling public, only one new route was opened, this being from Newcastle to Springwell via Wrekenton. This was to be short-lived, however, and was combined with Northern's New Washington - Springwell service after only a few months to provide a new through service. Northern also gained a share in a service from Stanley to Craghead via South Moor operated by Logan and Patterson and during May 1935 made an attempt to purchase the business of Robson Bros. Ltd. (Yellow Bus Service) of High Spen. This failed, however, and instead Robsons sold to Venture Bus Services Ltd. and Reed Bros Ltd. a few months later. A further development, taking place in 1935, was the introduction of the Bell Punch 'Automaticket' machine to the company.

Due to Northern's workshops at Bensham not being equipped to cope with mass production, the 31 SE6 three-axle chassis built in 1935 were constructed at AEC's works at Southall. Of these, 5 were placed in service in the Tynemouth & District fleet whilst of the others, 19 were given Short Bros. 44-seat bus bodies, 1 a Weymann 44-seat bus body and 6 were equipped with Short Bros. 28-seat coach bodies for the main fleet. The coaches, despite still being referred to as charabancs,

The NGT SE4 was a two-axle version of the side-engined SE6 and was powered by an AEC A172-type diesel engine instead of a Hercules unit. The prototype SE4, which made its debut in August 1936, was numbered 701 (AUP590) and was fitted with an English Electric 40-seat body which featured a new style of radiator grille. Seen here when brand new, it gave Northern eighteen years of service before ultimately being withdrawn in 1954.

One of three AEC Regents fitted with front entrance Brush bodywork purchased new by Sunderland District in 1933 is seen here before its entry into service. (K.A.Jenkinson collection)

were luxuriously appointed, and in addition to having sun roofs, had improved seating with double seats at one side of the gangway and single seats at the other, primarily for use on Northern's extended coach tours. Also joining the Northern fleet were 5 new oil-engined AEC Regal 34-seat buses with Weymann bodywork and 19 secondhand vehicles, all but 3 of which were acquired from Midland Red in the form of 4 SOS QC-type and 12 QLC-types all with charabanc bodywork. The remaining secondhand acquisitions comprised 2 BMMO QLC-type charabancs from Tynemouth and a former Leyland demonstrator, this being an oil-engined TD3c with Weymann 48-seat front entrance highbridge body. Built in 1934, this bus was fitted with a torque converter instead of a conventional 4-speed gearbox and was purchased to enable Northern to gain experience with an automatic form of transmission. Completing Northern's fleet changes for 1935, a pair of BMMO QLC-type charabancs were transferred to the company from Tynemouth & District, one of which carried Wakefield's fleet names, their replacements being 2 charabancs of the same type recently acquired from Midland Red. Sunderland District's fleet remained unchanged during this year with no new vehicles added, nor buses withdrawn, although this situation was soon to change, as in 1936 the company received 4 new Leyland TS7 single deckers fitted with Roe bodywork built to B.E.F. specification which, upon their arrival, allowed the withdrawal of the 4 Karriers. This was a new combination for the Northern Group who in recent years had begun to favour the AEC Regal as far as "bought-in" chassis were concerned and had never previously had any Roe bodywork within its fleet. The arrival of the TS7s began a link with Leyland and Roe which Sunderland District maintained for more than two decades and the adoption of its own buying policy can perhaps be explained by the fact that although it was under the control of Northern, unlike Tynemouth & District who shared its parent's General Manager and Chief Engineer, Sunderland District had its own management team who were thus able to work with some degree of independence.

Northern's intake of new vehicles in 1936 comprised 25 lightweight AEC Regal IIs with Weymann 34/36-seat bodywork, a pair of "home-built" SE6s fitted with luxurious 28-seat Beadle coach bodies and the prototype SE4. The latter, which was initially called an SE6 four wheel chassis, was a two-axle version of the successful SE6 and, whilst maintaining the side engine position, was powered by an AEC A172-type oil engine rather than the Hercules power unit fitted to its larger sister. Its 40-seat body with entrance alongside the driver was built by English Electric. Tynemouth & District also received 3 Bensham-built SE6s with Weymann 44-seat bodywork and additionally gained a front entrance lowbridge AEC Regent transferred from the Northern fleet. A spare Hercules engine was also purchased at a cost of $875.60.

One of fourteen Short Bros-bodied AEC Regents purchased by Tynemouth in 1932 as tramway replacement vehicles, T53 (FT2522) like its sisters carried lettering to this effect below its front destination screen. Seen here on a dismal winter's day enroute to Whitley Bay, it also carried 'tram route service' boards at the base of some of its nearside lower deck windows. (AEC)

New to Sunderland District in 1929, all-Leyland TS1 94 (UP2835) seen here at Houghton-le-Spring whilst working the Bishop Auckland service was fitted with a new Duple coach body in 1937. Given bus seats during the war, it had its coach seats restored in 1946 and retained its petrol engine until its final withdrawal in 1951. (K.Richardson)

TYNESIDE JOINS THE FOLD

During 1936, an important conquest was made when Northern, with Sunderland District, purchased 95% of the ordinary shares, 94% of the preference shares and 94% of the issued mortgages of Tyneside Tramways & Tramroads Company of Wallsend, so bringing it into the British Electric Traction fold. The Tyneside Tramways company was incorporated by Act of Parliament on 9 August 1901 in order to construct a street tramway on the north bank of the river Tyne from the Newcastle/Wallsend boundary to North Shields and from Wallsend to Gosforth with a branch from Wallsend to Walker. The line from Wallsend Boundary to North Shields which was formally opened on 29 September 1902 but in fact had been operational since 4 September, used standard gauge except for a short length of track at North Shields which was laid to dual 3ft. 6in./ 4ft. 8.5in. gauge where the company's line met with that of the Tynemouth & District system. A month later, on 18 October, the section from Wallsend to Gosforth was opened, with much of this running through open countryside on its own private right of way. To the west of Wallsend, connections were made with the Newcastle Corporation tramway at Shields Road and at Neptune Bank, and additionally the two systems met in Henry Street, Gosforth. Following the extension of the route to Gosforth Park on 18 June 1904, agreement was reached for the Corporation to operate its trams over the Henry Street - Gosforth Park section and into Wallsend in exchange for allowing Tyneside Tramways to run over the Corporation tracks to Stanhope Street, Newcastle.

By 1904, Tyneside Tramways' fleet totalled 24 open-top double deck cars, the first 18 of which had inaugurated the system two years earlier and had Milnes bodywork mounted on Brill trucks, 4 of which were bogie cars. The remaining 6, delivered in 1903, also had Brill trucks and Westinghouse electrical equipment but were on this occasion bodied by Brush, 4 of them seating 65 passengers and the remaining 2 having seated accommodation for 86. These were joined in 1911 by a pair of United Electric 59-seat open-top double deckers whilst the final additions to the fleet were made in 1920 in the form of 3 English Electric open-toppers.

Although a number of extensions to the track network were considered, as well as a line from Morpeth to Blyth via Ashington, none were ever constructed and the line remained with a total of just over eleven route miles until its final abandonment. Most of the route from Wallsend boundary to Gosforth was of single track with passing loops and in part used an old colliery wagonway, while the depot was situated at Neptune Bank, Wallsend. During 1929 the company took the decision to replace its trams with motor buses and later that year gained an Act allowing it to carry out its plans. This was a rather complicated Act however due to the agreement in force with Newcastle Corporation which permitted it to operate over the sections previously mentioned. Eventually, however, it was agreed that the track from Gosforth to Gosforth Park and from Neptune Bank to Wallsend be transferred free of charge to the Corporation and thus on 6 April 1930 Tyneside Tramways said farewell to electric traction. Newcastle Corporation, however, continued to operate trams to Wallsend for a further month, not withdrawing its service until 25 May. It is perhaps interesting to note that Tyneside had, as early as June 1905, considered the cost of running motor buses from Gosforth to Coxlodge but in July 1906 decided that they did not have the statutory powers to embark upon such a venture. However, bus operation was considered again in 1920 and once more in 1928 when it was stated that if they gained the powers to substitute buses for trams, even if they were not used they could bring about a settlement, good or bad, with Newcastle Corporation or alternatively they would have something valuable to offer to United Automobile Services, Northern General Transport Co. or any other likely purchaser. Indeed, when Mr.Stagg of Northern called upon them in November 1935 to inform them that Northern would like to make an offer for the share capital of the company, they were probably quite pleased to see him!

Tyneside's tram replacement vehicles were 6 new all-Leyland lowbridge TD1s with open-staircase bodywork and 6-cylinder patrol engines, which were followed by a further 2 later in the year, all of which wore the same dark leaf green and white livery as the erstwhile trams. Prior to their arrival, however, 8 elderly Tilling Stevens TS3A petrol-electric open-top double deckers which had previously been operated by Southdown Motor Services Ltd. were placed in service and these were later joined by 3 covered top double deckers provided by Newcastle Corporation under a working agreement, the latter being Daimler CF6s and AEC Regents with a variety of makes of highbridge

Tyneside Tramways Milnes car no.11 built in 1902 on Brill 21E trucks is pictured on the North Sheilds - Wallsend route. It remained in service until the abandonment of the system in April 1930.

One of Tyneside's original 1930 all-Leyland TD1s shows its route details in the top of each of its lower deck side windows. The company's 'boxed' fleet name was replaced by one of neater sans-serif lettering early in World War II.

The last of three front entrance highbridge Weymann-bodied AEC Regents purchased new in 1937 by Tynemouth, T95 (FT4222) was, along with its two sisters, given new bodywork by Pickering in 1949. After remaining in service for a further eight years it was sold to Gosport & Fareham Omnibus Co. (Provincial) of Hoeford for whom it operated until 1964. (K.A.Jenkinson collection)

Used by Northern's engineering department, Morris van M7 (CN8288) was purchased new by the company in 1937. Even Northern's ancillary vehicles were fully lined-out as can be seen in this pre-war view. (Go-Ahead Northern)

bodywork which were drawn from a pool of 6 vehicles for these duties. The 3 Daimlers were in fact all demonstrators, themselves on loan to Newcastle Corporation and which never became permanent members of that undertaking's fleet. All these buses quickly settled down to their duties on Tyneside's two services from Wallsend to Gosforth and Newcastle to North Shields, the latter of which was operated jointly with Newcastle Corporation. At the beginning of June, the original Newcastle Corporation double deckers were exchanged for 3 of that undertaking's English Electric-bodied AEC Regents in order that Tyneside Tramways could continue to fulfil its obligations, these remaining with the company until January 1931. Their replacements from that date were 3 all-Leyland highbridge TD1s which had been purchased by Newcastle Corporation at the request of Tyneside for fleet standardisation purposes for operation on that undertaking's share of the joint Newcastle to North Shields service. Tynemouth Borough Council had refused to issue Newcastle Corporation with hackney licences for the service, however, and as a result, the 3 TD1s, which had been painted from new in Tyneside Tramways livery, were instead passed to that company for operation, although they remained the property of the Corporation. Tyneside updated its fleet in 1933 with the purchase of a solitary all-Leyland highbridge TD2 as a replacement for a Tilling Stevens and a year later bought a petrol-engined all-Leyland highbridge TD3c. Further new buses appeared in 1935 in the form of 3 all-Leyland highbridge TD4c double deckers which were the first buses in the fleet to be fitted with oil engines and soon after the company's control was gained by Northern, that operator sold its solitary Leyland TD3c to Tyneside in whose fleet it replaced the last of the ex.Southdown Tilling Stevens petrol-electric open-toppers.

On 1 April Northern completely absorbed its General County subsidiary together with what was left of its fleet, i.e. 3 Albion PMB28s and 4 BMMO IM6s (of which all but 1 Albion had been transferred to it from the main fleet) after which General County was placed in liquidation on 12 May. Meanwhile, John Petrie, who had successfully guided Northern through its main period of development since he assumed the position of General Manager in 1926, decided that it was now time to hand over the reins and towards the end of 1936 took early retirement at the age of 56. Masterminding his company's progress through many difficult times, John Petrie was not only an engineer, but a supreme diplomat who led from the front and even conducted his

Numerically the last of the Brush-bodied AEC Regals delivered new in 1937, 750 (CN7965) looks immaculate in its lined-out livery as it rests at Scarborough whilst undertaking a private hire duty. (G.H.F.Atkins)

BET-style Brush-bodied AEC Regal 744 (CN7959) seen here when new in June 1937 was painted in an experimental livery of red with a cream waist band and flash above its side windows. Unfortunately its life was cut short when it was destroyed by fire in October 1942. (Go-Ahead Northern)

own cases in the traffic courts. His successor from 1 November was Northern's Chief Engineer, Major G.W.Hayter who himself had given so much to the company over the years. Having worked so closely with Petrie, it was not surprising that Major Hayter (who also retained his position as Chief Engineer) continued many of his predecessors policies after he took over as General Manager, and this led Northern to strengthen its position even further in the years ahead.

Fleet modernisation continued in 1937 with the purchase of new vehicles for the parent company as well as for its Tynemouth & District and Sunderland District subsidiaries, although the first of the year's arrivals (which made their debut in March) were secondhand rather than new, being 5 Brush-bodied BMMO QL-type single deckers purchased from Trent Motor Traction, another B.E.T. subsidiary. Despite being nine years old, they were of a type already owned by Northern, however, and thus soon settled down in their new home. The first of the "new" vehicles to arrive did so in May in the form of AEC Regals fitted with Brush and Weymann 34-seat bodies. A total of 35 were received, all of which were added to the Northern fleet, and delivery was completed in July. For Sunderland District came another 12 Leyland TS7s with Roe bodywork (purchased to replace the Leyland LT2s) whilst the only new double deckers were 3 front-entrance Weymann-bodied AEC Regents which were placed in service in the Tynemouth & District fleet. Northern had also ordered 10 Gardner-engined Daimlers, although these were cancelled before delivery in favour of further AECs. Meanwhile, Sunderland District's 6 1929 Leyland TS1s were all depatched to Duple's factory at Hendon later in 1937 where they were fitted with new 30-seat coach bodies before returning north to rejoin their original operator. Finally, on 20 July, following an agreement reached on 17 June, Northern purchased the business of Charlton's Blue Safety Coaches Ltd. of Hebburn-on-Tyne who operated one local route between Bill Quay Bridge and South Shields along with a number of workmens services on south Tyneside and two football services from Hebburn and Jarrow to Roker Park (Sunderland AFC). This acquisition added a further 26 buses and coaches to the Northern fleet including Leyland PLSC1s and PLSC3s, several Leyland TS1s, TS7s and LT7s, a Gilford, Albions of varying types and a pair of Maudslay ML5As, a number of which were immediately withdrawn and offered for sale. Charltons had originally been approached by Northern as early as June 1933 when their fleet comprised some 11 vehicles, but had declined the offer made to them. Three years later, however, on 18 March 1936 United Automobile Services Ltd. purchased Charlton's London service after expressing no interest in the company's other operations.

During 1937, the two-year old Short Bros-bodied SE6 coaches were rebuilt by Duple whilst two years later, they were again refurbished by this Hendon (London)-based coachbuilder and on the latter occasion were given fixed roofs to which a luggage pod was added towards the rear. Meanwhile, in 1938 the 3 ex.Charlton's Leyland-bodied TS1s were given new Duple 30-seat coach bodies for use on Northern's Limited Stop Pool duties.

Although Northern and its subsidiaries had now settled down to an established route network, during the latter years of the 'thirties several service modifications took place and, wherever a need was found, new routes continued to be introduced. In 1937 a number of new routes were inaugurated including that from Stanley to Greencroft which was operated jointly with the Annfield Plain Bus Association and lasted less than a year, and a service from Stanley to Tanfield Village jointly with Union Bus Service. Of the other new routes started during this year, one was commenced in July from Chester-le-Street to Ouston Housing Estate running on Friday, Saturday and Sunday evenings only whilst on the last day of that month a new circular service from Marlborough Crescent, Newcastle to Gateshead, Teams and Dunston was inaugurated as was a service from Gateshead to Heworth and a new peak hours route from Marlborough Crescent, Newcastle to the new Team Valley Trading Estate. In October 1937 it was reported that Venture & Reed was for sale, the company being partly in Northern's and partly in United's operating areas. Mr.Stagg held consultations with United and reports were given to the Board each month until March

Burlingham-bodied Leyland TS7 coach 798 (AUP575) was acquired by Northern from Charlton's Blue Safety Coaches along with that business in June 1937 when only one year old. It was, however, sold in the autumn of the following year to Hall Brothers of Hebburn-on-Tyne who ultimately rebodied it with a full-fronted ACB body.

Although Gateshead operated both double and single deck tramcars, it is perhaps the latter which are best remembered with their front exits and roof-mounted advertising boards. 47, built by Milnes in 1902 was originally built with an open cab and is seen here prior to its withdrawal in 1947 working the Teams service.

1938. Unfortunately, no details of these reports have been found and therefore one can only speculate on their contents. Also in 1938, the Avenue Hotel in Durham was vacated by its tenant after which it was then let to United.

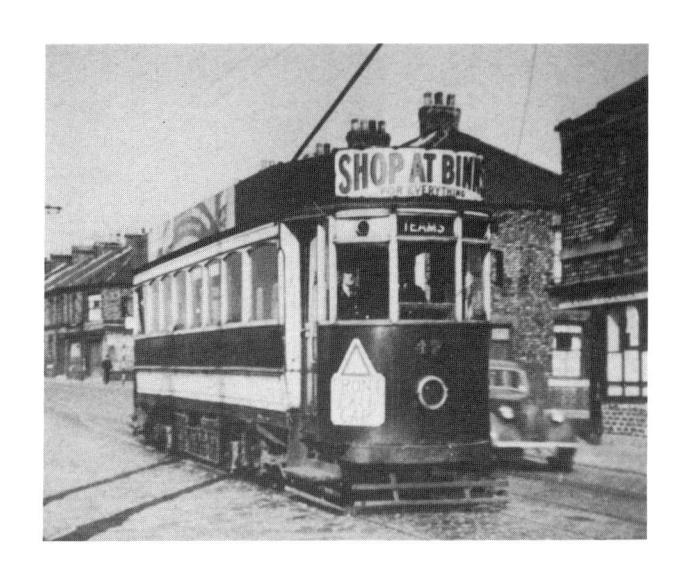

THE FINAL PRE-WAR DEVELOPMENTS

The final pre-war service developments came in 1938 when new routes were started from Boldon Colliery to Newcastle via Primrose Estate and Leam Lane; Hebburn, Jarrow and Primrose Estate; Sunderland to Newcastle via Washington and Wrekenton, and Houghton-le-Spring to Hetton via Hazard Lane, the latter being operated by Sunderland District while Tynemouth and United started a new joint service from North Shields to West Allotment via Billy Mill Estate on 7 May. Additionally, the South Shields to Esh Winning service taken over with the White & Nixon business in 1934 underwent some alteration in 1938 following the closure of part of the South Shields Corporation tramway system. The last new pre-war services, which were introduced in 1939, were from Newcastle to Lobley Hill and from Durham to Pity Me together with a new Sunderland District service in Sunderland from Union Street to Glenest Road via Tunstall Road, these bringing the total number of different routes across Northern's area of operation to more than 70.

The fleet modernisation programme started some years earlier escalated dramatically in the period leading up to the outbreak of World war II and during the two years 1938/9 witnessed the arrival of almost 160 new buses and coaches for Northern and its subsidiaries. For the parent company, 54 were received in 1938 comprising 16 bus (Weymann and Brush) and 12 coach (Brush and Duple)-bodied Leyland TS8s, a pair of Duple coach-bodied AEC Regals, 19 more SE4s fitted with 40-seat English Electric bus bodywork, and, for the first time for some years, 5 double deckers. These were Leyland TD5s with highbridge front entrance bodywork by Weymann. Still seeing the secondhand market as being useful source for additional vehicles, a further 6 BMMO QL-type buses were purchased from Trent Motor Traction whilst 9 buses of this type were gained from Tynemouth & District. Tynemouth replaced these with 8 new Leyland TD5 Weymann-bodied front entrance double deckers, needed for use on services on which passenger loadings had increased dramatically, whilst for Wakefield's came a batch of 4 Duple coach-bodied Leyland TS8s. Sunderland District continued to remain faithful to the Roe-Leyland combination however, purchasing 6 TS8s in 1938 and a further 8 in 1939 and additionally had 2 of its 1930 Leyland TS2s fitted with new Burlingham coach bodies. Also purchased in 1938 were 310 'Wallace tartan' coach rugs.

844 (GR5067), a BET-style Weymann-bodied Leyland TS8 new in 1938 is seen resting between duties near Worswick Street bus station, Newcastle in June 1955 shortly before it was withdrawn and sold. (K.A.Jenkinson)

Resting at Scarborough railway station in July 1954 whilst undertaking a private hire duty is Wakefields 104 (FT4544), a 1938 Duple-bodied Leyland TS8 with roof luggage carrier. Soon afterwards 104 together with its three sisters was given Northern fleetnames and operated for that company until its withdrawal in 1955. (G.H.F.Atkins)

Amongst the new touring coaches added to Northern's fleet during 1938 were a pair of 30-seat Duple-bodied Leyland TS8s, one of which (874 - CU3954) is seen here accompanied by its driver. Its double-length side window arrangement, roof-mounted luggage carrier and stylish livery give it a most luxurious appearance. (Go-Ahead Northern)

When acquired from Trent Motor Traction in 1938, Brush-bodied BMMO SOS QL-type 838 (CH7749) was already ten years old. In common with most buses of its type, it was not fitted with any destination equipment other than a route number box placed in its front bulkhead window. (Go-Ahead Northern)

All the new NGT SE4s delivered in 1938 were fitted with English Electric 40-seat bus bodies as illustrated by 810 (CPT910) which entered service in July of that year and survived until 1953 when it was withdrawn and scrapped. (Go-Ahead Northern)

Although the side-engined SE4 was still regarded as being "home-built", as mentioned earlier, most of their chassis were actually assembled at AEC's Southall factory due to an acute shortage of space at Northern's Bensham workshops. Northern's own design and specification had of course been strictly adhered to, and as a result AEC considered them to be non-standard, ultimately persuading Major Hayter to order AEC Regals for his future requirements rather than to continue with his own design. Whilst he acknowledged that the Regal was an acceptable substitute, he was less than happy that the seating capacity would thus have to be reduced to 36 at maximum, and as a consequence he sat down with AEC's designers in an attempt to find a way to increase the seating in a standard body on this type of chassis. This was eventually achieved by moving the driving position slightly forward in order to lengthen the body interior and thus squeeze in a further 2 seats. Following delivery of the last 6 SE4s early in 1939, subsequent deliveries during that year comprised modified AEC Regal chassis. No fewer than 53 arrived between May and July, the bodywork order having been split between Weymann, Brush and English Electric, all of whom built them to B.E.F. specification, and joining these were 6 conventional AEC Regals with Duple coach bodies and a conventional

1938 saw the arrival in the Northern fleet of five new Leyland TD5s, all of which carried front entrance Weymann highbridge bodywork. 856 (GR5079) along with the others of this batch was given new ECW bodywork in 1948 and in its new form remained in service until 1956. Sold to Cunninghams of Paisley, it gave a further four years service before eventually being scrapped in 1961. (Go-Ahead Northern)

Seen during the early 'fifties, Tyneside 19 (JR8619), a 1939 ECW-bodied Leyland TD5 had by that time had its original half-drop windows replaced by sliding ventilators. (J.Wyndham)

The last new coaches to enter service before the outbreak of World War II were six Duple-bodied AEC Regals which took up their duties in April 1939. Seen on a private hire duty in the early 'fifties, 931 (CN9231) carries 'Northern Tours' on its offside destination glass and still looks to be in pristine condition despite its advancing years. (T.Godfrey collection)

Regal chassis which was fitted with the Weymann 34-seat body from a 1936 Regal which had recently been withdrawn from service. Tynemouth & District also received 2 of the modified Regals with Brush bodies together with a pair of coach-seated examples for Wakefields and in addition gained a pair of BMMO QLC charabancs transferred from Northern.

Tyneside Tramways gained its first new buses since becoming a subsidiary of Northern when, in 1939, it received 9 Leyland TD5s with attractive ECW highbridge bodywork. Still rather surprisingly playing the secondhand market, Northern purchased a pair of 48-seat all-Leyland lowbridge TD1s from Ribble Motor Services in July 1939 and in addition received a BMMO QL-type single decker transferred from

In order to be able to accommodate seating for 38 passengers, the driving position of Northern's 1939 bus-bodied AEC Regals was moved forward slightly and as a consequence the cab was given a curved profile. Illustrating this is Weymann-bodied 880 (DUP130) which is seen here when new. Fitted with new Pickering bodywork in 1949, 880 was ultimately withdrawn in 1956. (Go-Ahead Northern)

Looking superb before its entry into service in 1936 is Sunderland District 135 (BPT951), a Leyland TS7 fitted with B.E.T.-style bodywork by Roe. These were the first vehicles in the Sunderland fleet to be fitted with oil engines and self-starters.

Wakefields. Also taken into stock, although immediately withdrawn, were a Bedford WLB 20-seat bus and a Maudslay ML3 coach acquired on 14 July with the small business of T.Cook of Consett. Cook, who had started his business in April 1926 was the last independent to succumb to Northern in pre-war years, although there were to be more after the hostilities ceased, as will be seen later. Cook's service from Consett to Stanhope created problems, however, due to it crossing the United/Northern demarcation line and at first it had been intended that the acquisition of this operator be undertaken jointly with United. In the event, after United was refused a licence to extend its Durham - Tow Law service to Stanhope, it pulled out of the deal and thus the service was truncated to operate from Consett to Tow Law with the section beyond being taken over by Baldwin & Barlow and O.S.Gibson.

THE DIFFICULT WAR YEARS

By the time that war was declared on 3 September 1939, the amassed fleet of Northern and its subsidiaries totalled some 666 motor buses and 78 electric tramcars. Of the buses, 479 were owned by Northern; 106 by Sunderland District; 64 by Tynemouth & District/ Wakefields and 17 by Tyneside Tramways, the 78 trams all being under the ownership of Gateshead & District. This total was soon to change however, for as a result of fuel shortages and service reductions etc., a quite large number of buses were taken out of service towards the end of the year and placed in store. Despite the service cuts and the suspension of the company's Limited Stop Pool operations, brand new buses continued to arrive during 1940 almost as if the war was not taking place. More double deckers were delivered for Northern in the form of 8 AEC Regents (of which 3 had originally been ordered for Tynemouth), this time with conventional rear entrance highbridge bodywork by Weymann, along with a further 32 Brush-bodied AEC Regal 1B 38-seaters, whilst Sunderland District received 5 Leyland TS8s and 5 Leyland TD7s, all of which carried Roe bodies. For the Tynemouth & District fleet came a pair of highbridge AEC Regents and 5 AEC Regal 1B 38-seaters similar to those supplied to Northern and for whose fleet they had originally been ordered. It is believed that Northern's second batch of AEC Regal 1Bs delivered in 1940 were painted in a dark green livery with red lettering although this cannot be substantiated.

As the hostilities began to bite, so too did the need by the Armed Forces for more vehicles and, almost repeating the events of World War I, the War Department began requisitioning buses and coaches for a variety of military purposes. Northern did not escape this wholesale commandeering exercise and by 1941 a total of 70 of its vehicles had departed. Although the vast majority of these were BMMO-type single deckers, included in their number were 6 AEC Reliances and 3 Morris trucks. Joining them were 3 BMMO-type single deckers from the Tynemouth fleet and 13 single deckers from Sunderland District, all except one, a BMMO IM6, being Leylands. In addition, Northern converted one of its AEC Reliances into a mobile operating theatre, presenting it to the Red Cross in September 1940 and modified 16 of its BMMO-type single deckers for use by the Civil Defence as ambulances. In addition, Gateshead Corporation hired 5 of Gateshead & District's parcel vans for four months for use as ambulances whilst in 1941 two were requisitioned by the War Department.

The reduction in its fleet size left Northern stretched to the extreme as more and more vehicles were required to provide essential services for those workers remaining on Tyneside and Wearside in jobs necessary to the success of the war effort. Employment on the Team Valley Estate increased from around 5,000 to 14,000 workers of whom 90% were carried on 500 journeys operated by Northern every day and

Amongst the last new buses built to pre-war standards to join the Sunderland District fleet were five Leyland TD7s which, fitted with Roe highbridge bodies, were received in 1940. One of these, 173 (EPT696), its destination screen surrounded by the customary advertising for Binns, the well-known north-east department stores chain, rests in Sunderland between its duties on the Houghton service.

*Seen whilst operating a private hire duty during the early post-war period is Sunderland District Roe-bodied Leyland TS8 168 (EPT691) which was new in 1940 and built to peacetime standards.
(K.A.Jenkinson collection)*

*Collecting homeward-bound workers at the old Reyrolles factory in 1942 are a selection of Northern, Tynemouth and Tyneside vehicles. Nearest the camera are, from left to right : Northern 435 (BR7024), a 1929 BMMO SOS M-type with Ransomes body; Northern 391 (CN3686), a Ransomes-bodied 1928 BMMO SOS QL-type; Tynemouth T92 (FT3905), a Weymann-bodied NGT SE6 and Northern 606 (CN6102), a Short Bros-bodied NGT SE6 whilst behind them are a Northern SE6, a Northern BMMO Q-type and a Tyneside open-staircase all-Leyland TD1.
(Go-Ahead Northern)*

in addition there was still the mining areas to serve in County Durham and the Royal Ordnance factory at Birtley which required 350 daily journeys. A further burden Northern had to contend with was the provision of 70 vehicles per day to transport workers to a new Royal Ordnance establishment under construction at Aycliffe, near Darlington in the heart of United territory. Buses were also often called upon at short notice to cover sections of the railway which had been damaged

*Fortunately, Northern and its associates suffered only a small amount of damage to its vehicles and properties as a result of enemy air attacks during Workd War II. One bus which was not so lucky, however, was Tyneside's ECW-bodied Leyland TD5 26 (JR8626) which was damaged in an air raid on 30 September 1941.
(Go-Ahead Northern)*

One of ten Short Bros-bodied BMMO SOS IM6 34-seat buses purchased new in 1933, 1027 (CN5476) was originally numbered 581. Transferred to the General County fleet in 1934, it returned to Northern two years later as no.732 and was in July 1940 commandeered by the War Department. Repurchased in 1942, it then took fleet number 1027 and remained in service until 1950 when it was finally withdrawn and sold after an extremely eventful life. (K.A.Jenkinson collection)

With its operator's name prominently displayed on its radiator header tank, 1934 Short Bros-bodied BMMO SOS ON-type CN6023 typifies vehicles of this type with their narrow cab which did not protrude above the radiator, thus giving a somewhat unbalanced appearance. Commandeered by the War Department in July 1940 and returned to the company in January 1943, CN6023 was renumbered 1044 (it originally having been 617). It is seen here in 1946 before being fitted a year later with a new Pickering body and AEC oil engine which enabled it to remain in service until 1954.

Although painted in Northern's fully lined-out peacetime livery, 1944 Massey-bodied Guy Arab II 1056 (FPT855) sported white wing tips and guard rails when new as illustrated by this view taken before its entry into service.

New to Tyneside in 1930, Leyland TD1 no.8 (TY7913) was fitted with a new NCB body of wartime styling in 1943. Here it passes Haymarket bus station, Newcastle on a journey from North Shields in June 1950, the year before its withdrawal from service. (Alan B. Cross)

by enemy bombing, thus stretching the company's resources even further! The shipyards around Tyneside were also working at full capacity and needed a large fleet of buses to transport the workers each day, and in order to achieve this, Northern was forced to cut back even further on its normal services. Those such as Newcastle to Lobley Hill and Durham to Pity Me introduced in 1939 had already been completely suspended in 1940 whilst several others had been truncated and numerous had their frequencies severely reduced. All those operated jointly with United were split into two and as a result Northern no longer ran south of Durham or Easington Village. Despite these moves and the additional strains on the company's resources, Northern managed to continue to serve all the differing sectors throughout its territory and, with a bare minimum of maintenance, its fleet struggled on. Mercifully, the only one of the company's premises to be damaged during the hostilities was the Tynemouth garage at Cullercoats which had been vacated in 1940 because of its exposed coastal position. This was struck by a bomb on 8 August 1942 which, in addition to causing severe structural damage also destroyed the adjoining Church. After being repaired it was requisitioned by the NFS who had been in partial occupation at the time of the air attack.

In order to assist with the increased demand for high capacity buses needed for the workers services, Northern received 11 AEC Regent double deckers from Sunderland District (5) and Tynemouth & District (6) in 1940/1 whilst a further Regent moved from Tynemouth & District to Tyneside Tramways at this same time. To slightly ease the

In this peak-hour scene at Gateshead railway station, three of Gateshead's single deckers and one of the company's ex.Sheffield double deck balcony cars almost hide two Newcastle Corporation trams from the camera. In the foreground, the single decker has just arrived from Teams whilst the double decker unusually shows Low Fell on its destination indicator. (Go-Ahead Northern)

burden on the hard-pressed fleet, a total of 44 of the buses requisitioned from Northern were returned to the company by the War Department in 1942 together with a further 3 single deckers which had been requisitioned from Midland Red earlier in the war, and all except for 8 which were SRR-type coaches were immediately put into service, the SRRs never being relicensed. Additionally, 1942 saw the arrival of the first new double decker to join the fleet since 1940. This was built to the austere specifications laid down by the Ministry of Supply and was based on a rugged Guy Arab I chassis. With its angular Massey highbridge body and painted dark green with red lettering, it looked somewhat out of place in the Northern fleet but nevertheless was a most welcome addition. During the following year it was joined by a further two dark green-liveried Guy Arab Is, one of which carried Weymann bodywork, the other a Massey body. During this same year, a further 4 BMMO single deckers were re-purchased by Northern from the Ministry of War Transport along with 2 buses of this same make by Tynemouth & District and a Leyland TS2, 2 BMMO IM4s and a BMMO ON by Sunderland District. The latter also received 4 austere Guy Arab IIs, this time fitted with Pickering highbridge bodywork and painted in a grey livery. The pair of BMMO IM4s were never returned to service however and were resold in 1944 whilst the BMMO ON was stored until its eventual re-entry to service in 1946.

Meanwhile, in similar fashion to operators in other parts of Britain, in addition to repainting a number of its buses into an olive-green livery, the cream roofs of most others were repainted grey in order to make them less visible to enemy aircraft. Wing tips and edges together with such items as step edges and lifeguards were painted white to assist passengers and other road users during the hours of blackout while headlights and interior lights were masked so as not to attract attention from the air etc. As can be imagined, the lack of street lighting coupled with almost non-existent vehicle headlights made driving at night an extremely strenuous task and similarly, the reduced interior lighting in buses placed enormous additional strains on conductors. The latter's duties were further hindered after Northern altered several of its single deckers to longitudinal perimeter seating in order to increase their carrying capacity (wartime regulations allowing up to 30 standing passengers to be carried), a feature which on occasions made the

collection of fares an almost impossible task. In an attempt to save precious fuel, and at the instruction of the Ministry of Transport, Northern also converted one of its diesel-engined and a number of its petrol-engined single deckers to producer gas operation, these pulling behind them strange looking trailers (of which 38 had been purchased) containing the gas producing equipment. Surprisingly, in view of the strains facing the company with the normal maintenance of its fleet, one of the "home-built" three-axle SE6 single deckers was rebuilt to two-axle configuration in the company's workshops at Bensham in 1942, and it is believed that this was the first 30ft.long two-axle bus to operate in Britain. It retained its seating capacity of 44 following its rebuilding however, and was thereafter designated SE6/4. Additionally, in order to extend the lives of several of the older pre-war double deckers of its own and its subsidiary fleets, Northern took the decision to fit a number of these with new bodies and to this end despatched 16 AEC Regents (12 from Northern and 4 from Tynemouth) and 5 of Tyneside's Leyland Titans to Northern Coach Builders at Newcastle who duly built their new highbridge bodies to Ministry of Supply specification in 1943. Despite being unable to purchase new buses other than via allocation by the Ministry of Supply, Northern's Board of Directors provisionally approved an order for 75 single deck and 50 double deck AECs for delivery after the cessation of the hostilities.

By now, the Guy Arab was becoming a familiar sight in fleets throughout the country and Northern was no exception. 12 more of these spartan double deckers made their debut in 1944, some with Massey bodywork, others with Northern Counties Motor & Engineering Co. bodies of a slightly less angular design, and on this occasion they received full Northern livery rather than being in the wartime dark green. Fitted with Gardner 5LW engines these Arab IIs soon settled down amongst the AECs and BMMOs which dominated the Northern fleet at that time and provided Northern with some much-needed additional double deckers. Not quite ending there, 5 more NCME-bodied examples were allocated to Northern in 1945 with an additional pair going to Sunderland District before the war officially ended. Despite the effects the war had had on many parts of Britain, Northern and its associates had been fortunate in suffering minimal damage to its vehicles or property as a result of enemy action, and despite fuel, staff and vehicle shortages, had served the population of Tyneside, Wearside and County Durham in an unbelievably efficient manner

Brush-bodied AEC Regal 928 (CU4268) was unusual in being the company's only diesel-engined bus to be converted to producer gas operation during World War II (all the other gas conversions being petrol engined). It is seen here connected to a gas-producer trailer early in 1943. (Go-Ahead Northern)

A typical scene at the end of a long day's work during the dark years of World War II shows a trio of Northern's 1938 Leyland TS8s and Tynemouth's Weymann-bodied NGT SE6 T91 (FT3904) collecting workers from the Tyneside factory of Hawthorn Leslie & Co. (Go-Ahead Northern)

Army personnel take their instructions at Newcastle's Worswick Street bus station during the strike of Northern and associate companies employees from 10th to 23rd March 1949. The Army general service trucks employed on these duties were mainly Canadian-built Chevrolets and Fords. (Go-Ahead Northern)

throughout those dark years. Before peace returned to Britain, however, a dispute between Northern's employees and management over new schedules led to the former withdrawing their labour with effect from 10 March 1945. As a result of this stoppage which rapidly spread from Bensham (where it began) to all depots of the Northern Group, the Army was called in to provide vital services for miners and war workers and for this purpose used a variety of its general service wagons in a manner reminiscent of the 'lorry-buses' immediately after World War I. Fortunately the grievances were soon settled and the strike was ended after thirteen days.

The 31st December 1945 saw a break with the past with the resignations of Mr.H.A.Stagg who had been Northern's Secretary since the company's formation and had previously been Secretary of Gateshead & District Tramways since 1910, and Mr.R.J.Howley, Northern's Chairman who had joined the board on 5 December 1913 and had taken up his current position on 7 June 1923. Mr.Howley remained a director, however, until 1946 and Mr.Stagg likewise until early 1947.

An interior view of one of Northern's Ransomes-bodied BMMO M-type buses. (T.Godfrey collection)

POST-WAR RECOVERY

With the war now ended, Britain was desperately struggling to return to a normal way of life as quickly as possible. Men demobbed from the armed services were returning home to resume their civilian occupations and re-united families were starting to enjoy their new found freedom. The desire to travel appeared to be high on their list of priorities and Northern, like bus and coach operators all over the country, soon found that demand was exceeding the availability of vehicles. Coupled with the fact that much of the fleet had lived on borrowed time over the past six years and given the minimum maintenance that it had received during this period, Northern and its subsidiaries were in desperate need of new buses and coaches. Orders were immediately placed for 50 Guy Arab and 18 AEC Regal II chassis, all fitted with Brush single deck bodies, 10 AEC Regents and 20 Guy Arabs with NCB double deck bodies and 18 AEC Regal IIs with Saunders single deck bodywork, but during this transitional period deliveries were painfully slow and it was not until November that the first of the new post-war buses made their debut. These comprised the first of the 18 AEC Regals with Saunders 36-seat bodywork, the remainder of which took up their duties in December along with the 10 AEC Regent IIs and 8 of the Guy Arab IIs fitted with locally-built NCB highbridge bodies. Although none of the Brush-bodied single deckers were received before the year ended, Sunderland District took delivery of 5 new Roe highbridge-bodied Leyland PD1s and as has been mentioned previously, received a further bus returning home from the War Department. Tynemouth & District gained no fewer than 18 new buses, all of which were double deckers (5 NCME-bodied Guy Arab IIs and 13 Weymann-bodied AEC Regent IIs, while Wakefields took delivery of 2 Weymann-bodied AEC Regents and 2 Tyneside Tramways received 3 all-Leyland PD1s. To further update its fleets, Northern continued the rebodying programme which it had started in 1943, with the fitting of a new NCB double deck body to its solitary BMMO REDD in 1945 and to 6 of Sunderland District's AEC Regents and in 1946 when a number of the 1936 AEC Regals and some BMMO IM6 and ON-types were given new 36-seat bus bodies by Pickering and several of Northern's ex.Tynemouth pre-war AEC Regents received new NCB highbridge bodies. In addition, a number of inter-fleet transfers also took place when Northern inherited 4 BMMO single deckers and 2 from Wakefields and 8 SE6s from Tynemouth & District. Far from increasing the fleet strength, however, these new arrivals nowhere near compensated for the number of buses withdrawn (53 by Northern and 20 by Sunderland District) and only Tynemouth & District with 20 new buses against 14 withdrawals and Tyneside Tramways with 3 new buses and no withdrawals actually gained an increase their fleet sizes. It must, however, be said that of the vehicles "officially withdrawn" in 1946, many of them had spent a long period in store towards the end of the war or had been used as ambulances or for other ancillary purposes and thus the situation was perhaps not as black as has been painted.

Northern, who since its inception had suffered low bridge problems throughout much of its operating area which precluded the use of double deckers on many routes, finally gained some success in persuading the highways authorities to widen the footpath at each side of the arched bridges on the approach to Worswick Street bus station at Newcastle and beneath the railway tracks at Tyne Dock, thus providing a narrow but clear passage beneath each to allow freedom for double deckers. This enabled the company's fleet of buses of this type to be strengthened and passenger capacity on some routes to be dramatically increased. Despite the above, however, the low bridge problem over the whole of Northern's operating territory was far from resolved and there was still a real need for maximum capacity single

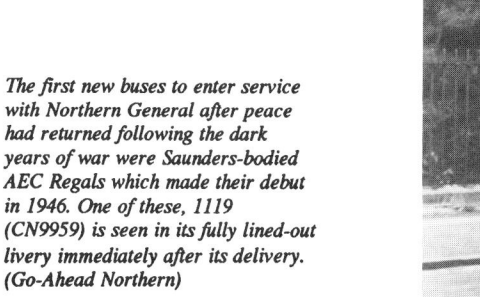

The first new buses to enter service with Northern General after peace had returned following the dark years of war were Saunders-bodied AEC Regals which made their debut in 1946. One of these, 1119 (CN9959) is seen in its fully lined-out livery immediately after its delivery. (Go-Ahead Northern)

Pictured before its entry into service in 1946 is NCB-bodied AEC Regent II 1169 (ACN169). One of the first double deckers to be added to the Northern fleet after the ending of World War II, it gave the company eleven years service before being withdrawn in 1957 and sold for further operation in Yugoslavia. (Go-Ahead Northern)

Seen at Newcastle's Haymarket bus station soon after their entry into service in 1946 are Tynemouth & District Weymann-bodied AEC Regent IIs 140 & 137 (FT5710/07). When new, these buses unusually had their destination screens over-panelled to leave only the route number apperture. Their destination was shown on removable boards in front of the lower saloon bulkead window. (K.A.Jenkinson collection)

The first of Northern's large fleet of specially adapted Guy Arab III single deckers made their debut in 1947. Fitted with Brush bodywork, these had their driving position moved slightly forward to enable 38 seated passengers to be accommodated. Seen when brand new is 1070 (GUP70) which took up its duties in April 1947. (Brush Coachwork Ltd.)

deckers within the company. To this end, the fleet of specially-modified Guy Arab IIIs ordered earlier began to arrive in February 1947 and, in similar fashion to the pre-war AEC Regal 1Bs, these had their driving position moved as far forward as possible to enable bodywork incorporating 38 seats to be fitted. All 50 of these Brush-bodied buses entered service during the course of the next five months followed in September and October by the 18 Brush-bodied 36-seat AEC Regals. Also joining the Northern fleet during 1947 were a further 14 NCB-bodied Guy Arab II double deckers whilst Sunderland District added 5 more Roe-bodied Leyland PD1 double deckers to its fleet.

By now, nationalisation of Britain's buses was looming on the horizon with the Government of the day pushing hard to bring all of Britain's transport under its control. The railways companies had already succumbed on 1 January 1948 and talks with the Tilling Group were at an advanced stage, these resulting in the sale of its interests to the state later that year, on 5 November, but the B.E.T., favouring the capitalist system, was totally opposed to any such Government offer. As the going began to get tough, almost all of the buses of the various B.E.T. subsidiaries throughout the country were adorned with anti-nationalisation posters and eventually they won the day, remaining independent and retaining their own identity. Although the Government gained a small stake in the Northern Group through its control of the railways, it was twenty more years before the State was able to accomplish its original dream and add the B.E.T. to its portfolio. However, more of that later.

The Limited Stop Pool service from Newcastle to Manchester and Liverpool had restarted by this time and, in addition, a service was resumed between Newcastle and Coventry under the Yorkshire Services 'Ten Cities Express' banner by Fawdon Bus Company. Northern undertook duties on both these routes, operating them with its pre-war coaches which were supplemented by stage carriage buses such as AEC Regals, Leyland Tigers and the new Guy Arab single deckers in the absence of any new coaches. Meanwhile, almost all the stage carriage services withdrawn or curtailed during the war had been reinstated and in addition, a few extensions were made to serve the numerous new housing estates which seemed to be springing up almost everywhere.

The delivery of new vehicles had by 1948 slowed down somewhat and Northern received only 18 NCB-bodied Guy Arab II double deckers during that year. Sunderland District fared a little better with 8 Strachan-bodied AEC Regal Is and 11 Brush-bodied Leyland PS1s

Seen during the late 'fifties wearing Northern's red livery with cream roof and centre band is 1947 NCB-bodied Guy Arab III 1214 (ACN514).

New in 1934 numbered 616, BMMO SOS ON-type CN6022 was impressed by the War Department in 1940 and was repurchased by Northern two years later. Renumbered 1043 upon its return, it was given a new Pickering body in 1947 and remained in service in its new form (as illustrated) until 1955 when it was sold to London dealer.
(Go-Ahead Northern)

Two of Sunderland District's post-war single deckers - Strachan-bodied AEC Regal 196 (GUP540) and Brush-bodied Leyland PS1 210 (GUP554) hide one of the company's Saro-bodied Leyland Tiger Cubs as they pick up their passengers in Sunderland in 1955. Both buses were new in 1948 and had bodywork built to BET Federation design.
(T.Godfrey collection)

whereas Tynemouth & District received a further 13 AEC Regent IIs with Weymann highbridge bodywork, and Wakefields one. Surprisingly, all the Weymann double deck bodies were built to what amounted to pre-war design, as were the Brush bodies on Northern's single deck Guy Arabs. The smallest of Northern's subsidiaries, Tyneside Tramways, added just 3 buses to its fleet, these being all-Leyland products based on the recently-introduced PD2 chassis.

Suffering from an acute shortage of buses with which to meet its increasing demands and replace those which were time-expired and recently withdrawn, Northern hired 25 Roe-bodied Leyland TS7 single deckers from Yorkshire Woollen District Transport during the second and third months of 1948. Yorkshire Woollen, also being a B.E.T. subsidiary, had purchased these buses in 1935/6 with bodywork built by Roe to B.E.F. specification and in many ways they were extremely

Originally fitted with a Brush body, Northern's 1939 AEC Regal IB 926 (CU4266) was rebodied by Pickering in 1949. Remaining in service until 1957, it is seen here in the early 'fifties still sporting its owner's fully lined-out livery.
(K.A.Jenkinson collection)

Due to the absence of new coaches, Northern in the early post-war years continued to employ pre-war vehicles on its long distance express services as is illustrated by this view of thirteen year old 1302 (HD5809) in Harrogate bus station enroute to Liverpool in December 1949. Acquired from Yorkshire Woollen District Transport in January 1949 after several months on loan, this Roe bus-bodied Leyland TS7 had recently been refurbished and fitted with rubber mounted windows by Picktree Coachworks of Chester-le-Street.

similar to those in the Sunderland District fleet and were therefore not total strangers to the Northern Group. At first retaining their Yorkshire maroon livery and fleet numbers, albeit prefixed with the letter 'Y', these buses were ultimately purchased by Northern in January 1949 after which they were renumbered into the company's standard system. Between May of that year and February 1950, despite provision having been made to rebody these, their structural condition was such that it was not found necessary and instead all 25 were rebuilt by Picktree Coachbuilders of Chester-le-Street (a company substantially owned by Major Hayter, though separate from Northern) and, although basically retaining their original appearance, were fitted with rubber-mounted windows etc. Meanwhile, Northern's vehicle rebodying programme continued with a number of its BMMO IM6 and ON-type buses and AEC Regal IIs receiving new Pickering bodies in 1946/7, the 5 1938 front-entrance Leyland TD5s being fitted with new ECW rear-entrance highbridge bodies in 1948, and the following year witnessing the provision of new Pickering 38-seat bodies for 2 BMMO IM6s along with a new Saunders body for one of the ex.Charlton's Leyland LT7s.

During the period 1947-9, the service network of Northern and its subsidiaries was enhanced by the inauguration of several new routes on Wearside, South Tyneside and in County Durham and of these, one (Durham - Brasside via Pity Me) had originated in May 1939 as a works service to a Government site at Brasside. Others included Consett to Elm Park and Consett to Oakdale Estate (both hourly), Gateshead to Heworth and Newcastle to Thornley (a small village near Tow Law), Newcastle to Seaburn, two summer services from Newcastle to Marsden via Jarrow and a Tuesday, Saturday and Sunday route from Consett to Allensford. All these were operated by Northern whilst Sunderland District added services from Houghton-le-Spring to Chester-le-Street via Herrington Burn and from Hetton-le-Hole to West Rainton to its network in 1947. Perhaps the most unusual service however, was that started by Northern on 5 March 1949, which was an all-night circular running from Newcastle's Central Station to Low Fell and Heworth.

Meanwhile, further expansion and consolidation was achieved in January 1949 when Northern made its first post-war acquisition of an independent operator within its territory. This was the old-established business of Dixon Brothers of Lanchester who traded as "The Witbank". Dixon's 13 buses (5 Leyland PLSC3s which had ironically started life with Sunderland District, 2 Maudslays and 6 Bedfords) were all added to Northern's fleet although only 4 each of the PLSCs and the Bedfords continued in service. Dixon Brothers had started their business in March 1922 and had always concentrated more on stage carriage services than on coaching, operating routes from Durham to Consett, Lanchester to Tow Law and Lanchester to Annfield Plain in addition to a number of works and church services. All these were continued by their new owner and that from Lanchester to Tow Law was extended by Northern back to Stanley.

Following the creation by the British Transport Commission in June 1949 of a Road Passenger Executive, it decided that a Northern Passenger Road Transport Board should be set up to establish effective working relations with the municipalities in the area which was to stretch from Ripon and Malton in the south to the Scottish border in the north. Almost all of United's operations would be placed under the control of the new board as would those of the eight municipal transport operators within the defined area, although it was accepted that if Northern and its subsidiaries were to be included, this could only be achieved by compulsory purchase, for which powers had been given to the BTC in the 1947 Transport Act. When all the independent companies were taken into account, a total of no fewer than 214 operators were to be included in the scheme which, in total, would maintain a fleet of some 4,400 vehicles. Despite encountering a vast amount of opposition to the scheme, especially from the municipalities and the BET, the BTC pushed ahead with its plans which got as far as being submitted to the Minister for approval. In the meantime, the Road

One of ten Windover-bodied Guy Arab III coaches purchased new by Northern in December 1948, 1217 (BCN17) was, like its sisters, painted in an attractive cream & maroon livery and powered by a Meadows engine. Stored until May 1949 before entering service, they all had their original engines replaced in 1954 by more economical AEC 7.7 litre units and remained in service until 1957. (Go-Ahead Northern)

Delivery of 38-seat Brush-bodied modified Guy Arab III single deckers continued into the summer of 1950 by which time more than 130 were in service in the Northern fleet. Those arriving in 1950 differed from their predecessors by having pan-mounted windows with radiused corners as illustrated by 1347 (LPT147).

*Two of the 1950 BET-style Roe-bodied Leyland PS2/1s supplied new to Sunderland District in 1950 were fitted with a small route number box alongside their front destination screen for operation on the Consett group of services from Sunderland for which just a single line destination display was considered inadequate. Illustrating this is 218 (JUP838) which is seen here in 1960 immediately prior to its withdrawal from service.
(K.A.Jenkinson collection)*

Passenger Transport Executive announced that it had similar schemes in hand for East Anglia and the South West, both of which subsequently met with the same response! The expectation that the Northern scheme would go ahead was sufficient in June 1950 to cause three local independents - Darlington Triumph Services Ltd., Express Omnibus Co. and ABC Motors (a consortium of three operators - Aaron, Binks and Coulson) to sell their businesses to the BTC. Initially it was intended that Darlington Triumph Services was to be taken over by United, but when the other two companies were added, the decision was taken to instead form a new company. Thus, a new company was set up on 1 August 1950 under the title of Durham District Services Ltd. to continue the services acquired from Triumph, Express and ABC. Although it had originally been intended that these company's buses would be owned by the proposed Northern Passenger Road Transport Board and that United would also disappear into this new body, no further moves were made in this direction and the scheme was eventually, and quietly abandoned.

Returning to the fleet, the first new coaches to arrive since before the war did so in May 1949, exactly two years after the date upon which they had been ordered. These, unusually, were Meadows-engined Guy Arab IIIs with Windover 30-seat bodies and were unique within the B.E.T. Although fast, they were heavy on fuel and thus, after five years in service, all were re-engined with more economic reconditioned AEC 7.7 litre power units removed from 1936 AEC Regals awaiting disposal. Until the arrival of these new coaches, all Northern's long distance services and tours had been operated by pre-war vehicles which, although luxuriously appointed, were now starting to show their age. Other new additions to the fleet in 1949 were 10 NCB-bodied highbridge Guy Arab IIIs and no fewer than 50 Brush-bodied 38-seat Guy Arab IIIs which, like their predecessors, were of the design in which the driving position was moved forward. Although it had rebodied two of its Leyland Tigers with coach bodywork in May 1939, Sunderland District broke new ground by purchasing its first ever new vehicles of this type, these being a pair of 30-seat Duple-bodied Leyland PS1/1s whereas Tynemouth & District confined itself to double deckers, receiving 6 NCB-bodied AEC Regent IIIs and 10 Pickering-bodied Guy Arab IIIs fitted with Meadows engines. The latter, like the Northern coaches, were also re-engined after three years. For Wakefields came 2 new NCB-bodied AEC Regent IIIs whilst only one inter-fleet transfer took place when Northern acquired a Leyland-bodied TD3c of 1934 vintage from Tyneside Tramways. This was immediately despatched to Burlingham's coachworks at Blackpool where it was given a new highbridge body before returning to the north-east to enter service with its "new" owner.

1949/50 saw more of Northern's pre-war vehicles gain a further lease of life when 28 AEC Regals were given new 38-seat bus bodies by Picktree, 56 were given new Pickering 38-seat bus bodies as were 7 Tynemouth Regals, and a 1940 AEC Regent was rebodied with the NCB body removed from a 1932 Regent. New buses continued to arrive in quantity during 1950 with Northern receiving a further 34 Brush-bodied 38-seat modified Guy Arab IIIs and 19 Guy Arab III double deckers, 8 of which were fitted with Brush and the remainder with NCB bodies. All the double deckers were of highbridge configuration and were 8ft. wide. Other than Gateshead, of which more

*New in 1950, Sunderland District Roe-bodied Leyland PD2/1 233 (KUP268) is pictured here in Fencehouses followed by 226 (KUP260), a Roe-bodied AEC Regent III of the same age.
(T.W.W.Knowles)*

47

later, the only one of Northern's subsidiaries to receive new buses was Sunderland District who gained 4 Duple coach-bodied Leyland PS1/1s, 6 Roe bus-bodied Leyland PS2/1s and 14 Roe highbridge-bodied double deckers of which 8 were AEC Regent IIIs and 6 were Leyland PD2/1s. Further consolidating its position, Tynemouth purchased Wallsend-based Hollings Garage & Engineering Works on 27 May 1950 and on that day took over the operation of their three services running between Wallsend and High Farm Estate. No vehicles were involved in the deal. Later in the year, in October, the extension of Northern's South Shields garage begun the previous year was completed to provide accommodation for an additional 43 vehicles.

THE TRAMS GIVE WAY

Perhaps the most important event at the start of the new decade was the re-entry into the field of motor bus operation of Gateshead & District Tramways who, since the beginning of 1914, had relied solely on electrtic traction. The original electric tramway fleet had been supplemented and partly replaced between 1920 and 1928 by a fleet of 25 new single deck bogie cars with seating for 48 passengers, the bodywork for all but seven of which was built in the company's own workshops. These were mounted on Brill trucks and fitted with Dick Kerr motors. Seven Brush-bodied double deckers were added to the fleet in 1923 and these proved to be the last trams to be purchased new, all those subsequently joining the fleet having had a previous owner. These comprised 6 double deckers purchased from Oldham Corporation in 1947 and 5 single deckers acquired from Newcastle Corporation in 1948 together with 8 double deck bodies from Sheffield Corporation and 3 double deck bodies from Liverpool Corporation in 1924.

A major development for Gateshead & District had come in December 1922 when powers obtained by Newcastle Corporation two years earlier for running across the Tyne via the High Level Bridge were invoked and through running began on 12 January 1923 from Dunston, Bensham and Low Fell to Newcastle (Central Station); Low Fell to Gosforth; Saltwell Park to the Museum; Heworth to Brighton Grove and the Monument and Wrekenton to Walker. All these services ran over the High Level Bridge and, just as Newcastle cars were then to be seen south of the river, so Gateshead cars ventured northwards into Newcastle. Six years later, in 1928, another bridge was opened across the river, this being the new Tyne Bridge upon which tram tracks were also laid, thus providing the tramway network with a second link between Newcastle and Gateshead and strengthening the inter-workings of the Gateshead company and Newcastle Corporation. The Gateshead system had by then settled down, affording the residents in and around that town a network of services which continued largely unchanged for the remainder of the system's life.

Had the second World War not intervened, the Gateshead tramway system might not have survived much beyond the early 'forties, however, for in 1938, as has been stated earlier, the company promoted the Gateshead & District Tramways and Trolley Vehicles Act which, if implemented, would have replaced the trams with trolleybuses in a similar manner to Newcastle Corporation. The intrusion of the hostilities halted these plans, however, and by the time peace returned, the political uncertainty in terms of possible nationalisation made the company reluctant to proceed with the conversion. Nevertheless, agreement was reached with Newcastle Corporation in October 1949 to abandon the trams, repeal the trolley vehicle powers and substitute motor buses, although at that point of time no further action was taken. Ultimately, the company promoted a new Bill in 1950 which, if passed, would allow the trams to be replaced by motor buses. On 12 July 1950 the Bill became law and consequent on this, the company changed its name from Gateshead & District Tramway Co. Ltd. to Gateshead & District Omnibus Co. Ltd. Prior to this, however, a start had been made on the conversion programme. Under the 1909 Act which allowed the use of buses as feeders to the tramway, the Wrekenton route was cut back to the junction of Belle Vue Terrace and Brunswick Street and buses took over from the trams on the cross-Tyne service to Heworth on 5 March 1950. Due to having insufficient buses, however, both routes remained open for rush hour and occasional tramcar workings from the foot of High Street and it was not until 22 September that the wiring was finally removed. Around 18 cars were withdrawn as a result of this closure, the remainder soldiering on until 3 March 1951 when the next conversion from tram to motor bus was undertaken, this involving the Saltwell Park and Bensham routes. This witnessed the demise of the remaining double deck cars, leaving the fleet entirely single deck for its final months of operation. Of the surviving routes, buses took over on that to Low Fell on 8 April 1951 with the Teams service following suit on 15 July. Completion of the conversion programme was achieved on 4 August 1951 when, following the raising of a railway bridge which had delayed the final abandonment, Gateshead's last trams made their final journeys on the Dunston service. The final two cars, 20 and 16 (the latter freshly repainted and carrying officials of the company and civic dignitaries) left Dunston for

Amongst the first buses to be purchased by Gateshead & District since 1913 was Guy Arab III 10 (BCN610) which was new in 1950 fitted with a Guy body built on a Park Royal metal frame. Seen here in its original livery, it was transferred to Northern in 1960 and during the following year was converted to a tree lopper.

Ordered by Gateshead & District but diverted to Northern before delivery in 1950, Brush-bodied Guy Arab III 1363 (BCN863) retained the three-aperture destination layout specified by Gateshead. After its withdrawal from service in 1962 it was sold to a contractor for use as a site office at North Shields.

Having now almost completed its rebodying programme which had involved a large portion of the pre-war fleet, Northern turned its attention to the building of new vehicles from the mechanical units removed from its remaining unrebodied pre-war AEC Regals. Built in its Bensham workshops using 1937 AEC Regal chassis frames and one from a 1932 AEC Regent lengthened to 30ft., these "new" chassis - which were classed as NGT rather than AEC - were then despatched to Picktree Coachbuilders at Chester-le-Street where they were given new 8ft wide bodies. 10 were fitted with full-front 35 seat coach bodies whilst the eleventh was built as a cheaper and lighter vehicle with 43-seat front entrance bus body of spartan half-cab design. The coaches were somewhat old fashioned in their appearance and underpowered with their AEC 7.7 litre engines, but nevertheless they gave eight years service before all were withdrawn and sold to Yugoslavia for further service. When new in 1951, three of these coaches were given experimental liveries, one being painted all-over white, one all black and one all red. Despite having diversified towards the complete reconstruction of pre-war vehicles, the previously-started more straight forward rebodying programme continued to trickle on with 7 of the 1944 Guy Arab IIs being given new Brush bodies during the year. This order was, however, originally for 8 such bodies, one of which was intended for fitting to pre-war AEC Regent 943 but in the event, this received the body from 568 whose chassis was being rebuilt

the last time at 11.22pm to make their way to Sunderland Road depot and thus, after 68 years, electric traction had come to an end, not only in Gateshead but throughout the whole of the B.E.T. empire. As far as the trams themselves were concerned, whilst the majority were scrapped in the depot yard, 19 of the single deckers were sold in 1951 to the Eastern Region of British Railways for use on its Grimsby & Immingham Light Railway where all but one continued in service until the closure of that line on 1 July 1961.

The buses purchased for the initial stage of the tramway conversion programme in 1950 comprised 20 Guy Arab III double deckers with bodywork built by Guy on Park Royal frames, but in view of the necessity of putting more buses on the Wrekenton and Heworth services at an early date, 6 8ft.-wide NCB-bodied Guy Arab IIIs were diverted from a Northern order as soon afterwards were 9 8ft.-wide Brush-bodied Arab IIIs. Supplementing these in 1951 were 37 new all-Leyland PD2s, all but 14 of which were also 8ft. wide. These were a special offer by Leyland at a reduced price and with an early delivery date, thus making it possible to convert routes more quickly. Four of the Leylands were, however, delivered in Northern livery and immediately wnt on loan to that company to whom they were ultimately sold in October 1952. In addition to the latter, Northern had also added 8 secondhand 1937/8 vintage Park Royal-bodied AEC Regents toits fleet in March 1950, these having been acquired from City of Oxford Motor Services Ltd.

One of eight Park Royal-bodied AEC Regents purchased by Northern from City of Oxford Motor Services in 1950, 1399 (FWL641) which dated from 1938 took up its duties in the north-east in August 1950. Fitted with a route number box on its front lower deck bulkhead (beneath the canopy), it is seen here working a Sunderland local service in 1952, two years before its withdrawal for scrapping. (K.A.Jenkinson collection)

Although bearing a strong resemblance to ECW's designs of that period, Northern Guy Arab III 1387, new in 1950, had a body built by Northern Coach Builders. Fully lined out, it looks immaculate as it poses for the camera prior to its entry into service. (Go-Ahead Northern)

49

Ten of Northern's 1938 Leyland TS8s were fitted with 30-seat coach bodies built by Brush which featured a stepped waistrail and had a roof-mounted luggage carrier. One of these, 869 (CU3949) seen resting in Wellington Street coach station, Leeds in July 1950 had been refurbished by Picktree who had replaced its original half-drop windows with sliding ventilators. It remained in service until 1954 and was scrapped during the following year. (G.H.F.Atkins)

All-Leyland PD2/3 38 (BCN889) was acquired by Tyneside from Northern in June 1951 when only three months old. Seen here in looking immaculate in its original lined-out livery, it remained in service until 1964. (J.Wyndham)

and lengthened (as mentioned above) and thus the 8th body was cancelled.

The only genuine new vehicles to enter service with Northern in 1951 were 5 all-Leyland PD2/3 double deckers although 4 buses of this same type were delivered to Tyneside Tramways whilst 10 Brush-bodied underfloor-engined Leyland PSU1/9s were added to the Sunderland District fleet. The original order placed for these - in November 1947 - was for 6 Leyland single deckers with Roe bodywork for delivery in 1949/50, but on 20 September 1950, due to their non-delivery, it was agreed to replace the order with one for 10 "flat-engined" Leylands fitted with Brush 43-seat bodies. In addition, Tyneside Tramways received a new all-Leyland PD2/3 transferred from Northern in exchange for an NCB-rebodied 1932 AEC Regent.

Before the year ended, Northern agreed on 15 November to purchase the stage carriage services from Washington to Birtley and to Chester-le-Street, and excursions and tours licences of J.Nicholson & Sons (New Washington) Ltd. of Birtley who traded as Crown Coaches, and also to take over the excursions and tours licences of Marshall & Co. Ltd. from the Haymarket, Newcastle. In both instances no physical assets such as vehicles or property were involved.

In 1951, having now reached 99 in its route numbering system, Northern found itself faced with a problem due to the route number boxes (on the buses which had them) only having two-track blinds. Although in the past the numbers of services which had ceased running had been reused, with the company now having 98 services, this practise was no longer possible. Instead, this difficulty was overcome by using a single number with a letter suffix and as a result services such as 1A and 3B were soon to become familiar. After a comparatively quiet year in 1950, several new services were introduced in 1951 and included amongst these were Sunderland (Park Lane) to Pennywell (which was opened after strong opposition from Sunderland Corporation who considered that their housing estates should be served by their buses!); Durham to Consett via Lanchester and Delves; South Leam Estate to Jarrow and a circular service in Stanley all operated by Northern whilst Sunderland District extended its Newcastle to East Herrington route to Fence Houses Station in December of that

One of five all-Leyland PD2/3s purchased new by Northern in 1951, 1392 (BCN892) looks immaculate in its lined-out livery as it awaits its departure to South Shields from Worswick Street bus station, Newcastle in August 1954. (G.H.F.Atkins)

Having been rebuilt in 1939 with a fixed roof and given a roof-mounted luggage carrier, Short Bros-bodied NGT SE6 653 (CN6612) was still employed on holiday tour duties when caught by the camera in George Street, Nottingham in October 1951. As can be seen, its original all-red livery had given way to Northern's post-war coach scheme and during its earlier rebuilding it had also gained an enlarged front grille. (G.H.F.Atkins)

year. Following in January 1952 were a pair of services from Sunderland (Park Lane) to Red House Estate and at the end of the year two to Plains Farm which were run jointly with Sunderland Corporation.

Further expansion was achieved in August 1951 when Northern acquired the business and fleet of J.W.Hurst & Sons Ltd. of Winlaton. Hurst had entered the bus business by October 1923 and in the latter years had concentrated mainly on stage carriage services with routes operating from Newcastle to High Spen; Newcastle to Winlaton via two different routes; Blaydon to Winlaton Mill and from Winlaton to Blaydon Haughs, all of which passed to Northern (and were numbered 8, 8A, 8B, 8C and 8D respectively) together with Hurst's garage and all-single deck fleet which comprised 1 Maudslay ML3; 1 Leyland TS6; 5 Dennis Lancets and 5 Guy Arab IIIs. One of the Dennis buses, a Lancet J3, was only a month old whilst four of the five pre-war buses had been rebodied by ACB during the 1947-9 period and at the time of takeover, a further new body was on order.

By now, the Northern Group was the only large bus operator in

Sunderland District's 1945 NCME-bodied Guy Arab II 181 (FPT999) swings out of its home-town bus station on a journey to New Silksworth during the early 'fifties. Still looking every inch a wartime bus, it remained in service until 1958.

Amongst the vehicles acquired by Northern with the business of J.W.Hurst & Son of Winlaton in August 1951 was KPT136, an ACB-bodied Guy Arab III 35-seat bus dating from 1949. Seen here at Marlborough Crescent bus station, Newcastle after gaining its new owner's livery and fleet number 1453, it remained in service until 1961. (K.A.Jenkinson collection)

Britain to still maintain 1d fares and whilst the cost of everything it used to carry on its business was nearly three times what it was in 1939, its fares had only increased by 25% since that date. This was without doubt a proud record and one which the company was reluctant to change, although as a result of subsequent cost increases, it had eventually to do so.

Although the underfloor-engined single decker had already appeared in the Sunderland District fleet, it had yet to make its debut with Northern where in 1952 it was still conspicuous by its absence. Indeed, the only single deckers to enter service with the parent company during that year were a further 11 rebuilt pre-war AEC Regals which, after having their chassis lengthened and widened, were fitted with new Picktree full-fronted coach bodies. It was reckoned that in post-war days, Major Hayter became almost obsessed with fuel economy, hence the rebuilding of older AECs instead of purchasing large numbers of Leyland Royal Tigers, and the continuance of Gardner 5LW-engined Guys right up to his retirement, although presumably small-engined Tiger Cubs were considered economic, as were the lighter, integral AEC Monocoaches that Hayter purchased in 1954. Also arriving during 1952 were 40 new Guy Arab III double deckers for which the bodies were built in equal numbers by Park Royal and Weymann (and of which 10 of the former were diverted from a Gateshead order) whilst Tynemouth received 10 Weymann-bodied Guy Arab IIIs and Wakefields 6 Beadle integrally-constructed coaches which employed pre-war AEC running units. Sunderland District meanwhile added to their fleet a further 8 underfloor-engined Leyland Royal Tiger buses, the bodies of which on this occasion were built by Roe and were of 8ft. width, being the first vehicles of this dimension to be operated by that company. 1952 also brought an end to the Northern company's rebodying programme and saw only two buses treated in this manner, these being Massey-bodied wartime Guy Arab Is which were given new Roe highbridge bodies. Amongst the buses withdrawn by the Northern Group was the unique BMMO REDD double decker, the chassis of which was scrapped after its 1945 NCB body had been transferred to one of the ex.City of Oxford AEC Regents. Meanwhile, one of the 1933 BMMO IM6-type single deckers was decorated with coloured lights and used as an illuminated vehicle at Seaburn during 1952.

1953 witnessed the rebuilding of 12 of the 1936 AEC Regal II chassis which were then fitted with new Picktree 43-seat front entrance, half-cab bus bodies and a further 3 which re-emerged with full-fronted Picktree coach bodywork. In addition, 10 integrally-constructed Beadle 35-seat coaches were received, built using unidentified pre-war AEC running units together with 20 new Weymann Orion-bodied Guy Arab IV double deckers. Initially, 30 of the latter had been ordered, but of these 10 were diverted to another B.E.T. subsidiary, Potteries Motor Traction, before their arrival in the north-east. During 1953, the only one of Northern's subsidiaries to gain any new vehicles was Sunderland District who took delivery of 2 Leyland Royal Tigers fitted with Duple 37-seat centre entrance coach bodywork and also had its 4 1943 vintage Guy Arab IIs fitted with new Roe highbridge bodies. On the property front, Sunderland District's Philadelphia premises were extended to provide new fitting shops and stores.

Seeking further consolidation, Northern in March 1953 acquired the business of Hunters Omnibus Company Limited of Great Lumley which had been established by S.F.Hunter early in 1928. Included in the deal was Hunters' hourly service from Chester-le-Street to Great Lumley Council Houses (which was supplimented during 1954 by an additional new service extended to Houghton-le-Spring) and 4 vehicles (2 Bedford OBs, a Commer Commando and a Leyland PS1/1), all of which continued in service with their new owner. 1953 also witnessed the extension of the Gateshead services to the new Leam Lane, Ellen Wilkinson and Wardley estates.

Having exhausted its stock of pre-war chassis, 1954 saw Northern and its associates discontinue its rebuilding programme and concentrate wholly on the purchase of completely new vehicles. The final two rebuilds, which were allocated to the Wakefield's fleet, were both integrally-constructed Beadle coaches which used reconditioned pre-war AEC components acquired from NGT and, following their arrival, all the subsequent additions to the various fleets were brand new. Northern's intake was a massive 103 vehicles which included double and single deck buses and 13 coaches. The latter, 5 of which were intended to inaugurate continental touring with the remaining 8 being replacements for SE6s, were based on underfloor-engined Guy Arab LUF chassis which were given the last Picktree bodies to be built, that manufacturer thereafter concentrating solely to the construction of caravans and commercial vehicles. The new double deckers comprised 10 Weymann-bodied Guy Arab IVs which replaced those diverted to PMT during the previous year whilst the single deckers were 15 Saro-bodied and 40 Weymann-bodied Leyland Tiger Cubs and 25 AEC-Park Royal Monocoaches, one of which was first exhibited at the 1954 Commercial Motor Show along with the first of 2 integrally-

Wearing its original dark blue & white livery complete with gold lining, Sunderland District's 1951 Brush-bodied Leyland Royal Tiger 240 (LUP391) was one of the first underfloor-engined vehicles in the Northern group fleet. It is seen here passing through Sunderland enroute to Herrington Burn.

Sporting a smaller-style fleet name, Tyneside 37 (ENL683), an all-Leyland PD2/3 of 1951 vintage leaves Newcastle on its way to North Shields during the late 'fifties. As can be seen, Tyneside did not use route numbers and thus overpainted the number apperture at the side of the destination screen.

The only new vehicles to join Sunderland District during 1952 were Roe-bodied Leyland Royal Tigers which, incidentally, were the first 8ft. wide vehicles in the fleet. Illustrating this batch is 251 (MPT319) which is seen here heading towards Sunderland on the 49 service.

One of the vehicles taken over by Northern with the business of J.W.Hurst & Son, Winlaton in August 1951 was GPT537, a Duple-bodied Guy Arab III dating from August 1946. Seen here when new, it was given fleet number 1452 by Northern whom it continued to serve until 1960. (Go-Ahead Northern)

Awaiting its North Shields Ferry-bound passengers on the seafront at Whitley Bay in 1953 is Tynemouth 187 (FT7387), a Weymann-bodied Gardner 5LW-engined Guy Arab III which had been delivered new during the previous year. (J.Wyndham)

This integrally-constructed Beadle coach, new in 1952, used running units removed from a pre-war AEC Regal. One of six added to the Wakefields fleet during that year, 180 (FT7280) is seen here at Scarborough railway station in July 1953. All six were withdrawn from service in 1960 and were immediately sold for further use in Yugoslavia. (G.H.F.Atkins)

1940 Weymann-bodied AEC Regent 960 (CN9560) followed by 943 (CN9543) fitted with the 1945 NCB body transferred from 568 pass through a Sunderland suburb whilst working a special service to the County Show during the early 'fifties.

New to Midland Red in 1925 and purchased by Northern in 1927, BMMO SOS S-type HA2435 was transferred to Wakefields Motors in 1931, returning to Northern two years later. Its chassis was then rebuilt and lengthened and fitted with a new Short Bros. 36-seat body and unbelievably it remained in service until 1955, its last few months being spent on driver training duties.

Built by Northern General in 1952 using pre-war AEC mechanical components and fitted with a new 35-seat coach body by Picktree, 1404 (CCN404) had shallower windscreens than the similar coaches built later in that year and featured a cream waistband and surround to its front grille. Following its withdrawal from service in 1959 it was sold for further use to Yugoslavia. (K.A.Jenkinson collection)

Partly home-built, the mechanical units used in the construction by Northern General of 1461 (CCN681) were those removed from 1937 AEC Regal 752 (CN7697). The new 35-seat coach body was built by Picktree and the completed vehicle was placed in service in March 1953. Initially used on Northern's holiday tours and fitted with curtains to its side windows, it is seen here at Glasshouse Street, Nottingham in July 1953 enroute to the Isle of Wight. 1461 enjoyed a comparatively short life, however, and was withdrawn in 1959 and sold to a Surrey dealer. (G.H.F.Atkins)

Built by Beadle in 1953 using pre-war AEC running units, Northern's coach-seated 1489 (DCN89) gave seven years service before being withdrawn and sold to an operator in Tenerife in the Canary Islands. (Go-Ahead Northern)

1478 (DCN78) was one of a number of buses whose chassis were built by Northern in 1953 using the mechanical units removed from 1936 AEC Regal IIs. Its 43-seat Picktree body had a stepped waist rail and shallow side windows, giving it a somewhat old-fashioned appearance. Remaining in service until 1962, 1478 was scrapped during the following year.

The Guy Arab IIIs delivered to Tynemouth & District in 1954 bore Weymann bodies of a less attractive design than their predecessors as illustrated by 193 (FT7893) seen here in the early 'sixties-style red livery which was only relieved by a cream roof and band at upper deck floor level.

constructed 44-seat Beadle-Commer TS3 buses which were delivered to Northern in 1955. The Saro-bodied single deckers had originally been ordered with Weymann bodywork, this being changed due to the latter's inability to maintain their delivery schedule. 1954 brought the first underfloor-engined vehicles into the Northern fleet and thus signalled the start of a new era for the company. Added to these 103 buses and coaches were a further 29 for Northern's subsidiaries. These comprised the 2 Beadle coaches (mentioned earlier) for Wakefields, 4 Weymann-bodied Guy Arab IV double deckers for Tynemouth & District and 9 MCCW-bodied Leyland PD2/12s for Tyneside Tramways whilst Sunderland District benefitted with 16 Saro-bodied Leyland Tiger Cubs, 5 of which were fitted with 2-speed rear axles for use on the Consett service. Additionally, Northern further

All Sunderland District's new buses delivered in 1954 were Saro-bodied Leyland Tiger Cubs of which 267 (OUP664) is seen here painted in its original lined-out dark blue & white livery.

One of 25 AEC-Park Royal Monocoaches bought in 1954, 1601 (DCN901) in its unrelieved red livery served Northern until 1969 when it was withdrawn and sold to a dealer. It was, however, fortunate enough to find a new home in South Wales where it gave a further three years service before finally being consigned to the scrap yard. (T.W.W.Knowles)

New to Tynemouth in 1938, Duple coach-bodied Leyland TS8 107 (FT4547) ended its days on loan to Northern whose fleet names were applied along with an all-red livery. Seen here in Harrogate bus station in 1955 a few months before its withdrawal from service, it was still being used on long distance limited stop duties such as that from Newcastle to Liverpool. (K.A.Jenkinson collection)

enhanced its fleet with 2 AEC-Picktree 38-seat rebuilds being transferred from Tynemouth & District from whom they had been on loan since November 1952.

The arrival of such a large number of new buses inevitably caused the demise of a quantity of older members of the combined fleet and marked the withdrawal of the final examples of several types including the last 39 side-engined SE6s and the ultimate ex.Charlton's vehicle. In total, 111 buses and coaches ran their final journeys with Northern, Tynemouth, Sunderland District and Tyneside Tramways during 1954, leaving only a handful of "genuine" pre-war vehicles to soldier on for a further couple of years. Meanwhile, like Northern's 1949 Windover-bodied Guy Arab IIIs, all but one of Tynemouth's 10 Pickering-bodied double deck Guy Arab IIIs had their Meadows engines replaced by reconditioned AEC 7.7 litre engines whilst the odd man out gained a Gardner 5LW power unit.

CONTINENTAL DEVELOPMENTS WHILE CONSOLIDATING AT HOME

Having operated extended tours to a wide variety of places within the British Isles since 1922 when a 7-day tour of Scotland was started, Northern now decided to expand these activities to a number of overseas destinations and in 1954 introduced a programme which included Denmark, Holland, Belgium, Germany, France and Switzerland. Employing the Picktree-bodied underfloor-engined Guy Arabs on these new duties, these tours quickly gained in popularity and some years later Northern, in conjunction with Sheffield United Tours and Midland Red added a small number of air-coach tours to their expanding programme whilst at one time one of the company's coaches was outstationed in Switzerland during the summer months for a tour on which both the passengers and driver were flown out to Basle! During the spring of 1954, J.Wilson, W.Barker, G.H.Wilson and M.C.Vickers who traded as Bee-Line Continental Tours Ltd. of Newcastle offered their business to Northern General and, after agreeing a figure of £3,000 for the goodwill, the company was maintained by its new owner as a subsidiary. No vehicles were involved in the transaction, and as a result of its new acquisition, Northern placed all its continental tours under the Bee Line title. Prior to this acquisition, Northern had opened a new bus station at Jarrow on 9 February 1954 in an attempt to centralise bus traffic in that town. Built at the request of Jarrow Council and costing around £15,000, this new bus station had four platforms, each of which incorporated shelters and in return for this new facility, the Council agreed to the re-routing of two services which had previously been restricted to single deck operation. Further consolidation was achieved in July 1954 when Northern

The last bodies to be built by Picktree were a batch of thirteen for Northern General in 1954, all of which were mounted on Guy LUF chassis. 35-seat coaches with a front entrance, glazed cant panels and front roof dome and swept-back wings, these were initially used on tours duties upon which they replaced the last of the pre-war SE6s. All thirteen, including 1531 (DCN831) which is seen here when new, were withdrawn and sold in 1960 after which no fewer than nine ended their days with Samuel Ledgard of Leeds.

1625 (PUP625), one of a pair of 44-seat integrally-constructed Beadle-Commer TS3 buses added to Northern's fleet in February 1955, this particular vehicle had first been exhibited at the Commercial Motor Show in London in October 1954. Never particularly popular, these two lightweight buses had but a brief life with their original owner and were both withdrawn in January 1959. (Go-Ahead Northern)

New in 1955, Northern's MCCW-bodied Guy Arab IV 1647 (CU7647) was one of several fitted from new with rear platform doors for operation on the company's longer stage carriage services. It remained in service for thirteen years before being ultimately withdrawn in 1968. (T.W.W.Knowles)

purchased the Whickham to Ryton via Winlaton stage carriage service of Dale's Coaches (Swalwell) Ltd. together with that company's three colliery services whilst on the property side, the lease of the Westgate Road, Newcastle premises was not renewed after 29 September.

Figures published by the B.E.T. during the summer of 1954 showed the issued capital in ordinary shares and fleet totals for each of its subsidiaries, these as far as the Northern Group was concerned being as follows : Northern General Transport - issued capital £2,077,702 (held by B.E.T. £918,277; held by B.T.C. £918,275) with 704 vehicles; Bee-Line Continental Tours £10,000 (all held by NGT) with no vehicles; Sunderland District £400,000 (all held by NGT) with 110 vehicles; Gateshead & District £152,390 (£150,740 held by NGT) with 66 vehicles; Tyneside Tramways £133,900 (£131,320 held by NGT) with 19 vehicles; Wakefield's £75,000 (all held by NGT) with 19 vehicles; Tynemouth & District £208,845 (£174,060 held by NGT) with 79 vehicles; Fawdon Bus Co. £3,030 (controlled by Northern General, Yorkshire Woollen District, Yorkshire Traction, West Yorkshire Road Car Co., East Yorkshire Motor Services and North Western Road Car Co.) with no vehicles, and Omnibus Stations Ltd. £42,000 (held by Northern General, North Western, Ribble, Yorkshire Woollen District, BMMO, Yorkshire Traction, Trent, West Yorkshire and Crosville).

A milestone was reached in the history of Northern General Transport on 31 December 1954 when Major Gordon W.Hayter O.B.E. retired from his position as General Manager, thus ending an era spanning some 33 years. Having joined the company as Chief Engineer in 1922, Major Hayter became General Manager in 1936 and eleven years later also became a director of Gateshead & District and Sunderland District. During his period with Northern he had been responsible, together with the Assistant Chief Engineer, Donald Sinclair, for vehicle design, and particularly the side-engined SE4 and SE6 single deckers, as well as for the overall development of the company before, during and after World War II. His contribution to its success and that of its associates had been enormous and it was difficult to imagine someone else at the helm. His successor, James Forster was, however, no stranger to Northern having started his career with the company in 1922, and becoming traffic superintendent

Numerically the last of five BET-style Weymann-bodied Leyland Tiger Cubs purchased in 1955 by Sunderland District, 283 (PUP555) is seen here in its owner's dark blue & white livery working the 38 service to Laurel Grove.

Fitted with BET-style Weymann 44-seat bus bodywork, Guy LUF 1661 (SPT61) was purchased new in 1955. Seen here wearing its original red & cream livery, it operated for Northern for only eleven years and was withdrawn and sold in 1966. (Go-Ahead Northern)

No fewer than six new cream & maroon-liveried Weymann Fanfare-bodied AEC Reliance coaches were added to Wakefields fleet in 1955, one of which - 199 (FT8999) - poses for the camera before entering service. (Go-Ahead Northern)

Pictured in Harrogate bus station enroute to Liverpool in 1957 is Tynemouth's 1939 Duple-bodied AEC Regal 110 (FT4910). Painted in all-red livery, it was being used by Northern, whose fleet names it carried, and was withdrawn from service later that same year. (K.A.Jenkinson collection)

at Consett in 1926 and at Stanley in 1929 before aspiring to the position of personal assistant to John Petrie in 1933. After leaving to take up the position of Traffic Manager with Lincolnshire Road Car Co.Ltd. on 30 November 1935, he returned to become Traffic Manager of Northern General on 1 November 1936, a role he performed until his departure in 1949 when he became General Manager of Trent Motor Traction. He returned to Northern on 1 January 1955 from which day he took over the helm as General Manager, a position he retained until his retirement on 31 December 1968 after which time General Managers came and went in quick succession. At the same time as

Tynemouth's only new additions in 1956 were eight Park Royal-bodied Guy Arab IVs, one of which - 215 (FT9415) is seen here in the mid-'sixties awaiting its Wallsend-bound passengers. Withdrawn in 1968, it was then transferred to Northern General whom it served for around nine months before being sold.

*One of fifteen new Willowbrook-bodied AEC Reliance semi-coaches received by Northern in 1956, 1716 (FCN716) is seen here in July 1959 at Manchester's Lower Mosley Street bus station awaiting its return to Newcastle on the limited stop service. Its predomianantly red livery relieved only by a cream waist band gives it a smart appearance.
(G.H.F.Atkins)*

Seen resting at Jarrow is Northern 2166 (FT9408), a Park Royal-bodied Guy Arab IV which began life with Tynemouth in 1956 and was transferred to Northern twelve years later.   (C.Dean)

Northern's Park Royal-bodied Leyland PD2/12 1762 (VUP762) leaves Newcastle on a journey to Washington during the late 'sixties.

Major Hayter retired, so did Sunderland District Omnibus Company's General Manager, Ernest Mountain. Having replaced the original Tramway Manager of that company, George Stratton, in September 1927, Ernest Mountain's role with SDO was as important, if not more so, than that of Major Hayter at NGT, particularly as Sunderland District adopted its own vehicle policy during those years. In addition to becoming General Manager of Northern General, James Forster, following Ernest Mountain's retirement, also took over this position at Sunderland District, thus bringing the two companies even closer together.

As far as the fleet was concerned, in a similar manner to the previous year, the delivery of new buses continued apace in 1955 with 55 taken into stock by Northern, 2 by Gateshead & District, 5 by Tynemouth & District, 6 by Wakefield and 12 by Sunderland District. Those for Northern comprised 22 Weymann-bodied Guy LUF underfloor-engined 44-seat buses; 31 MCCW-bodied Guy Arab IV double deckers and the 2 integrally-constructed Beadle-Commer TS3 44-seat buses mentioned earlier. Of the double deckers, several incorporated features new to the company with 16 having rear platform doors to improve internal heating and 15 being equipped with flashing direction indicators, although surprisingly the latter had these removed after only a few months in service! Tynemouth & District also received 5 MCCW-bodied Guy Arab IVs with open rear platforms while Wakefields took delivery of 6 Weymann coach-bodied AEC Reliances. Sunderland District remained faithful to Leyland with the purchase of 5 MCCW-bodied PD2/12s and 5 Weymann bus-bodied Tiger Cubs, although they did stray to AEC for a pair of Reliances with Park Royal 41-seat centre entrance coach bodies built to that manufacturer's Royalist design. As a result of the arrival of these new vehicles, the withdrawal of older members of the fleet was able to continue with 1955 witnessing the demise of the last side-engined SE4 and the final buses of BMMO manufacture.

The route network had now settled down to the extent that few changes were to the existing services during the 1954-6 period and only a handful of new routes were started. Amongst these was one operated by Sunderland District from Sunderland to Fatfield which commenced on 24 July 1954 and one operated jointly by Northern and Sunderland Corporation from Sunderland to Grindon Village Estate which began on 2 November 1954. Similarly, three new services were inaugurated during 1955, one of which operated infrequently on Saturdays only from Durham to Nettlesworth and began in May only to be discontinued some ten months later whilst in 1956 only one new service was introduced, this running from Sunderland to Deneside Mission.

1955 also saw a start made on the reconstruction of Chester-le-Street depot which was by now extremely overcrowded. Designed to house and maintain 70 vehicles, Chester-le-Street depot's allocation had risen during the early 'fifties to some 125 buses and 22 coaches and for some time it had been necessary to park 56 buses on a rubble compound a short distance away from the main buildings. This had originally been leased in 1928 from Leedale Garage and was requisitioned by the military authorities in 1940. During the following

The only Albion Aberdonians to be purchased by Northern and its associates comprised a batch of five which took up their duties in the early autumn of 1957. Fitted with BET-style 44-seat Weymann bodywork, they gave a mere ten years service before all being withdrawn in 1967 and sold to a London dealer. One of them, 1759 (CU9759) is seen here when new. (Go-Ahead Northern)

year its roof collapsed and, not wishing to reapir this, its owners sold the freehold to Northern later in 1941. Although proposals for the rebuilding and extension of Chester-le-Street depot were laid in 1953, it took almost two years before these were implemented and it was not until towards the end of 1956 that this work was completed. In addition to the reconstructed depot being now able to accommodate 167 vehicles, it also carried out full dock duties for Murton and Sunderland depots in addition to its own fleet as well as housing the uniform stores for the whole company. Also in 1956, Northern constructed and opened a new bus station and adjoining 55-vehicle garage in Park Lane, Sunderland close to the street loading points formerly used by the company. Incorporated into its design was a two-storey building, almost

1744 (GCN44) was one of a number of Willowbrook-bodied Leyland Tiger Cub semi-coaches purchased by Northern in 1957. Painted in a predominantly cream livery with red roof and waistband, this particular vehicle gave the company seventeen years service and was not withdrawn until 1974. (Go-Ahead Northern)

During 1957 Northern took delivery of both Willowbrook dual-purpose and coach-bodied Leyland Tiger Cubs. Amongst the latter was 37-seat 1752 (GCN52) which was in 1962 refurbished by Plaxton and converted for dual purpose use. Its life ended in 1970 when it was withdrawn from service and sold for scrap. (Go-Ahead Northern)

One of a pair of Duple Midland-bodied Leyland Tiger Cub coaches purchased by Sunderland District in 1958 for use on touring and private hire duties, 300 (10BPT) looks most atractive in its cream and light blue livery. Equipped for one-person-operation in 1969 and repainted in bus livery two years later, 300 survived in service until 1973 and was sold during the following year for scrap. (Go-Ahead Northern)

Awaiting its North Shields-bound passengers at its terminus in Croft Street near Newcastle Central railway station is Tyneside MCCW-bodied Leyland PD3/4 50 (NNL50) which was new in 1958. After its withdrawal in 1971 it passed to Northern for use as a driver training vehicle.

triangular in shape, on the southern platform which housed the administrative offices for the district traffic superintendent and his staff and an employee's canteen. Costing £92,000 in total, it was originally intended that the new garage would replace a much smaller 14-vehicle unit inconveniently placed at Holmeside in another part of the town, but in the event, the old depot was retained for a short period before eventually being leased to a car dealer. Meanwhile, in the early summer of 1955, Northern replaced its cramped booking and enquiry office at Worswick Street bus station, Newcastle with a new office in Pilgrim Street where in addition to providing facilities for private hire and tours bookings etc., the chart room for the whole of the company's activities was relocated.

The years 1956/7 continued the fleet modernisation programme with the arrival of 111 new buses and coaches for Northern and 16 for Tynemouth & District. Those for the parent company comprised 10 Weymann 'Fanfare' coach-bodied Guy Arab LUFs, 20 Park Royal-bodied Guy Arab IV and 10 Leyland PD2/12 double deckers, 31 AEC Reliances with Willowbrook semi-coach and MCCW bus bodies, 15 Willowbrook semi-coach/coach bodied Leyland Tiger Cubs, 20 Weymann bus-bodied Tiger Cubs and, more unusually, 5 Weymann-bodied Albion Aberdonian 44-seat buses, the latter being originally ordered as Leyland Tiger Cubs but changed due to a saving in price! For Tynemouth & District came 8 Park Royal-bodied Guy Arab IVs, 5 Willowbrook-bodied Leyland PD2/12s and 3 semi-coach Willowbrook-bodied AEC Reliances and with the arrival of so many new vehicles, this enabled the last of Northern's pre-war buses to be withdrawn and sold together with a quantity of wartime and early post-war vehicles.

Obtained new by Northern in 1945, NCME-bodied Guy Arab II 1062 (FUP62) survived in passenger service until the early spring of 1958 when it was rebuilt to full-fronted configuration and fitted with dual controls (including a second steering wheel) for driver training duties. Seen here in its new guise in 1960, it was not until 1964 that it was finally withdrawn and sold. (T.W.W.Knowles)

Pictured when new in 1958, Tynemouth's MCCW-bodied Leyland PD3/4 229 (AFT929) was transferred to Northern in 1975 upon the winding up of the Tynemouth company only to be withdrawn and sold later that year. (Go-Ahead Northern)

Although starting life with Tynemouth, 1958 MCCW-bodied Leyland PD3/4 229 (AFT929) spent a short period with Gateshead & District whose fleet name it had gained when photographed here. Note its destination display which quaintly shows 'Foot of High Street'.

Meanwhile, although Sunderland District received no new vehicles during the years 1956/7, 4 1946 NCB-bodied Guy Arab IIs were received on loan from Northern and were painted into Sunderland District colours whilst Northern's 1956 Willowbrook dual-purpose AEC Reliances entered service in a new predominantly cream livery. At this same time, Sunderland District began to experiment with its colour scheme and in March 1956 repainted one of its Roe-bodied Leyland PD2/1s into an all-over dark blue livery relieved only by a single white band and without the familiar SDO scroll. This proved to be extremely short-lived, however, although no sooner had it reverted to standard livery in May 1956 than one of the Roe-bodied AEC Regent IIIs was given an all-blue front and also omitted the SDO scroll! This remained thus painted until September 1957 when, together with a Saro-bodied Leyland Tiger Cub, it was given the new mid-blue and cream coach livery which both retained until being returned to standard dark-blue and white fleet colours in November 1959. Immediately prior to this, Northern had also made alterations to its livery by starting to eliminate the ivory window surrounds on double deckers from February 1956 and on single deckers from October of that year. A further modification was made in May 1957 when Northern began to paint the roofs of all its buses red, this resulting in double deckers being relieved with only a cream band above the lower deck windows and single deckers being all-over red.

On 1 July 1956, the registered office of Tynemouth & District was moved from 88 Kingsway, London to 117 Queen Street, Gateshead whilst 1957 witnessed the demise of Bee-Line Continental Tours Ltd. when that company was placed into voluntary liquidation and its operations passed to Northern. Meanwhile, Northern had increased its share capital to £3,116,553 of which the B.E.T. held £1,377,913 and the B.T.C. held £1,377,912, whilst Sunderland District increased its share capital to £440,000 and Northern increased its shareholding in Tynemouth & District to £174,170. The fleet totals of Northern and its associates were at that time quoted officially by the B.E.T. as being : Northern 692, Wakefields 19, Gateshead & District 73, Tyneside 20, Sunderland District 103 and Tynemouth & District 82 making a combined total of 989 buses and coaches.

The final two years of the 'fifties brought with them 102 more new vehicles for the Northern fleet, these comprising 52 AEC Reliances with bus bodywork by Burlingham and Willowbrook, 20 Willowbrook bus-bodied Leyland Tiger Cubs, 10 Willowbrook-bodied AEC Reliance coaches and 20 MCCW-bodied Leyland PD3/4s, these being the first 30ft long double deckers in the fleet. Tynemouth & District, Wakefields and Tyneside Tramways also received 30ft long MCCW-bodied Leyland PD3/4s in the quantity 10, 2 and 3 respectively while Sunderland District took delivery of 13 Burlingham-bodied Leyland PD3/4s fitted with rear platform doors, and a pair of Duple Midland-bodied Leyland Tiger Cub coaches, one of which was

Looking immaculate in the dark blue & white livery of its owner Sunderland District is 1958 Burlingham-bodied Leyland PD3/4 288 (YPT288) seen here in the late 'sixties.

The first Leyland PD3s to join the Gateshead & District fleet were five MCCW-bodied examples which took up their duties in 1958. Looking immaculate in its brown livery relieved by two cream bands, one of these buses, 75 (HCN475) is seen here operating a cross-Tyne service. (K.A.Jenkinson collection)

exhibited when new at the 1958 Commercial Motor Show. The most spectacular of the new buses, however, were the 10 Alexander-bodied Leyland Atlanteans received by Gateshead & District in 1959, these being the Northern Group's first rear-engined double deckers. When ordered early in 1957, all the double deckers for Northern and its associates were specified as Leyland PD3/4s, but, following the examination of a prototype Atlantean, it was decided in October 1957 to change these to the new rear-engined model which it was believed had the advantage in that the front door could be supervised by the driver to allow the conductor more time to collect fares (OMO was not considered for double deckers in those days!). In the event, it proved too late to change the order as far as Tynemouth was concerned as the Leyland PD3/4 chassis were already under construction, so instead it was decided to fit these with front instead of rear entrance bodies.

Resting in Newcastle's Marlborough Crescent bus station in 1958 a few months after its entry into service is Northern's Burlingham-bodied AEC Reliance 1824 (HCN124). After giving seventeen years service, this bus - by then renumbered 4013 - was sold in December 1975 for scrap.

New in 1959 as a 37-seat coach, Willowbrook-bodied AEC Reliance 1853 (JCN453), together with its sisters, was rebuilt by Northern in 1965 and fitted with a new front which incorporated raked windscreens and a destination indicator in its front roof dome. Retaining its glazed cant panels and coach-type seating which was increased to accommodate 41 passengers, it was repainted in a predominantly red livery relieved only by a cream waist band. Renumbered 4524 in 1975, it was withdrawn from service during the following year. (Go-Ahead Northern)

This too proved to not be possible and thus when they arrived in 1958 they were to the specification of the original order. Gateshead's new Atlanteans joined the 5 MCCW-bodied Leyland PD3/4s which had entered service with the company during the previous year and their arrival together with further new buses received in 1960 allowed the transfer of 26 Guy Arab IIIs to the Northern fleet. Additionally, 3 Leyland PD1s and 3 Leyland PD2s, all with Leyland bodywork, were transferred on loan to Tynemouth & District from Tyneside Tramways in 1958, one of the PD1s having previously been on loan to Gateshead & District earlier that same year.

Continuing to expand and improve its garage and maintenance facilities, and in an attempt to overcome overcrowding at its existing depots, Northern during the latter months of 1957 constructed a new garage at Cromwell Place, Winlaton, high on the hills overlooking the

The first rear-engined double deckers to be placed in service by the Northern Group were ten Alexander-bodied Leyland Atlanteans delivered to Gateshead & District in 1959. One of these was 87 (KCN187) seen here in its original livery operating the Bensham and Saltwell Park circular service 54. Withdrawn in 1972, it then travelled half way around the world to join Kowloon Motor Bus Co. in Hong Kong to whom it gave yeoman service until its final demise in 1977.

upper reaches of the River Tyne in the Blaydon area. Replacing the small 8-vehicle depot in Hood Square which had been acquired with the business of J.W.Hurst & Sons in 1951, it was designed to act as a sub-depot to Bensham and, relieving the latter of some 40 vehicles, it incorporated a maintenance area for running repairs, although all major work (referred to by Northern as 'docking') continued to be undertaken at Bensham. Following the opening of this new depot, the old Hurst premises were sold to Blaydon Urban District Council. At around this same time, an extension was added to the Tynemouth & District depot at Percy Main in the form of an unheated 40-vehicle "dormy shed". To gain access to this, buses entered the main service garage, passed through the new Dawson washer, and thence cut diagonally across the garage to a ramp leading along the side of the building and across the new road to the "dormy shed". Meanwhile, a start was made on the extension of Sunderland District's garage at Philadelphia which, when completed in 1959 enabled a further 40 vehicles to be accommodated, whilst a rebuilding scheme was agreed in principle for Murton depot to allow it to house an additional 40 vehicles, although in 1959 this figure was modified to 23.

1958 found Northern in conflict with Consett Urban District Council who had without warning increased its charges for the use of its bus station. Feeling that having to pay 35% more for this facility was unreasonable, to say the least, the company together with Venture Transport, the bus station's other main user, asked the Minister of Transport to intervene and fix the fees. After much consultation between all the parties concerned, a compromise was reached which although not to Northern and Venture's total satisfaction was at least acceptable. Also in 1958, the sad news was received of the death of Major G.W.Hayter at the age of 70. After his retirement from Northern General in 1954, in addition to retaining his connection with the bodybuilding concern, Picktree, he had worked in a consultative capacity and had also been a director of Guy Motors Ltd.

Although the service network throughout the Northern Group's territory had remained constant with only minor modifications throughout the mid-late 'fifties, a new service had commenced early in 1957 from South Shields Market Place to Whiteleas Estate, this being operated jointly with South Shields Corporation. More revolutionary, however, was the introduction on 5 September 1959 of four new limited stop "Express" services, each of which was operated on an hourly frequency. Numbered X1 to X4 respectively, these ran from Newcastle to Durham stopping only at Chester-le-Street; Newcastle to South Shields with an intermediate stop at Tyne Dock Gates only; Sunderland to Durham with a stop at Houghton-le-Spring and Sunderland to Newcastle via the Boldons with no stops enroute. As a result of the success of these new express services, a fifth was added in 1961 numbered X6 (X5 didn't appear until 1966) running from Sunderland to Consett. This was thus numbered to avoid passenger confusion due to the parallel Sunderland - Consett stopping service being numbered 5 - would that this could happen in the 'nineties! Meanwhile, in July 1959 the decision was taken to place the Fawdon Bus Company into voluntary liquidation and to transfer the licence for that company's solitary service - the Ten Cities Express - to Northern General. To this end, the final meeting of the Fawdon company was held on 4 July 1960 and on 14 December of that same year the licence for Fawdon's service was ultimately transferred to Northern.

Although painted in a predominantly red livery in 1965 and fitted with a roof-level destination box, 1959 Willowbrook-bodied AEC Reliance 1853 (JCN453) still retained its glazed cant panels and coach-type seating. (Go-Ahead Northern)

INTO THE 'SIXTIES

The new decade opened with fewer new vehicles joining the fleet than had done during the late 'fifties, although all execpt Tyneside Tramways benefited on this occasion. Northern's share of the new intake comprised 18 Leyland Atlanteans - its first rear-engined double deckers - bodied by Roe and MCCW and 10 Harrington-bodied AEC coaches. Atlanteans were also received by Gateshead (10 with Roe bodywork), Tynemouth & District (5 with Roe and and 8 with MCCW bodies), Wakefields (1 with MCCW bodywork) and Sunderland District (11 bodied by Roe and Alexander) whilst the latter company also gained 2 MCCW semi-coach bodied Leyland Tiger Cubs. Whereas the majority of the new vehicles delivered in 1960 were double deckers, only 18 of the 60 arriving in 1961 were of this type - 12 Roe-bodied Atlanteans for Northern and 6 for Gateshead & District. Of the remainder, 10 Harrington Cavalier-bodied Leyland Leopard coaches and 20 Alexander semi-coach bodied AEC Reliances were added to the Northern fleet, 4 Burlingham-bodied AEC Reliances to Wakefields and 8 Leyland Tiger Cubs were allocated to Sunderland District, 3 each having Alexander bus and semi-coach bodies and two fitted with Burlingham coach bodies. 1962 brought a further 63 vehicles into the combined fleet with Roe-bodied Atlanteans for Northern, Sunderland District and Tynemouth & District, and the first 36ft long vehicles for the Group in the form of 10 Willowbrook bus-bodied Leyland Leopards for Northern and 2 semi-coach Willowbrook-bodied Leopards for Tynemouth & District. The new-length Leylands had all originally been ordered as AEC Reliances, but as the latter could not be fitted with an engine larger than a 7.75 litre unit, this was changed to the more powerful 9.8 engined litre Leopard. Of Northern's new Atlanteans, two were exhibited at the British Exhibition in Oslo, Norway in August 1962 before entering service in the north-east. The customary cascading of vehicles from the subsidiary fleets to that of their parent continued during 1960-2 and in this manner Northern received 2 Leyland PS1/1s, 3 Tiger Cubs and 8 AEC Regent IIIs from Sunderland District, 29 Guy Arab IIIs from Gateshead & District and 3 AEC Reliances and 3 Leyland PD2/1s from Tynemouth & District, all of which had been

Sunderland District's first rear-engined double deckers made their debut in 1960 in the form of Leyland Atlanteans with Weymann and Roe bodywork. One of the latter, 308 (308GPT) sporting an illuminated offside advertising panel passes through Sunderland on service 14 in the early 'sixties. Transferred to Northern on 1 January 1975 upon its absorption of Sunderland District, it was renumbered 3168 and was repainted into NBC poppy red livery, remaining in service until 1978.

New to Northern in 1961, Alexander semi-coach bodied AEC Reliance MCN992 was loaned to Tynemouth in May 1968 before being permanently transferred to that company in 1971. Originally numbered 309 by Tynemouth, it was renumbered 314 upon the arrival of that company's Leyland Panthers in 1969. Despite at first only being on loan, it nevertheless immediately gained Tynemouth fleet names and numbers as seen by this July 1968 view.

Sunderland District 319 (2519PT), a dual purpose-seated BET-style Alexander-bodied Leyland Tiger Cub new in 1961 is seen enroute to Consett wearing a light blue & cream livery used by its owners on its dual purpose vehicles.

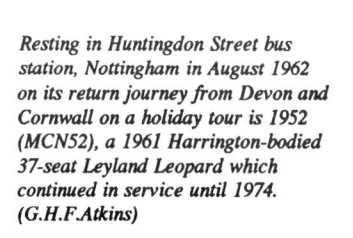

Resting in Huntingdon Street bus station, Nottingham in August 1962 on its return journey from Devon and Cornwall on a holiday tour is 1952 (MCN52), a 1961 Harrington-bodied 37-seat Leyland Leopard which continued in service until 1974. (G.H.F.Atkins)

65

After spending the whole of its working life with Gateshead & District, 1951 all-Leyland PD2/3 38 (CCN138) was overhauled and repainted and given Northern fleet names at the start of 1967 in preparation for its departure to its new owner, Universal Tours of California, USA. This posed view alongside a signpost for Washington shows Hollywood on its destination blind. (Go-Ahead Northern)

One of a pair of Burlingham-bodied Leyland Tiger Cub coaches purchased by Sunderland District in 1961, 321 (2521PT) stands in the entrance of Philadelphia depot prepared for its next duty.

Amongst the least attractive of Northern's Leyland Atlanteans were the Roe-bodied variants which joined the fleet in 1960-2. One of these buses, 1967 (1967PT) although still wearing the company's BET-style red livery has already gained an NBC side poster, indicating that this view was taken in 1973/4.

replaced by the new arrivals. In the meantime, all the Atlanteans delivered prior to 1962 had their centrifugal clutches replaced by fluid flywheels to bring them into line with the new deliveries of this type of bus. 1962 also witnessed the introduction of a new fleet numbering system for Northern which segregated the various types of vehicles from each other. Under this new scheme, double deckers were to be numbered 2001 upwards, single deck buses from 2251, semi-coaches from 2501 and coaches upwards from 2601. This was applied, however, only to new additions to the fleet and those already in stock were not renumbered into the new scheme. Meanwhile, Gateshead & District experimentally repainted one of its 1951 all-Leyland PD2/1s in a lighter shade of maroon in June, although this remained unique as all subsequent repaints were undertaken in the established dark maroon and cream colour scheme. At Chester-le-Street, Northern proposed in 1961 to purchase some land to the south of the depot from Chester-le-Street CWS and to sell the old Leedale Garage site which was still vacant.

Surprisingly, there were still extremely few service changes except for those of a minor nature and during 1962/3 only five new routes were started by Northern and one by Sunderland District. On 21 January 1963, however, the service from Usworth Colliery to Waterside operated by J.& T.Hunter (Washington) Ltd. was purchased, together

This scene at Marlborough Crescent bus station, Newcastle in May 1964 shows the vehicles of three different operators. From left to right is United's ECW-bodied Bristol MW5G 928JHN, Northern's Weymann-bodied Guy LUF 1663 (SPT63) and Venture Transport's Willowbrook-bodied Atkinson PM745H 173 (RUP434). The latter did not survive long enough to pass to Northern's control following the purchase of Venture by the NBC, being withdrawn in 1967, a year after Northern sold its 1663. (K.A.Jenkinson)

The only new single deckers to join the Tynemouth fleet in 1962 were a pair of Willowbrook-bodied Leyland Leopards. Although fitted with 49 coach-type seats, these were painted in bus-style red livery relieved only by a cream waistband as illustrated by 263 (FFT813).
(Go-Ahead Northern)

Tynemouth's first Daimler Fleetlines made their debut in 1963 when 10 Weymann-bodied examples were received. Painted in its owner's attractive red & cream livery, 270 (HFT370) is followed here by Wakefields Roe-bodied Leyland Atlantean 255 (FFT755) which was new in 1962. All ten of the Tynemouth Fleetlines were sold in 1972 to East Yorkshire Motor Services Ltd. in exchange for 6 Park Royal-bodied AEC Bridgemasters.

with one vehicle (a 1949 Bedford OB) which was resold almost immediately for the princely sum of £30! This newly-acquired service was instantly altered to run from High Usworth to Waterside, and maintaining a hourly daytime frequency with no evening operation, it was not until 22 November 1973 that it was finally discontinued. A further development of 1963 followed the retirement on 31 March of J.W.King, Manager of Gateshead & District. Rather than appoint a new successor, Northern's General Manager, James Forster added this position to his existing duties whilst L.M.Parker, Chief Engineer of Northern additionally took over this role with Gateshead & District. Indeed, the only "new" appointment made by the Gateshead concern was that of a Traffic Manager in order to ensure the existing liason with Gateshead and Felling Councils was continued, - a legacy of the days when Gateshead proposed to purchase the tramways.

On the property front, a scheme was approved in March 1961 for the extension and modernisation in three stages of Northern's Bensham premises. Stage one was to involve a new paint shop which was to be designed for brush painting due to four fleet colours being used (red, maroon, green & blue, plus black and white). Stage two would enable the main workshops to be extended by the covering of part of the open yard whilst stage three would improve the pits and surrounding area. Work commenced almost immediately and upon the completion of stage one in 1962, Tynemouth's Cullercoats depot which had latterly been used solely as a paint shop was able to be closed and sold. During the following year, on 26 April, the parcels service operated by Gateshead & District was sold to Larkswood Motors Ltd. who were a subsidiary of Hanson Haulage (Leeds) Ltd., The latter company had initially approached Gateshead with a view to purchasing the business in September 1962, although before serious negotiations could begin, Gateshead & District were obliged to first ascertain that British Road Services Ltd. did not wish to purchase their parcels operations which dated back to 1907 and was motorised from 1915.

Following three years during which time fewer new vehicles had been purchased that in previous years, 1963 saw a greater number arrive and two more new makes join the combined fleet. Of the latter, 12 were coach-bodied Bedford SB5s with 8 Harrington Crusader-bodied examples joining Northern and the others, all with Plaxton coachwork, being allocated 2 each to Sunderland District and Wakefields. The purchase of lightweight coaches was a new departure for the Northern Group and although these vehicles occasionally saw service on the company's long distance Limited Stop Pool services, they were primarily acquired for private hire and touring duties. The other newcomer to the fleet was the Daimler Fleetline, of which 10 Weymann-bodied examples were bought for Tynemouth & District. Conventional heavyweight coaches came in the form of 5 AEC Plaxton Panorama-bodied AEC Reliances for UK touring duties and 5 Harrington Grenadier-bodied Leyland Leopards for use on Northern's continental tours whilst the remainder of the new arrivals comprised 22 MCCW-bodied Atlanteans and 19 Willowbrook 53-seat bus-bodied AEC Reliances for Northern, 10 MCCW/Weymann-bodied Atlanteans for Gateshead & District and 6 Willowbrook bus-bodied Leyland Leopards for Sunderland District which allowed it to cascade 6 of its Roe-bodied Leyland PD2/1s to Northern. During 1962, the 5 1957 Willowbrook coach-bodied Leyland Tiger Cubs were all refurbished by Plaxton, returning as 41-seat dual-purpose vehicles whilst the 10 Weymann-bodied Guy LUF 37-seat coaches of 1956 vintage were refurbished at Blackpool, by Duple, retaining their 37-seat layout in the process.

If 1963 had been a year of surprises as far as the arrival of new types was concerned, then what can be said of 1964? Of the 63 new buses to make their debut during this year, 40 were of types already

One of a pair of Plaxton-bodied Bedford SB5 coaches purchased new by Sunderland District in 1963, 330 (3730UP) was used mainly on private hire and local excursion duties. After giving only five years service, it was withdrawn in 1967 and sold to a Co.Durham coach operator.
(K.A.Jenkinson collection)

One of five Harrington-bodied Leyland Leopard coaches purchased by Northern in 1963, 2617 (PCN17) awaits its passengers in Chester-le-Street whilst working a duty on the X1 service. Renumbered 5008 in 1975 and converted for one-man-operation during the following year when stencil route number holders were also fitted, it was ultimately withdrawn from service in 1977 and was sadly sold for scrap. (C.Dean)

1963 Plaxton-bodied AEC Reliance 2611 (PCN11) basks in the sunshine at Nottingham's Huntingdon Street bus station in July 1964 whilst its tour passengers enjoy their lunch break enroute to Devon and Cornwall. (G.H.F.Atkins)

familiar in the north-east with B.E.T.-style Marshall-bodied AEC Reliances for Northern, Atlanteans for Gateshead & District and Tyneside Tramways with Alexander and Weymann bodies respectively, 7 more Leopards for Sunderland District and 5 Daimler Fleetlines together with 2 Leopards for Tynemouth & District. The remaining 23 were, however, something completely different, being Park Royal-bodied Routemasters powered by Leyland engines, and of a type until now operated only in London. Northern specified the 30ft. long variant with front entrance bodywork, of which only one had previously been built. Although purchased for use on Northern's longer stage carriage

Northern in 1963 purchased eight lightweight 41-seat Harrington-bodied Bedford coaches for use on local excursion and private hire duties. All were withdrawn in 1967 after which three, including 2602 (PCN2) which is seen here wearing its attractive cream & maroon livery soon after entering service, were sold to another BET subsidiary, Mexborough & Swinton, for continued use. After passing to Yorkshire Traction in 1969, they were ultimately sold to a dealer who exported them to Sarawak in January 1971. (Go-Ahead Northern)

The first Marshall bodies to appear in the Northern fleet did so in 1964 when fifteen 43-seat AEC Reliance buses made their debut. Of standard BET design with double curvature windscreens and rear windows, these buses were painted in an unrelieved red livery as illustrated by 2286 (BPT286B). (Go-Ahead Northern)

Joining the Tynemouth fleet in 1964 were five Weymann-bodied Daimler Fleetlines, one of which was 277 (JFT277) pictured here. This particular bus had an eventful life, being sold in 1972 to United Automobile Services who, early in 1973 returned it to Northern. Renumbered 2877, it was after only a few days despatched back to Tynemouth in whose fleet it reverted to its original number (277), but two years later, upon the demise of the Tynemouth company it was transferred to Northern where it took up fleet number 3194. After receiving NBC-style Tyneside PTE yellow livery in September 1975, it was finally withdrawn in 1977. (Go-Ahead Northern)

services, the first fifteen of this new breed took up their duties at the start of April on the not-so-long Sunderland - Pennywell service. The Daimler Fleetlines were ordered in place of Atlanteans upon the recommendation of Northern's General Manager and Chairman who similarly reported upon the Routemaster on 20 November 1962 stating that although it was more expensive, it was around one ton lighter in weight than current rear-engined double deckers and would thus be more economical on fuel and other running costs. As a result, no further Fleetlines were ordered by Northern and instead, the Routemaster was favoured. Continuing the theme of "unusual" vehicles, Northern in the autumn of 1964 converted one of Tynemouth & District's 1952 NCB-bodied Guy Arab IIIs into a permanent driver training bus, fitting this with a full width cab and dual controls as a replacement for one of Northern's Guy Arab IIs which had been similarly treated in 1958. Taking up its new duties in November, it was to serve in this role until August 1972, being supplemented by conventional older members of the fleet only when occasions necessitated the use of additional training vehicles. During 1963, a pair of Guy Arab IVs were transferred from Gateshead & District to Northern who also received 6 Roe-bodied Leyland PD2/1s from Sunderland District whilst at the start of 1964 5 all-Leyland PD2s were transferred to Northern from Gateshead & District.

A further 27 Routemasters were added to the Northern fleet in 1965 together with 8 semi-coach Weymann-bodied AEC Reliances while Gateshead & District and Tyneside received 15 and 2 Alexander-bodied Leyland Atlanteans respectively, Tynemouth & District gained 7 Alexander-bodied Daimler Fleetlines and Sunderland District took delivery of 8 semi-coach Weymann-bodied Leopards. During this year, Northern undertook its own rebuilding of a number of its older coaches rather than despatch them to an outside coachbuilder

New in 1958, Burlingham-bodied AEC Reliance 1797 remained in service until 1974. Seen here leaving Marlborough Crescent bus station in Newcastle at the start of its journey to Lanchester, its front panels had been rebuilt to eliminate their original curved profile and winged Burlingham motif.

Prospective passengers hide the identity of one of the two Routemasters resting in Worswick Street bus station, Newcastle in May 1964. This was operating the 45 service to West Hartlepool while 2097 (RCN697) was awaiting its departure time to Crook on the 42 route. (K.A.Jenkinson)

69

Leyland PSUC1/1 1873 in June followed in August by AEC Reliance 1976 while on the final day of 1969 a similar fate befell AEC Reliance 2277. Fortunately, no injuries were sustained in any of these incidents, although except in the case of 2270, all the vehicles were so badly damaged that they were subsequently scrapped rather than any attempt being made to rebuild or rebody them. A temporary departure from the Northern fleet involved one of its Routemasters which was displayed at an exhibition at Gutersloh, Germany during September and October.

During January 1965, the General Manager reported to the Tynemouth board that the company had been offered the goodwill of

New to Gateshead & District in 1964, Alexander-bodied Leyland Atlantean 117 (ACN417B) survived with its original owner until the company was absorbed by Northern on 1 January 1976. Already in NBC-style yellow livery when it was transferred to Northern on this date and renumbered 117 (becoming 0117 in 1978), it continued in service until 1980 when it was despatched to the NBC Eastern Region Disposal Pool at Lincoln for cannibalisation and ultimate dismantling.

Starting life in 1952 in the fleet of Tynemouth & District, Weymann-bodied Guy Arab III FT7383 was withdrawn in 1964 and transferred to Northern for conversion to a driver training vehicle. After being rebuilt with a full-width cab and given dual controls, it was numbered 42 and took up its new duties in May 1965, continuing these until August 1972. (K.A.Jenkinson collection)

Heading towards Worswick Street bus station, Newcastle in 1969 soon after being repainted into Tynemouth-style red & cream livery is Northern's four year-old Routemaster 2114 (FPT584C).

and transformed its 10 1959 Willowbrook bodied AEC Reliances into semi-coach type vehicles by increasing their seating from 37 to 41, fitting destination screens to their front roof dome and equipping them for one-man-operation. One other vehicle worthy of mention is a 1963 Willowbrook bus-bodied Leyland Leopard (2270), the body of which was destroyed by fire in May 1964. After holding its remains in store for several months, its chassis (which luckily had not been seriously damaged in the blaze) was eventually overhauled and despatched to Marshall of Cambridge who fitted it with a new 53-seat bus body built to standard B.E.T. specification. In its new form it re-entered service during 1965. Sadly, this turned out to be the first of six of Northern's single deckers which were to suffer fire damage before the decade ended. Willowbrook-bodied Leyland PSUC1/1 1880 was destroyed on 16 June 1964 whilst in service and three years later, during the summer of 1967, Willowbrook-bodied AEC Reliance 2272 burnt out whilst travelling empty. 1968 witnessed the destruction by fire of

the Priory Motor Coach Co. of North Shields consisting of excursions and tours from North Shields and Wallsend, minor express services and private hire work but with no vehicles or other assets. It was stated that any purchase could be joint with United Automobile Services Ltd. and although authorisation to offer up to £600 was given, nothing came of this and Priory continued to operate under its then current ownership. Later in January, on the 28th, Tyneside moved from its depot at Neptune Bank into new premises at Hadrian Road, Wallsend, built on land leased from Wallsend Corporation. As the lease on the former, which had expired on 29 June 1959 but had been renewed for its maximum term (until 29 June 1974) did not afford the company any long-term security, it had been decided in January 1963 to seek a new site from which to base its operations and on the opening of its new garage the remaining period of the lease of the Neptune Bank depot

New to Sunderland District in 1965 fitted with BET-style Weymann dual purpose bodywork, Leyland Leopard 347 (HUP947C) is seen in Philadelphia depot wearing its original light blue & cream livery. Transferred to Northern upon its absorption of Sunderland District on 1 January 1975, it was repainted into NBC poppy red and renumbered 4304. It was withdrawn and sold in 1978.

Pictured outside Wallsend depot, Tyneside 55 (ENL355C), one of a pair of Alexander-bodied Leyland Atlanteans purchased new in 1965, shows its single line destination indicator which, without a route number apperture, typified the Tyneside fleet. Loaned to Northern and painted in that company's red livery in 1974, it was permanently transferred on 1 January 1976 upon the demise of the Tyneside company and remained in service until 1978. (Go-Ahead Northern)

was sold to Thermal Syndicates Ltd. A more notable event during 1965, however, was the registering of both Gateshead and Tyneside under the Companies Act 1948 in order that they could obtain the benefits of internal regulation under modern Memorandas and Articles of Association with interalia powers of capitalisation of reserves. Both companies thus added "Limited" to their titles and acquired new seals. That of Tyneside Tramways & Tramroads Company Limited, which had surprisingly retained its title even though it had not operated trams since 1930, was only used once, however, being impressed on the appropriate page of the minute book, and was then destroyed following the reforming of the company on 14 March 1965 under the name Tyneside Omnibus Company Limited. Apart from the application of revised legal lettering to its buses, its new identity was not made obvious with the company retaining its existing livery and "Tyneside" fleet name. Another change, made during the previous year, was more visible, however, this involving the livery of the Gateshead & District fleet which, since the reintroduction of motor buses in 1950 had been maroon with cream bands. With the delivery of the 1964 Alexander-bodied Atlanteans, an attractive green colour scheme similar to that used by Tyneside was adopted and all future repaints were undertaken in these colours. Before 1965 ended, a transaction which passed almost unnoticed was the sale in November of Hall Park Garage, Hetton-le-Hole. This had been acquired by Northern in 1930 with the purchase of part of Eastern Express Motors Ltd. and in 1932 was leased to a firm of corn merchants (Hall & Sumerbell) to whom it was now sold. November also witnessed a heavy snowfall which began on the 14th and was followed by a thaw which caused much flooding and then more snow which paralysed West Durham. Several vehicles had to be abandoned in this snow and dug out when the thaw began, this harsh weather resulting in some 60,000 miles of operation being lost.

1966 brought a further 63 new vehicles into the combined fleet with Northern receiving 41 Leyland Leopards with coach, semi-coach and bus bodywork, one of which despite being bus-seated was exhibited at the 1966 Commercial Motor Show painted in semi-coach livery, and 10 Alexander-bodied Atlanteans. Sunderland District enhanced its fleet with 3 bus and 2 coach-bodied Leopards whilst Gateshead & District and Tyneside received 5 and 2 Alexander-bodied Atlanteans respectively. The year also witnessed the arrival of another front entrance Routemaster, this being acquired in November from London Transport in whose fleet it had been numbered RMF1254 and had remained unique. Upon its arrival with its new owner it was fitted with a plaque in its lower saloon stating that it was a former London bus, although in truth it had never operated in normal service in the metropolis!

Deliveries in 1967 were similar to those of the previous year with Northern receiving 19 bus and 12 semi-coach bodied Leopards and 8 more Alexander-bodied Atlanteans, Sunderland District taking 6 OPO-equipped Leopard buses, Tynemouth & District 3 Alexander-bodied Fleetlines and Tyneside 2 Alexander-bodied Atlanteans. Of the Leopards delivered to Northern, the 12 Marshall-bodied semi-coach examples fitted with luxurious seats for 47 passengers were painted in a predominantly cream livery with a red skirt, mainly for long distance express operations to Leeds, Manchester, Liverpool, Keswick, Blackpool and the Potteries whilst one of the bus-seated Leopards was fitted with the prototype Marshall Camair body which featured standee-type windows and was also surprisingly painted in a version of

Numerically the last of the 1966 Alexander-bodied Leyland Atlanteans, 2144 (MUP144D) is seen here in pre NBC-style livery during the early 'seventies. Renumbered 3128 in the 1975 scheme it outlived most of its sisters and was not withdrawn until 1981. Sold in February of the following year to APT, Lincoln, it then passed to PVS, Carlton on 3 March 1982 for dismantling.

Seen prepared for participation in Durham University's Rag Parade in February 1966 carrying promotional material for Northern's continental tours is Hillman Husky estate car BCN804C. (Go-Ahead Northern)

the dual purpose colour scheme. Additionally, 2 Weymann Fanfare-bodied AEC Reliance coaches were transferred to Northern from Wakefields whilst 6 modern rear-engined single deckers were evaluated (a Leyland Panther, Panther Cub, AEC Swift, Daimler Roadliner, Albion Viking and Bristol RE). All except the Albion were used on service 39 between Newcastle and Thornley.

Although the service network had continued to remain fairly static throughout the mid 'sixties, following the success of the X-numbererd express services which, incidentally, had had their Saturday frequency doubled in 1960, two more routes of this nature were introduced in 1965/6, one starting on 6 November 1965 from Newcastle to Winlaton (X7), the other (numbered X5), operated jointly by Northern, Sunderland District and United, commencing on 28 February 1966 from Newcastle to West Hartlepool via Washington and Peterlee with more stops than the other X-services. A more unusual service started on 28 February 1966 was that from Sherburn (Grey Horse) to Pity Me (Kirkham Road), this effectively being a Durham local service which, as a result, was operated jointly with United. Following this came a new long distance service from Newcastle (Haymarket) to Hanley, Staffordshire which, numbered X95, was inaugurated on 27 May and was operated jointly by Northern, United, West Yorkshire, Yorkshire Woollen District, LUT, North Western and PMT. Later, on 27 August 1966 a special service was started between Stanley and Harperley Hill (Zoo), this being operated on summer Saturdays and Sundays "to suit traffic requirements" while four days later a second "summer special" service was launched from Boldon Colliery to Seaburn. This latter operation was so short-lived that it was never even incorporated into Northern's timetable booklet!! A more dramatic development, however, was implemented by Northern and Sunderland District following the introduction by Sunderland Corporation of a flat fare system using tokens. As this affected Northern's and SDO's operations in the town, they both introduced a 4d flat-fare together with a special 3/4d 12-journey ticket in order to retaliate against the municipality's new form of competition. In an attempt to "mend fences", during November 1967 steps were taken to negotiate with Sunderland Corporation for a co-ordination of services in the town but these were hampered by the resignation of that undertaking's General Manager following the collapse of the flat-fare system. As a consequence of the opening of the new Tyne Tunnel in 1967, Northern's service 60 (Sunderland to Jarrow) was, on 21 October, extended through this new passage beneath the river to Blyth and was operated jointly with Tynemouth & District and United. Similarly, a new service started by Northern on 2 September 1967 from Hebburn (Lukes Lane Estate) to Jarrow was also extended through the Tunnel on 21 October to continue to Killingworth, this too becoming jointly operated by Tynemouth & District and United and a year later was further extended to Cramlington.

The year which followed brought with it massive changes for Northern and its subsidiaries, for it was during 1968 that the B.E.T. finally agreed to sell its British road passenger transport interests to the State. Following her appointment as Minister of Transport on 23 December 1965, Barbara Castle M.P. quickly made her vision of an integrated transport system known and set about to bring her dream into reality. In the belief that local authorities should be responsible for public transport planning, she further decided that the Transport Holding Company, which a few years earlier had taken over from the British Transport Commission, should be dissolved and that in its place, as far as road passenger transport was concerned, should be a National Bus Company. With this in mind, she believed that the B.E.T. must be brought under State control - and indeed she is quoted as saying "I will not rest until the B.E.T. has been wholly absorbed in the T.H.C. and the two throughly integrated under new transport authorities". The B.E.T. however, obviously holding a different view, refused to sell out voluntarily. Despite at first being adamant in its resolve to remain independent, the B.E.T. entered into a series of talks which were to continue throughout the summer of 1967 and ultimately, on 22 November of that same year, announced that agreement had been reached for the sale of its bus interests to the State. The sale was formally completed on 14 March 1968, albeit back dated to 1 March 1968, and from that date Northern and its subsidiaries became part of the Transport Holding Company. No sooner had news of the agreement been announced, than the Govenment published its new Transport Bill which, on 25 October 1968 after its passage through Parliament, became the 1968 Transport Act. Amongst the provisions of this new Act were : (i) That Passenger Transport Authorities were to be set up for Merseyside, Manchester, Tyneside and the West Midlands under whose control Passenger Transport Executives would take over the municipal transport undertakings within those areas. Other operators could continue to operate within those areas subject to PTA approval. (ii) The National Bus Company was to be set up to take over the control of the T.H.C's bus subsidiaries in England and Wales (i.e.the former T.H.C. and B.E.T. companies). (iii) A new bus grant scheme was to be set up which would provide 25% of the cost of new buses which provided facilities for one-person-operation and conformed to standardised specifications. (iv) Provision was to be made for subsidisation of rural services by local authorities where judged essential, with Government support. A list of the latter was being prepared by Northern in September 1970 and it was noted that if applications for grants were rejected, the services would be withdrawn.

Fitted from new for one-person-operation and equipped with forced ventilation (note the absence of any opening windows etc.), 364 (WPT364F) was one of five Willowbrook-bodied 53-seat Leyland Leopards purchased by Sunderland District in 1968.
(Go-Ahead Northern)

Sunderland District 257, one of two Duple-Britannia-bodied Leyland Royal Tigers purchased in 1953 is seen here in its owner's light blue & cream coaching livery. Like its sister, 257 was exported to Australia after its withdrawal by its original owner.

Sunderland District Guy Arab II 178 (FPT207) began life in 1943 fitted with an austere Pickering body. This was replaced by a new Roe highbridge body in 1953 thus giving it a much more stylish appearance.

Having gained a cream centre band to its previous rather drab unrelieved dark red livery is Tynemouth's NCB-bodied AEC Regent III 160 (FT6560).

Painted in the dark blue & white livery of its owner Sunderland District, 312 (312GPT) seen here outside Philadelphia depot was one of a pair of MCCW-bodied Leyland Tiger Cubs which joined the fleet in 1960.

After losing its roof in a low bridge accident in 1967, Sunderland District Burlingham-bodied Leyland PD3/4 293 (YPT293) was fitted with a new upper structure by Willowbrook and in January 1969 following another mishap it gained an MCW front roof dome.

74

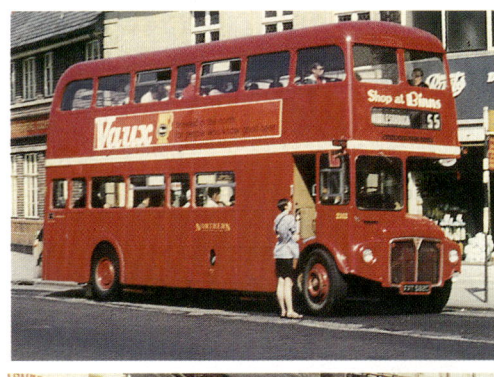

75

Seen on a private hire duty when only a few weeks old in 1968, Northern's coach-seated Alexander-bodied Leyland Leopard 2637 (FCN637F) was during the following year repainted into the company's predominantly cream coach livery.

Meanwhile, Northern and its subsidiaries had updated their fleets in 1968 by the purchase of a further 52 new vehicles of which 20 were Leyland Leopards with semi-coach or coach bodywork together with 12 Alexander-bodied Atlanteans were for Northern and 7 bus-bodied Leopards were for Sunderland District. The remaining 13 were divided between Tynemouth & District, Wakefields and Tyneside, the first named receiving 10 Alexander-bodied Daimler Fleetlines, Wakefields gaining 2 Alexander coach-bodied Leyland Leopards, and Tyneside a solitary Alexander-bodied Atlantean. In order to serve the growing needs of the company in the new-town area to the south of Gateshead, Northern built a new depot at Washington, opening it on 7 September 1968 with an initial allocation of 33 vehicles, although surprisingly on this occasion no office facilities were incorporated, these instead being provided at the new-town's bus station which was built by the Development Corporation.

Page 74, left column, top to bottom :

Adorned with Gateshead & District's green & cream livery is 75 (HCN475), an MCCW-bodied Leyland PD3/4 delivered new in 1958. (Photobus)

Although still wearing Tyneside's dark green & cream livery, Alexander-bodied Leyland Atlantean 58 (KNL58E) lacked fleet names when photographed during the early 'seventies on a journey to Newcastle. (Photobus)

One of thirteen Bristol LD6G Lodekkas purchased in 1970 from Crosville, 2197 (VFM629) was repainted into dark green & cream livery and given Northern fleet names and was at first operated by Tyneside, moving to Northern's Consett depot in February 1971. It was withdrawn from service early in the following year. (T.Godfrey collection)

Page 74, right column, top to bottom :

The conductress of Routemaster 2112 (FPT582C) which still wore Northern's pre-NBC dark red livery converses with the driver as it momentarily pauses on its way to Middlesbrough on the 55 service. (B.Newsome)

Tynemouth's red & cream-liveried Alexander-bodied Daimler Fleetline 292 (DFT292E) leaves Haymarket bus station, Newcastle at the start of its journey to Cullercoats in 1969. (B.Newsome)

Northern's MCCW-bodied Leyland Atlantean 1893 (893EUP) was hired to Gateshead & District from January 1970 and was painted in that company's green & cream livery as illustrated here whilst operating a Northern service. Following its withdrawal in 1972 it was sold to Kowloon Motor Bus Co., Hong Kong for further service. (T.Godfrey collection)

Leaving Darlington bus station at the start of its return journey to Newcastle on the 723 service is NBC corporate-liveried ECW-bodied Bristol VRT 3411 (JPT911T). (T.Godfrey collection)

Painted in the original style of Go-Ahead Northern's Expresslink livery. Willowbrook 003-bodied Leyland Leopard 5083 (TUP583V) rests at Lanchester whilst working the X30 service in April 1985. (S.A.Staddon)

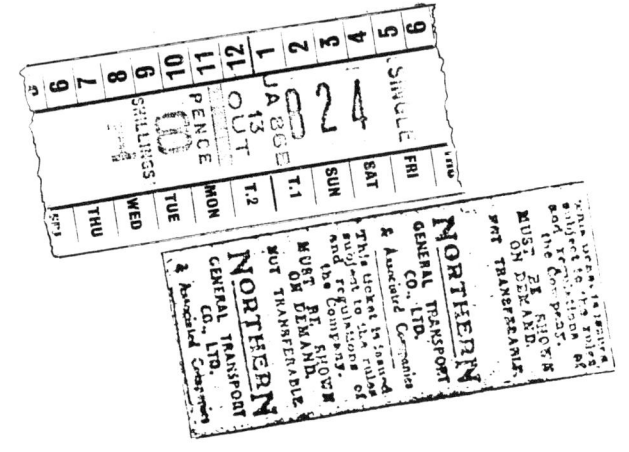

Page 75, left column top to bottom :

Corporate National Express-liveried 1981 Willowbrook 003-bodied Leyland Leopard 5089 (LFT89X) shows off its National and Northern fleet names as it works a journey on the X6 service to Consett. (T.Godfrey collection)

Northern's Willowbrook-bodied Bristol VRT which was delivered new in 1978 painted in NBC's corporate poppy red & white livery rests between duties at Chester-le-Street. (T.Godfrey collection)

This crowded scene at Sunderland bus station in 1967 shows a host of Northern buses including MCCW-bodied Leyland PD3/4 1832 (YPT832), Routemaster 2118 (FPT588C) and a pair of Atlanteans all sporting pre-NBC dark red livery. (B.Newsome)

Illustrating Sunderland District's dark blue & white livery, new Leyland National 1K (MCN151K) stands at the front of Philadelphia depot in 1972. (A.Staddon)

Page 75 right column, top to bottom :

Still wearing the attractive livery of its original owner, Venture, Alexander dual purpose-bodied AEC Reliance 258 (CPT258B) was given fleet number 2833 when it joined the Northern fleet and became 4267 under the 1975 renumbering scheme. (B.Newsome)

Looking smart as it heads to Castletown in 1970 is Northern's MCCW-bodied Leyland Atlantean 2066 (4266UP) painted in pre-NBC red & cream livery. (T.Godfrey collection)

Adorned with Northern fleet names following its transfer from Gateshead & District in 1970, MCCW-bodied Leyland PD3/4 1838 (YPT838) still wore its Gateshead green & cream colours for a few months before gaining Northern's red livery. (T.Godfrey collection)

Pictured wearing its pre-NBC unrelieved dark red livery, Newcastle-bound 2252 (HCU52), a 1962 Leyland Leopard was fitted with Willowbrook bodywork built to standard BET design. (B.Newsome)

FROM B.E.T. TO N.B.C.

The sale of the B.E.T. to the state together with the implementation of the new 1968 Transport Act had a direct effect on the Northern General Transport Group who not only found itself with new masters, but also in the midst of one of the newly created PTAs. Now being under the same control as United Automobile Services, the "dividing line" separating the two companies was no longer necessary. Discussions took place between Northern and United in September 1969 with a view of the transfer from United of its properties in Sunderland and certain of its operations in order that the services of the two companies in this town could be more closely and economically integrated. Although no developments were forthcoming with regard to properties, on 26 October Northern applied for, and were granted, licences for two Durham District Services routes, these being the Sunderland-Peterlee-Wingate-Sunderland and that from Sunderland to Middlesbrough, both of which continued to be held for several years. The first new service to be introduced after the passage of Northern to state ownership, however, was one of a somewhat unusual nature running on Sundays only. This operated from South Shields to North Shields via the Tyne Tunnel and was a replacement for the river ferry service between these two points. Additionally, the X1 Newcastle to Durham service was extended to Middlesbrough jointly with United on 27 October. As far as the new Tyneside PTA was concerned, this had

Fleetlines, 2 were Alexander coach-bodied Leopards which were the last vehicles to be allocated to the Wakefield's fleet before that company was wound up, and 3 were Alexander-bodied Atlanteans for Sunderland, these being the first new double deckers for that company for seven years. An unusual secondhand purchase was that by Tynemouth & District of a three-year old Hillman Super Minx 4-seat car which it is believed was obtained for use on a feeder service for Northern General excursions and tours. Throughout this period, the customary inter-fleet transfers continued unabated, mainly with cascaded subsidiary fleet vehicles joining Northern, although during the final month of the year 6 of that company's Roe-bodied Atlanteans were hired to Gateshead & District in order to ease a temporary vehicle shortage there. Surprisingly, although they were only to remain with Gateshead for four months, they were all repainted into that operator's green livery. Perhaps more momentous was the withdrawal of the last Guy vehicle in the fleet (1697, 1 1953 Park Royal-bodied Arab IV), the first of which made its debut in 1942 after which 481 were operated. Meanwhile, Northern, who had first introduced one-man-operation in 1966 on a very limited scale, began to convert more of its single deckers for this type of use and towards the end of the year started to conduct a number of livery experiments which were to continue into 1970. Introducing a much brighter image to the company, albeit sadly

Sporting Wakefield's fleet names and legal lettering, 305 (GFT805G) was one of a pair of 47-seat Alexander-bodied Leyland Leopard coaches delivered new to the company in 1969. Both passed to Northern in 1975 and, renumbered 4346, GFT805G gave a further six years service before finally being withdrawn and sold. (Go-Ahead Northern)

been established on 1 April 1969 with the Tyneside Passenger Transport Area (Transfer of Undertakings) Order 1967 coming into force on 1 December 1969 transferring to the Tyneside Passenger Transport Executive on 1 January 1970 the two municipal fleets within its area, Newcastle-upon-Tyne and South Shields Corporations who between them operated 386 buses whilst the company buses running within its bounds numbered 542. Of these, 207 were operated by Northern, 80 by Tynemouth & District/Wakefields, 68 by Gateshead & District and 15 by Tyneside, the remainder comprising 164 with United and 8 with Hunter & Son of Seaton Delaval. However, more of these later.

After spending less that a year under the control of the T.H.C., Northern and its subsidiaries were transferred to the National Bus Company upon its formation on 1 January 1969 and thus a new era began. In the initial months, little change could be observed and the flow of new buses continued to reflect previous B.E.T. policy. Joining the fleet during this year were 50 vehicles, of which half were of a new single deck type, the rear-engined Leyland Panther. Fitted with Marshall Camair 48-seat dual-door bodywork, these were allocated to Northern (18), Sunderland District (2), Tynemouth & District (3) and Tyneside (2), the latter being the first ever single deckers for this operator. The trio received by Tynemouth were actually delivered as Gateshead vehicles but were repainted and renumbered before their entry into service and were almost immediately hired to Northern. One of Northern's new Panthers had been exhibited at the 1968 Commercial Motor Show before its delivery to the company and was the first dual-door vehicle to be operated by the Northern Group. Of the remaining 25 new arrivals, 8 were Alexander coach-bodied Leopards for Northern who also received 12 Alexander-bodied 77-seat Daimler

The first of a trio of Weymann-bodied Leyland Atlanteans purchased by Tyneside in 1964, 51 (BTY151B) seen here wearing its original dark green & cream livery was transferred to Northern in January 1976 by which time it had been repainted into the NBC yellow scheme. After giving a further four years service it was withdrawn and sold for scrap in 1980.

54
Gateshead
3761
GO-AHEAD NORTHERN
GO-AHEAD NORTHERN
C761 OCN

GO-AHEAD NORTHERN
D233 URG

My Mum's a Great Knit!
56
NORTHERN

188 SUNDERLAND
Park Lane
WEAR BUSES
K860PCN

DRIVER UNDER INSTRUCTION
LEARN TO DRIVE A BUS.
091-460 5144.
LEARN TO DRIVE A BUS
091 460 5144

Our Strength Depends On The Company We Keep
57 HEWORTH
Q.E. Hospital

530 COTSWOLDS ESTATE
BT
It's good to talk
Pause for talk.
Telephone
3468
VFM BUSES
mean value for money
VFM BUSES
AUP 368W

804 SOUTH STANLEY
NORTHERN
JTY 383X

79

Marshall Camair-dual door-bodied Leyland Panther 2342 (GCN842G), seen working a Sunderland local service in 1971, like several of its sisters was later rebuilt without its nearside standee windows.

only temporarily, several Routemasters, a Leyland PD3 and a number of Atlanteans were repainted into Tynemouth-style colours of red with cream window frames and roof (this almost being the old Northern livery) while two Atlanteans appeared in all-over red, one in red with a broad cream band and one red with three narrow cream bands. In a similar manner several single deckers were given a new paint scheme comprising red below the windows with cream above in place of the all-over red adopted a couple of years earlier. Additionally, the fleet name which since 1969 had been applied in lower case lettering on the lower deck side panels was in 1970 moved to a forward position above the lower deck windows on double deckers. On the service front, a new long distance express service (X67) was started on 6 June from Newcastle to Southport while on 25 October a more local express route (X8) was inaugurated from Peterlee to Jarrow via Sunderland.

Although March 1968 had marked the start of a new era for Northern and its subsidiaries, it was not until 1970 that the effects of State ownership, and in particular the National Bus Company, really began to bite and old policies started to change. Although Northern and its associates had placed orders for 48 new vehicles for delivery in 1970, all were delayed until the following year and in their place came a mixture of secondhand vehicles drawn from within the Northern Group or from other NBC subsidiaries. The first of these to arrive, in January, were a trio of Burlingham coach-bodied AEC Reliances which were transferred to Northern from Wakefield's whilst following between March and July were 13 Bristol LD6B Lodekkas acquired from Crosville, 10 of which were for operation and three for cannibalisation for spares. In the event however, one of these buses suffered a mechanical failure enroute from Crosville to its new owner and instead of being repaired or towed to Gateshead, it was instead immediately sold for scrap. Not particularly quick to enter service in their new home, 8 of these Lodekkas were initially loaned to Gateshead & District with whom they made their debut between April and September and 1 entered service on loan to Tyneside in December whilst the remaining example took up its duties with Northern in July 1971. All except the solitary example allocated to Northern, which was painted in that company's red colour scheme, wore a green livery, one with cream

Page 78, left column, top to bottom :

Although still wearing corporate Tyne & Wear PTE livery, MCW Metrobus 3761 had gained Go-Ahead Northern fleet names when caught by the camera at Gateshead Metro in June 1986.   (S.A.Staddon)

Adorned with Tyne & Wear Transport fleet names and NBC logos on its side panels and a Northern fleet name below its windscreens, corporate Tyne & Wear liveried former PTE Leyland Atlantean 3533 and MCW Metrobus 3486 stand between duties at Gateshead Metro. (T.Godfrey collection)

Leaving Gateshead Metro in September 1993 is Northern Group driver trainer T513 (XSD598T), an ex.Western Scottish Alexander-bodied Seddon Pennine VII.   (K.A.Jenkinson)

VFM Buses Roe-bodied Leyland Atlantean 3468 (AUP368W) rests in the yard of South Shields depot in 1994.   (B.Newsome)

Page 78, right column, top to bottom :

Passing Sunderland's Park Lane bus station in December 1989 whilst working a local service is Go-Ahead Northern 233 (D233URG), an Alexander-bodied Mercedes Benz L608D fitted with coach-type seating. (K.A.Jenkinson)

Approaching Gateshead MetroCentre in November 1995 enroute to Sunderland is Wear Buses Wright-bodied Dennis Dart 8060 (K860PCN), one of ten delivered to the company in 1993.   (K.A.Jenkinson)

Wearing the red, blue & white livery of Go-Ahead Gateshead, MCW Metrobus 3629 (A629BCN) leaves Gateshead Metro on route 57 to Heworth in September 1993.   (K.A.Jenkinson)

Stanley bus station is the location of this November 1995 view of Northern's ECW-bodied Leyland Olympian 3583 (JTY383X) painted in 'Proud of our Routes' livery.   (K.A.Jenkinson)

Page 79, left column, top to bottom :

Pictured in Leeds bus station whilst working an excursion from the north-east is coach-seated ECW-bodied Bristol VRT 3406 (JPT906T) which carried Go-Ahead Northern's early style of stripy livery. (T.Godfrey collection)

One of two Roe-bodied Leyland Royal Tiger Doyen coaches purchased by Northern in 1983, 7012 (A212XJR) is seen here painted in corporate National Holidays livery.   (T.Godfrey collection)

New to Northern in 1986, ECW-bodied Leyland Olympian 3657 (C657LJR) seen here during the following year with Go-Ahead Northern fleet names was transferred to Sunderland District in 1991 and now sports Wear Buses livery.   (W.Counter)

Painted in Tyne & Wear PTE Care Bus livery is Go-Ahead Northern Leyland National 4748 (UUP830K) which had been fitted with wheelchair access immediately forward of its rear nearside wheel arch. It is seen here at Gateshead MetroCentre in June 1990.   (T.G.Walker)

Page 79, right column, top to bottom :

Off-loading its passengers on Tynemouth's sea front whilst operating Coastline service 333 in September 1993 is Go-Ahead Northern's open-top Park Royal-bodied Leyland Atlantean 3285 (RCN111N). (K.A.Jenkinson)

Acquired by OK Motor Services Ltd. from Hunter, Seaton Delaval in 1991 is NCME-bodied Leyland Atlantean HNB35N which began life with Greater Manchester Buses. It is pictured here at Team Valley depot in April 1995.   (K.A.Jenkinson)

Although transferred to Tynemouth in 1991, ECW-bodied Leyland Atlantean 3540 (MBR440T) still carried Go-Ahead Northern fleet names and livery when photographed leaving Gateshead Metro on Tynemouth's 302 service to North Shields in September 1993.   (K.A.Jenkinson)

Several of the Optare Delta-bodied DAF SB220s delivered to Go-Ahead Gateshead were painted in Supershuttle livery for operation on the M66 service from Gateshead Metro to the MetroCentre. One of these, 4758 (K758SBB) is seen carrying its additional Supershuttle fleet number S2 above the driver's side window in April 1994.   (K.A.Jenkinson)

One of a pair of Marshall-bodied Leyland Leopards bought new by Tynemouth in 1964, JFT282 was transferred to Northern in August 1969. Seen enroute to Winlaton during the early 'seventies, it survived in service until 1975 when it was sold for scrap.

window surrounds and roof (i.e. Tyneside style), the remainder with a cream centre band which ultimately became the standard Gateshead NBC livery for several years. Transferred to Northern from Gateshead & District between June and December 1970 were 12 single-door Alexander-bodied Atlanteans which were exchanged for 12 of Northern's dual-door Atlanteans (6 of which on transfer were converted from single door by Northern and 6 by Alexander) which it was thought would be better utilised on the high traffic density routes operated by Gateshead and their ultimate conversion to one-person-operation. Further vehicles to move to Northern, albeit on loan, were 2 Alexander coach-bodied Leyland Leopards of Wakefields for use on the new X8 Jarrow - Sunderland - Parkside service, these being returned to Tynemouth & District during 1970 as a result of Wakefields having then ceased trading. Lastly, in November the company received 3 Park Royal-bodied AEC Reliances and an Alexander-bodied Leyland Leopard from Venture Transport, an operator purchased by the NBC earlier in the year, and about which more later. This, however, was far from the end of the story, for in addition to these new arrivals, Northern also hired a large number of vehicles for various short periods of time during the year to help it overcome temporary shortages. The first of these strangers came from East Kent Road Car Co.Ltd, in February in the form of 12 Park Royal-bodied AEC Reliance coaches and during their brief stay, which lasted for only around six weeks, 4 were operated by Sunderland District whilst the remainder gave service to Northern. At around this same time, 5 ECW-bodied Bristol LS5G buses were hired from United Automobile Services, of which all except one were initially used by Sunderland District. Although the first of these returned home in June, the others gave several more months service with the last not being sent back to its rightful owner until February

Wearing an experimental livery in 1970, Gateshead & District Alexander-bodied Leyland Atlantean 138 (CCN638D) seen here on circular service 52 at The Eagle on Leam Lane Estate, 138 was transferred to Northern later in that same year. (C.Dean)

Seen outside its depot in 1970, Gateshead & District Alexander-bodied Atlantean 133 (CCN333C) wore one of the experimental liveries applied during that year. Like several of its sisters, it was soon to pass to Northern in whose fleet it gained standard colours. (C.Dean)

Painted in an experimental scheme of dark green with three narrow cream bands in 1970, Gateshead & District Alexander-bodied Leyland Atlantean 131 (BCN131C) gained standard Northern livery after its transfer to that company later in the year. (C.Dean)

One of twelve AEC Reliances hired from East Kent in 1970, Park Royal coach-bodied 524FN picks up its passengers at Houghton-le-Spring whilst working the X5 service from Newcastle to West Hartlepool. (C.Dean)

2189 (VFM601) and 2192 (VFM626), two of the Bristol LD6G Lodekkas purchased from Crosville in 1970, are seen here in dark green & cream livery with Northern fleet names despite being operated by Gateshead & District. (T.W.W.Knowles)

Acquired from Crosville in 1970, Bristol LD6G 2191 (VFM610) was the only one of these buses to receive a green livery with cream window surrounds and roof. Although operated by Gateshead & District, it carried Northern fleet names and, of course, 'Shop at Binns' front and rear adverts. (T.W.W.Knowles)

1971. Hired by Northern from its subsidiaries were a Leyland PD2/12, 2 Leyland PD3/4s and 2 Leyland Panthers from Tynemouth & District, 3 Atlanteans from Gateshead & District and a Leyland Panther from Tyneside, most of these remaining with Northern for several months, while more unusually, a Plaxton coach-bodied Ford R226 was borrowed from its manufacturer for around three weeks for evaluation purposes in July. The only new vehicle to be taken into stock by the company was a Plaxton-bodied Leyland Leopard coach which made its debut in January whereas no new vehicles were delivered to any of its subsidiaries during 1970. Other than the 12 Atlanteans mentioned earlier which were transferred to Gateshead, the only other company to receive any permanent additions to its fleet was Tynemouth & District who acquired the 6 Alexander semi-coach bodied AEC Reliances which had been on loan from Northern since May 1968.

With the newly-created Tyneside Passenger Transport Executive taking control of the Newcastle and South Shield Corporation's fleets on 1 January 1970, Northern and its subsidiaries now found that they had a different partner on the services they had previously operated jointly with these municipalities, although this made no difference to the routes concerned which continued to run as before. Partly as a result of the creation of the PTA, comparatively few new services were started during 1970, and those that did were generally outside the PTA area. One new route however, which was inaugurated jointly by Northern and United on 27 April, brought the buses of both companies into unfamiliar territory. This was the X30 express service which, although officially running from Newbiggin to Greencroft Road Ends via Ashington, Newcastle, Gateshead, Stanley and Annfield Plain, actually

Venture Transport 221 (1884PT), a 1961 Weymann-bodied AEC Reliance seen here leaving Marlborough Crescent, Newcastle enroute to High Spen survived long enough to come under NBC control, although it never joined Northern's fleet. Taken out of service in 1972, it was sold for scrap during the following year.

Although numbered VC1 by Venture Transport, the 'VC' prefix was not carried on Duple-bodied Bedford VAM14 SUP201E seen here on an excursion duty. New in 1967, it remained in service until 1974 when it was sold to a dealer before passing to a Bolton coach operator. (K.A.Jenkinson collection)

had only one journey per day to Newbiggin, the remaining operation being between Ashington and Greencroft Lane Ends on an hourly frequency. A further change taking place on 1 January 1970 was the transfer of Wakefield's Motors Limited's service licences, goodwill and rolling stock to Tynemouth & District who had effectively operated the company since January 1932.

Perhaps the most important development of 1970, however, was the purchase by the National Bus Company on 30 April of the old-established business of Venture Transport Company (Newcastle) Limited. The Venture company was incorporated on 10 March 1938 to acquire the businesses of Venture Bus Services Ltd., Reed Brothers Ltd. and Robson Brothers Ltd. whose origins dated back to 1912 when five brothers, W., E., R.M., G. and J.R.Reed of Sunniside began a service from the Bensham terminus of Gateshead & District Tramways to Burnopfield with an Iris charabanc. Abandoned soon after the start of World War I and not restarting afterwards, a new service was instead commenced in September 1918 running from Newcastle to Chopwell via Rowlands Gill and Hamsterley and employing 2 Albion buses, and in 1919 the company was reformed as Reed Brothers Limited. Some years later, in 1924, two brothers-in-law, G.R.Harrison and W.J.Richardson purchased a share in an old-established carriers business, Harper & Lockey of Shotley Bridge and commenced a bus service from there to Newcastle via the Derwent Valley under the title "Venture" using a 14-seat Chevrolet. Both businesses prospered and in 1925 Harrison and Richardson approached the Reed Brothers with a view to them co-operating in the operation of the Shotley Bridge to Newcastle service. Agreement was quickly reached and almost immediately the service was extended westwards to Consett which was later to become the headquarters of the company which became Venture Bus Services Ltd. in 1929. After both companies had gained further expansion by the acquisition of other small operators, it was agreed in 1930 that both would letter their vehicles "Venture and Reed Bros", adopt a common livery, and share a new depot at Blackhill, near Consett, although each would remain independent. Venture was, at this time, still at Hamsterley. Further strengthening their relationship, in 1933 they jointly formed a third company under the title of Robson Brothers Limited to take over two of the services run by the old-established operator of that name, and two years later added a service previously run by a Mrs Amy Bessford. By the time Venture Transport Company (Newcastle) Limited was formed in 1938, the company was operating twenty-two different services radiating from Consett, Chopwell and High Spen to Newcastle and Hexham and had a fleet of over 50 single deck buses and coaches. Further expansion was gained in 1951 when the company purchased the C. & E. Bus Company Limited of Oxhill, Annfield Plain, and although 5 vehicles were included in this deal, all were quickly laid up whilst C. & E's depot at Oxhill continued to be used until 1967. The company remained in existence, however, with services operated by Venture buses 'on hire to C & E Bus Co. Ltd.' Venture's final acquisitions were made in 1965 with the purchases of Motor Services (Consett) Ltd. and a garage and filling station at Annfield Plain, all of which were included in the company's sale to the NBC and placed under Northern's control.

Although the company continued to prosper, the closure of many of the pits in the north-west Durham coalfield during the 'fifties caused some retrenchment and forced Venture to embark upon some one-man-operation of its services as early as 1959. Some diversification had by this time taken place, however, and in addition to maintaining its bus operation, a subsidiary company had been formed in the property field whilst a car and mobile caravan concern was also operated as an offshoot of the transport company, as was a taxi business. Despite having refused offers from the B.E.T. for the purchase of its business during the 1950s, and one from Northern General Transport in January 1966 when they were asking for £700,000, Venture, perhaps being wary of the powers granted to Tyneside PTA which might in the future have some effect on its services and due to the increasing age of its directors, accepted an offer of £540,000 made for its purchase by the National Bus Company in 1970 and on 1 May of that year it became a subsidiary of Northern General Transport Co. Although its head office was immediately transferred to that of Northern at Queen Street, Bensham, the Venture fleet name continued in use, as initially did its attractive yellow, cream and maroon livery with slight modification. Included in the deal was Venture's all-single deck fleet comprising 13 Albion Aberdonians, 2 Leyland Tiger Cubs, 36 Leyland Leopards, 27 AEC Reliances and 6

Sunderland District's new buses delivered in 1971 comprised seventeen Alexander-bodied dual-door single deck Daimler Fleetlines, all of which remained with the company until its demise on 1 January 1975 when they were transferred to Northern. 379 (LUP379J) which is seen here in its original dark blue & white livery soon after entering service, was renumbered 4328 by its new owner who operated it until 1981 when it was sold for scrap. (Go-Ahead Northern)

Pictured when new in 1971, Gateshead & District 155 (LCK105K) was one of 6 dual-door ECW-bodied Bristol RELL6G added to the fleet. After only a few months, all were transferred to Northern who renumbered them (155 becoming 2839 and, in 1975 being renumbered again to 4268). In March 1979 4268 was rebuilt to single door configuration and remained in service thus until 1983 when it was sold to APT, Lincoln. It ended its days in February 1984 when it was dismantled by PVS, Carlton on behalf of APT.

New in 1964 as a conventional front-entrance 30ft. long Routemaster, 2085 (RCN685) was experimentally rebuilt in 1971 following an accident in which it suffered serious frontal damage. To make it suitable for one-person-operation, it was converted to semi-normal control layout with its cab and driving position being set back to enable it to be more adjacent to the front passenger entrance. Named the 'Wearsider', it entered service in its new form in August 1972 and was not withdrawn until 1978, a year after many of its conventional sisters. (Go-Ahead Northern)

Built by Northern in 1972 from Tyneside 49 (NNL49), a 1958 MCCW-bodied Leyland PD3/4, 3000 (MCN30K), which was given the name 'Tynesider' was of normal control configuration to enable it to be one-person-operated. An experimental project which proved to be less than successful, 3000 saw little use after the end of 1972 and spent most of the remainder of its life as a staff bus at Percy Main depot. Withdrawn in 1978 it then passed via a succession of owners to a preservationist whose intention is to restore it to its rebuilt condition. (K.A.Jenkinson collection)

Bedford VAMs.

After such an unconventional year, it was wondered what 1971 might hold as far as Northern and its subsidiaries were concerned. Would it perhaps be another year in which the only additions to its fleets would be those cascaded by other operators, or would some brand new vehicles arrive? This question was soon answered when, in February, the first of 24 rear-engined Daimler SRG6 single deckers were delivered to Northern. These had originally been ordered with 48-seat Marshall bodies, this being changed by the NBC to Willowbrook and then to Alexander who equipped them as dual-door

44-seaters. Joining them were 8 ECW-bodied 44-seat dual-door Bristol RELL6Gs of which a further 15 were to arrive before the year ended whilst two months later, 6 Alexander-bodied single-door Daimler Fleetline double deckers made their debut. Venture received what turned out to be its last new buses, these being 6 Alexander dual purpose-bodied Leyland Leopards, the order for which had been placed by the company immediately before its sale to the NBC. The arrival of the Bristol RELLs was the first visible sign that Northern was now part of the NBC and that in future it would be subject to that organisation's buying policy rather than continue in its previous B.E.T. manner. New vehicles were also received by Northern's subsidiaries, with Gateshead & District and Tynemouth & District receiving 6 and 4 dual-door ECW-bodied Bristol RELL6Gs repectively and Sunderland District taking delivery of 17 Daimler CRG6s with Alexander 44-seat single deck dual-door bodywork. Of Tynemouth's new Bristol RELLs, 3 were despatched on loan to Northern in April prior to being permanently transferred during the following month whilst the fourth was delivered direct to Northern and thus never operated for its intended owner. In exchange, Tynemouth gained 5 Alexander-bodied Daimler SRG6 saloons from Northern and 2 Marshall Camair bodied Leyland Panther Cubs from Sunderland District. A further 29 Bristol RELLs had been allocated to Northern by the NBC for delivery during 1971, but in the event these were instead diverted to Gosport & Fareham and United Automobile Services prior to leaving the ECW factory at Lowestoft. Similarly, it is minuted by Northern that 10 ECW-bodied Daimler Fleetlines were to be received from an order placed by East Yorkshire Motor Services Ltd., although these too never arrived at Gateshead. During this period, 2 Sunderland District Leyland PD3s and 11 assorted Venture vehicles were transferred to Northern who also temporarily gained numerous vehicles on loan from other members of the Group.

Early in 1971, a new chronological fleet numbering system was introduced starting at 2700, this including all the vehicles taken into stock during that year and eventually embraced the whole Group. No renumbering of the existing fleet was planned however, and thus to the casual observer it appeared that the fleet was numbered in a somewhat haphazard manner. Meanwhile, following the transfer of Wakefields licences and vehicles etc, to Tynemouth & District at the start of 1970, the use of the Wakefields fleet name had been abandoned and all the vehicles sporting it were transformed by the fitting of Tynemouth lettering whilst operations in the name of Venture's subsidiary, C. & E. Bus Company Limited ceased as from 11 September 1971 when its routes from Stanley to Dipton and Flint Hill were taken over by Northern. Later in the year, on 22 December, Durham bus station was transferred from Northern to United at the decree of the National Bus Company who had approved this move on 22 February. Development of the bus station had been in the pipe line since 1960 when property owned by J.H.Veitch & Sons Ltd. in North Road was purchased and an attempt had been made to buy the Methodist Chapel (which, incidentally, still survives today). Little progress was made, however, prior to the site's transfer to United except for demolishing the printing works when its derelict buildings became dangerous, although presumably in the transaction of December 1971 the Avenue Hotel which was rented to United as their offices was also included in the development plan. Earlier in the year, the Gateshead Transport Advisory Committee had held its last meeting on 23 June when it was noted that the Tyneside PTA was now in existence.

Although no further secondhand vehicles were purchased, 1971 saw the transfer of a large number of vehicles between Northern and its subsidiaries and included amongst these were several of Venture's single deckers which were taken into stock by Northern. Further loans were made throughout the year to Northern by Gateshead & District, Sunderland District and Tynemouth & District to ease continuing vehicle shortages and two more vehicles were borrowed from their manufacturers for evaluation. The first of these was a Willowbrook bus-bodied 53-seat dual-door Ford R226 painted in West Midlands PTE livery which spent a few weeks with Northern in February and March, whilst for a couple of weeks in December came a Willowbrook dual purpose-bodied Bedford YRQ in Ulsterbus colours.

Changes within the Northern Group continued apace during 1972 and as far as the fleet was concerned brought into it yet more NBC influence with the introduction of the Leyland National. Prior to the arrival of the first buses of this type however, further rear-engined Daimler SRG6 single deckers took up their duties, these being diverted from an order placed by Maidstone & District Motor Services and fitted with Willowbrook 44-seat dual-door bodywork. Although all 30 were legally owned by Northern, 6 were allocated from new to Gateshead & District in whose livery they were painted whilst 6 were given Tynemouth fleet names. Also making their debut with Northern were 5 Plaxton coach-bodied Leyland Leopards which were finished in a cream livery with red waist band.

Surprisingly, having only evolved a new fleet numbering system during the previous year, Northern changed this at the end of April 1972 and in its place introduced a new Group series starting at '1' to which the year suffix of the registration number was added (i.e. the remainder of the 1972 deliveries were 1K to 12K and 13L to 31L), although following past traditions, vehicles already in the fleet were not included in the new scheme! The first buses to be numbered in this new series were Leyland Nationals, the first 3 of which arrived in May, and although delivered in Northern General livery, they were immediately repainted into Sunderland District colours before entering service with that company. In total, 31 Leyland Nationals, all of which were dual-door 44-seaters, took up their duties during the year with all but the first three being allocated to the Northern fleet. Joining these in the autumn were 14 ECW-bodied Leyland-engined Bristol RELH coaches, 5 dual-door ECW-bodied Leyland-engined Daimler Fleetline double deckers and 18 dual-door ECW-bodied Leyland Atlanteans. Despite all being legally owned by Northern, 13 of the Atlanteans were painted in Gateshead & District livery for operation in that fleet whilst the remaining 5 were put to work in the Tyneside fleet.

In addition to receiving the above large quantity of new buses and coaches, Northern also gained a number of single deckers transferred from its subsidiaries with 6 Bristol RELLs from Gateshead & District, 3 AEC Reliances from Venture and 2 Leyland Leopards from Sunderland District. These were joined by 12 dual-door Marshall-bodied Daimler SRG6 single deckers obtained from Maidstone & District in exchange

During 1972, Tynemouth exchanged some of its Daimler Fleetlines with East Yorkshire Motor Services for a number of Park Royal-bodied AEC Renowns. One of the latter, 335 (GAT822D) is seen operating the 408 service to Whitley Bay before passing to Northern on 1 January 1975 following the demise of the Tynemouth company. Repainted into NBC-style yellow livery in June 1975, 3213, as it had then been renumbered, remained in service until 1978.

One of a number of Bristol FLF6G Lodekkas purchased by the Northern group from United in 1972, 2864 (RHN951F) is seen here sporting Tynemouth fleet names on its NBC corporate poppy red & white livery. Along with all the other ex.United buses of this type, it was sold to the Scottish Bus Group in 1973/4.

Although owned by Northern General, six of the dual-door Willowbrook-bodied Daimler SRL6 single deckers diverted from a Maidstone & District order and delivered in 1972 were painted in Gateshead & District livery for operation by that company. One of these, 2824 (NCN64L) is seen here soon after its entry into service operating the Leam Lane Estate circular route 52. Renumbered 4258 in 1975, it was at the start of the following year transferred to Northern upon the absorption of the Gateshead fleet and was later repainted into NBC-style yellow livery. After its withdrawal in 1978, 4258 was sold to Citybus, Belfast for further service, being withdrawn in November 1979 after being maliciously attacked.

for Northern's 12 Alexander-bodied double deck Daimler Fleetlines of 1969 vintage, and by 11 front entrance Bristol FLF6G Lodekkas acquired from United Automobile Services Ltd., although three of these were immediately placed in service in the Tynemouth & District fleet. Tynemouth also received 6 Park Royal-bodied front entrance AEC Renown double deckers from East Yorkshire Motor Services gained in part exchange for 20 Daimler Fleetlines, and in addition disposed of 6 Alexander-bodied Fleetlines to United Automobile Services along with 5 of Northern's buses of this same type. As will be seen later, the 11

The only ECW bus-bodied Bristol RELL6G to be purchased by Northern was a batch of 23 which arrived during 1971 although a further 19 had been ordered but were diverted to Gosport & Fareham and United before delivery. Seen in its original red & cream livery is 2740 (KCN240J) which began life as a dual-door bus but was converted to single-door configuration in March 1979. Withdrawn in 1982 when only eleven years old, 2740 which by that time had been renumbered 4213 was sold to APT, Lincoln in April of that year and passed to PVS, Carlton for dismantling on 4 May 1982.

Sporting a 'Shop at Binns' advert above its front destination screen which was not on a cream background, 1955 MCCW-bodied Leyland PD2/12 PUP548 still carries Sunderland District livery in 1970 despite it having been transferred to Northern General's driver training fleet during the previous year. (K.A.Jenkinson collection)

New to Northern in March 1971 numbered 2728 (KCN28J), this Alexander-bodied Daimler SRG6LX was transferred to Tynemouth in August of that year, becoming 328 in that fleet. Returning to Northern in January 1975 when it absorbed its Tynemouth subsidiary, it already wore NBC-style yellow livery and, renumbered 4356 it continued in service from Percy Main depot until its withdrawal and sale in 1981.

Fleetlines were returned to their original owners after only a few months following the rescinding on 13 March 1973 of the original authorisation for their exchange for Lodekkas given on 15 October 1972. Never having actually been sold, the Fleetlines regained their original fleet numbers when they returned, whereas all previous returns to the fleet had been renumbered (one BMMO single decker having carried three different Northern numbers in its lifetime!).

Without doubt, the most unusual vehicles to be placed in service during 1972, however, were two experimental double deckers constructed by Northern General to enable them to be used for one-person operation. The first of these was rebuilt from one of Tyneside Omnibus Co's 1958 MCCW-bodied Leyland PD3/4s, whose chassis was converted to normal control configuration and its body modified accordingly. With its entrance door placed at the front adjacent to the driver, and named the "Tynesider", it was not particularly attractive in its appearance. Plans were laid for it to be tested in service in different parts of the company's area of operation and after only a couple of weeks in service with Northern, it was despatched on loan to Gateshead & District in May, moving a month later to Tyneside Omnibus Co. by whom it was operated until November. Although not officially withdrawn until 1978, it saw little use after the end of 1972, however, except as a staff bus at Tynemouth's Percy Main depot. Sold in July of that year to a preservationist, it was in 1992 purchased by London & Country for spares, and, after being heavily cannibalised, rather than being scrapped it surprisingly found yet another new owner, Blue Triangle of Liverpool who had intended to rebuild for an unbelievable re-entry to service in a passenger carrying capacity! In the event, this task was never completed and when Blue Triangle was purchased by MTHL in 1994, the Tynesider returned to preservation. The second conversion involved one of Northern's Routemasters which had been seriously damaged in an accident in 1971. This was converted to semi-normal control layout thus necessitating the substantial rebuilding of its front end to allow the entrance door to be adjacent to the driver. Being slightly more attractive in its overall appearance than the "Tynesider", it re-entered service with Northern in August 1972 named the "Wearsider", and remained in use at Sunderland depot until 1978 when it was withdrawn and sadly sold for scrap.

Amongst the first Leyland Nationals to be purchased by Northern was dual-door 17L (MCN817L) which entered service in August 1972. Seen here in its original pre NBC-style livery, it was renumbered 4418 in 1975 and in December 1979 was converted to single-door layout. Nine months later it received NBC-style yellow livery and a year later was sold to United Automobile Services for continued use.

1972 saw the arrival of twelve ECW coach-bodied Bristol RELH6Ls which were delivered in BET-style red & cream livery as illustrated by 80L (MCN880L). Soon after its entry into service, however, 80L together with its sisters, was converted for one-man-operation and fitted with a 'Pay as you enter' sign in the top of its nearside windscreen for use on some of the company's longer inter-urban services such as the X3 to Sunderland. In May 1973 it was repainted into NBC's corporate white coaching livery and in October 1979 gained NBC's red & white dual purpose colours. Two years later (in October 1981) it was repainted yet again, this time into NBC-style yellow livery which it retained until its withdrawal during the following year.

CORPORATE IDENTITIES

Visually, as far as the fleet was concerned, 1972 marked the start of a new era, as it was in that year that the first of Northern's vehicles appeared in the new National Bus Company corporate livery. The first to be thus treated were coaches which shed their cream & red colours in favour of an all-over white scheme adorned with large "National" fleet names applied in alternate red and blue letters. These were followed by the first of the semi-coach and stage carriage vehicles to be transformed, the former becoming poppy red below the waist and white above, the latter being painted all-over poppy red, relieved by a white band at upper deck floor level on double deckers. Additionally, all were given new corporate-style fleet names in 6 inch high white letters together with NBC's "double-N" symbol. Although it was decreed that the poppy red/white colour combination was ultimately to be applied to the whole of the Northern General fleet and to its subsidiaries, one exception was Sunderland District who adopted a version of the NBC corporate livery using blue with white relief. Surprisingly, however, Northern, Gateshead & District and Tyneside Omnibus Co. continued to receive new vehicles painted in pre-NBC liveries and it was not until 1974 that visible changes began to escalate.

A further development of 1972 was the closure of Northern's operational depot at Bensham to allow the expansion of overhaul and maintenance facilities, the buses concerned being transferred to Gateshead & District's Sunderland Road garage which was extended with the erection of a prefabricated building. The reason behind this move was that the company's Chief Engineer had seriously depleted his staff by some 120 men, particularly at depot maintenance level, in anticipation of a productivity scheme which did not materialise. As a result, he was left with the choice of expanding the activities of the central workshops at Bensham or engaging more men at the depots and as the former proved to be cheaper, this was the option he took!

1973 witnessed the arrival of more new vehicles and although all were legally owned by Northern General, several were allocated to its subsidiaries with whose fleet names they were adorned. Of the 76 vehicles received, all except 10 were Leyland Nationals which apart from 2 which were 49-seat single door variants, had dual doors and seating for 44 or 46 passengers. Although the bulk of these were placed in the Northern fleet, six joined Tynemouth and 5 were allocated to Sunderland District. The remaining 10 vehicles were Plaxton-bodied, Leyland-engined Bristol RELH coaches of which 8 were for Northern and 2 for Sunderland District.

Although the secondhand additions to the fleet were minimal during 1973, they were nevertheless unusual. The first of these, received in the opening month of the year, was an ECW-bodied Bristol VRT acquired from Scottish Bus Group subsidiary, Central SMT in exchange for one of the ex.United Bristol FLFs under the SBG/NBC exchange agreement involving these types of buses. Although this particular VRT was repainted into Sunderland District's NBC-style blue livery, it never entered service with that company and instead, after briefly returning to

The only former Scottish Bus Group Bristol VRT to join the Northern Group was ex.Central SMT NGM174G which arrived at Bensham in January 1973, was painted into Sunderland District NBC-style blue & white livery and numbered 2873, and then departed back to its original owner in February 1973 without ever having been used in the north-east. Later that month it was despatched to Eastern Counties Omnibus Co. Ltd. in whose fleet it became VR319.

Central SMT, it ended up with Eastern Counties after a decision had been taken to replace the Bristol FLFs purchased from Northern by the Scottish Bus Group with the Daimler Fleetlines transferred to United in 1972. In exchange for these, United would receive the cascaded SBG Bristol VRTs instead of Northern, thus standardising its double deck

Wearing the NBC version of Tyneside PTE's yellow livery is Tynemouth's Leyland National 45L (MCN845L). New in 1973, this bus, like its sisters, was legally owned by Northern General and upon the demise of Tynemouth & District on 1 January 1975 it became 4446 in the Northern fleet to which it was transferred.

During 1973, the Northern group purchased a number of Plaxton coach-bodied Bristol RELH6Ls including 122L (NCN822L) which was allocated to Sunderland District. Seen at Harrogate wearing corporate NBC white coach livery, it was transferred to Northern in January 1975 and numbered 5050. It was withdrawn in 1981 after being severely damaged by fire.

Still wearing Northern's pre-BET style livery but having gained a corporate NBC fleet name with 'double-N' symbol on its cove panels, dual purpose-seated Marshall-bodied Leyland Leopard 2525 (ECN125E) fitted with a 'pay as you enter' panel below its windscreens hurries towards Newcastle on the 97 service.

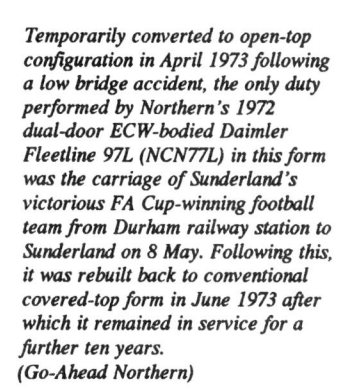

Wearing an unrelieved red livery complete with Northern fleet names and NBC's 'double-N' logo, dual-door Leyland National 73L (NCN972L) is seen here in 1973 when only a few months old operating service 8 to Blaydon.

Temporarily converted to open-top configuration in April 1973 following a low bridge accident, the only duty performed by Northern's 1972 dual-door ECW-bodied Daimler Fleetline 97L (NCN77L) in this form was the carriage of Sunderland's victorious FA Cup-winning football team from Durham railway station to Sunderland on 8 May. Following this, it was rebuilt back to conventional covered-top form in June 1973 after which it remained in service for a further ten years.
(Go-Ahead Northern)

fleet on the Bristol chassis. To this end, 3 of the Alexander-bodied Fleetlines "returned home" in 1973 with a further two following in 1974. One was immediately despatched on loan to Sunderland District whilst the remainder re-entered service with Northern. Also returning to their original owner at this same time were the 6 ex.Tynemouth Fleetlines.

A further surprise was the appearance of an open-top double decker in the Northern fleet. This was one of the company's 1972 ECW-bodied Daimler Fleetlines which, after suffering damage sustained in a low bridge accident in April 1973 was converted to open-top configuration. Its only duty in its new form appears to have been the carrying of Sunderland AFC's FA Cup-winning team from Durham railway station to Sunderland on 8 May on their triumphant return from Wembley, and during the following month it was rebuilt to its original covered-top format prior to returning to normal service.

After a comparatively quiet period during which few new routes had been introduced, 1973 witnessed a number of service changes and saw the start of a reorganisation of route numbering in the North East into district sequences. Under this new scheme, local services in the Newcastle and Gateshead areas were numbered up to 99, those in Sunderland, Seaham and Houghton-le-Spring areas were given numbers between 100 and 199, Durham, Peterlee and those operating south to Durham were placed in the 200s, North Tyneside (including all Tynemouth and Tyneside services) in the 300s, the 400s were used for routes in Northumberland north of Newcastle, the 500s for those around South Shields and Jarrow, 600s in the Tyne Valley including the Whickham, Winlaton and Ryton areas, 700s for the Chester-le-Street, Stanley and Consett areas including the services from Newcastle to Crook and Bishop Auckland and 900s for workman's services. This affected not only the services operated by Northern and its subsidiaries, but of all the companies serving the north-east. Although there was also an 800 series, this was used entirely by Northumberland area independents and thus did not involve the Northern group. Several new and revised routes were inaugurated during 1973 including two running between Jarrow and Hedworth Lane Estate, one via Bede Burn Road, the other via the pedestrian Tyne Tunnel (through which one could walk to Howden and get a bus to Wallsend); a new circular route in each direction serving Newcastle, Teams and Dunston; one from Washington to Jarrow via Heworth and one from Chester-le-Street to Houghton-le-Spring via Lumley. Three new services were started in Consett on 29 September whilst on 22 November, in connection with the opening of the new bus station at Washington, a

Painted in NBC-style dark blue & white livery and sporting a 'double-N' logo in front of its Sunderland District fleet name is 174M (OTY407M), a Park Royal-bodied Leyland Atlantean which was, numerically, the last new bus purchased by that company before its demise in January 1975.
(Go-Ahead Northern)

As part of a nationwide campaign to promote National Holidays, most NBC subsidiaries painted one or more buses in an all-over advertsing livery for this purpose. This is illustrated by Northern's Park Royal-bodied Leyland Atlantean 3282 (RCN108N) pictured here at Gateshead Metro (S.A.Staddon)

Purchased new by Venture Transport in 1971, Alexander-bodied Leyland Leopard RPT295K was transferred to the Northern fleet on 1 January 1975 and numbered 4400. Losing its original owner's colours in favour of NBC corporate poppy red, 4400 gained NBC's local coach red & white livery in August 1977 only to revert back to local coach colours in March 1979. In December 1980 it was repainted yet again, this time into NBC-style yellow livery which it retained until its withdrawal from service in 1981. Here it is seen at Marlborough Crescent bus station, Newcastle in 1974 whilst still in the Venture fleet working the 33 service to Chopwell.

massive revision of services in that area resulted in the commencement of no less than seven new routes. 1974 witnessed a further two new services being introduced in Consett on 9 February and on the following day, five new routes were started in the Gateshead district where those previously operated had been largely based on the old tram routes, and in Winlaton, and in addition the new circular route launched in May of the previous year was revised and operated jointly by Gateshead & District and Tyne & Wear PTE. A few more new services were launched during the spring and summer including one by Tynemouth in March (X38 Whitley Bay - Newcastle) which operated only at peak times whilst in May Venture's solitary X-service (X1 Consett to Newcastle via Shotley Bridge) was renumbered X11 so as not to clash with Northern's X1. Finally, on 30 November, services in the Consett area were reshuffled and no fewer than nine new services were introduced. This latest upheaval allowed a rationalisation of the former Northern and Venture services in that area to provide greater economies without any loss to passengers. 1973 also witnessed the opening of two new bus stations, one on 26 February provided by the local authority at Seaham Harbour, the other at Stanley coming into use on 4 July whilst one proposed at South Shields never materialised.

Despite continuing to receive the Leyland National in quantity, this model was not without its problems and being dissatisfied with certain of its design features, Northern set about modifying it in an attempt to make it more reliable. One of its Sunderland District examples which was barely a year old was severely damaged by fire whilst in service in June, and, after being towed to the Leyland hospital at Chorley for repair, it returned to Northern in December 1974 and was then used for experimental purposes at the Telma retarder depot at Scarborough. Upon completion of this work it was ultimately returned to Sunderland District's Philadelphia depot where it was stripped for spares without ever re-entering service. Meanwhile, one of Northern's 1972 Leyland Nationals was extensively rebuilt incorporating numerous modifications such as the repositioning of its batteries from the rear to a position at the front and improvements to its heating/ventilating system, after which it was returned to service.

1974 was to become a milestone in the history of the Northern General group as it was at the end of that year that three of its subsidiaries ceased trading. However, looking first at the fleet, this was updated by the addition of 64 new vehicles comprising 13 single-door Leyland Nationals, 26 Park Royal dual-door Leyland Atlanteans, 4 ECW-bodied dual-door Bristol VRTs and 2 Plaxton-bodied Leyland Leopard coaches. Of the Leyland Nationals, 2 were loaned from new to Venture with 2 going to Sunderland District whilst 2 of the Atlanteans were loaned to Tynemouth and 16 were operated by Gateshead & District. The remaining new vehicles were 12 dual-door Park Royal-bodied Atlanteans for Tynemouth and 7 similar buses for Sunderland District. A further 9 Leyland Nationals had been ordered for Northern but these were instead diverted to United Counties Omnibus Co. An unusual, albeit temporary, addition to the Gateshead & District fleet was an NCME-bodied Daimler Fleetline fitted with Sevcon automatic transmission. Borrowed from SELNEC, Manchester from December 1973 to February 1974, it is believed that it was used as a "test-bed" for Sevcon - whose factory was in Gateshead - and during its stay it became a familiar sight on local services in its distinctive ivory & orange livery.

Although the NBC corporate livery was now becoming more common on the vehicles of Northern and its subsidiaries, another new livery had made its debut (during 1973), this being yellow with a white relief band. This began to be applied to Gateshead, Tynemouth and Tyneside's buses operating on services within the Tyne & Wear PTE area in order to create a corporate image (Tyne & Wear PTE's livery being yellow & cream) and at a later date, to a number of Northern and Sunderland District buses. Ultimately United Automobile Services followed suit but painted its Tyne & Wear area fleet into the then

Rebuilt by Northern with a half-width roof pod, Leyland National 4441 (MCN840L) shows its unusual appearance at Felling in 1976. (T.W.W.Knowles)

The last new buses to enter service with Tyneside were five dual-door ECW-bodied Daimler Fleetlines, all of which were legally owned by Northern but were given Tyneside fleet names. 90L (ETY90L) seen here at North Shields wearing the yellow & white NBC-style Tyneside PTE livery was transferred to the Northern fleet in January 1976 upon the demise of the Tyneside concern.

Wearing NBC-style yellow & white livery in 1974 is Tynemouth 309 (HCN45G), a 48-seat Marshall Camair-bodied Leyland Panther which was delivered new to Gateshead & District in 1969 but was transferred to Tynemouth before entering service.

standard PTE livery of yellow with white window surrounds and roof, blue beadings and blue wheels!

As stated earlier, 1974 witnessed the demise of three of Northern's subsidiaries : Sunderland District, Tynemouth & District, and Venture Transport, all of which ceased to trade at midnight on 31 December as a result of their purchase by Northern General Transport Co.Ltd. No money changed hands in this transaction, however, and instead the purchase price remained outstanding as an inter-company balance repayable upon demand without interest by agreement between the companies concerned. From the following day, all the vehicles owned or on loan to Sunderland District, Tynemouth and Venture passed to Northern as did their services and depots etc., and as a result a new fleet numbering scheme (yes, another one!) was implemented at this same time. This placed all the double deckers in the 3000 series, single deckers and semi-coaches in the 4000 series and coaches in the 5000 series. Vehicles were renumbered in strict numerical order within the three blocks (except for 4523/4 which got overlooked) starting with the original Northern fleet and then following on with those received since 1971 when the corporate numbering scheme was introduced, then the vehicles transferred from Sunderland District (90, of which 3 were already withdrawn); Tynemouth (72 of which 8 were withdrawn), and Venture (50) respectively. Out of the 874 vehicles involved, only one retained its former number, this being the converted "Tynesider" double decker 3000! Despite this massive renumbering programme being introduced at the start of 1975, a number of buses operating from Murton and Consett depots still carried their old identities as late as the summer of 1976, whilst Gateshead & District continued to use its existing scheme for its pre-1971 buses until December 1977 after which an '0' prefix was added to three digit numbers and an '01' prefix to buses with two digit numbers (of which there was only one - 91 which became 0191.

Northern's remaining two subsidiaries - Gateshead & District and Tyneside - continued to operate throughout 1975, a year during which only a handful of service changes were undertaken and fewer new vehicles were added to the fleet. Of the latter, 8 were Plaxton-bodied Leyland Leopard coaches painted in NBC's corporate National white livery, 5 were Leyland Nationals and 27 were dual-door ECW-bodied Leyland Atlanteans. A further new dual-door ECW-bodied Bristol VRT was also received in February, this being the Series III prototype which had been exhibited at the Commercial Motor Show in October of the previous year. Before its arrival in the north-east, it had in January been demonstrated to Cardiff City Transport (although it was not used in service by that undertaking) and in December 1975 it was despatched on loan to Tayside Regional Council for a short period of evaluation. To cover for its temporary departure, Leyland Motors loaned Northern one of its Leyland National demonstrators, this being a 49-seat single door example whilst, joining the fleet in December, on a permanent basis, were 5 semi-coach Willowbrook-bodied Leyland Leopards from East Yorkshire which had been on hire since October.

The only secondhand Routemaster to be acquired was 2145 (254CLT), a 1962 example which was purchased from London Transport in November 1966. Being unique - and thus non-standard - in the London fleet, it had never operated in normal service in the metropolis although it had been evaluated by several provincial operators during the first couple of years of its life. Easily recognisable due to being the only one of Northern's Routemasters to have opening front upper deck windows, it is seen here at Gateshead depot in May 1980 after being renumbered 3129. Withdrawn later that year, it was quickly - and happily - sold for preservation. (K.A.Jenkinson)

Owned by Tyne & Wear PTE but operated on its behalf on the Tyne Commission Quay service by Northern, former Standerwick ECW coach-bodied Briatol VRLL 34 (OCK64K) seen here outside Percy Main depot carries a 'Norway Denmark Quay' board below its windscreens. (K.A.Jenkinson)

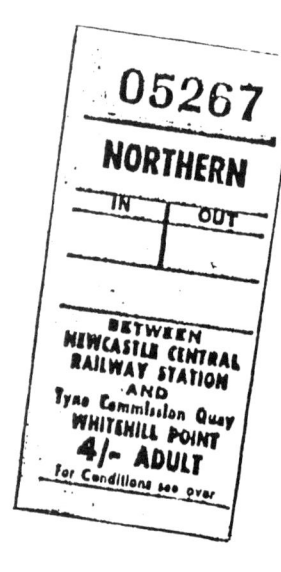

Also hired during the year were 2 Park Royal-bodied AEC Reliance coaches from East Kent and 2 Harrington-bodied Reliance coaches from Maidstone & District, these operating for Northern from January to May, a United ECW-bodied Bristol MW5G for one week in January and, for evaluation purposes, a Ford R1014 with Plaxton bus bodywork was borrowed for a month during the early summer. Perhaps the most unusual newcomer, however, was an ECW coach-bodied Bristol VRLLH6L which was hired from Standerwick during July/August for evaluation on the Tyne Commission Quay service. Although no vehicles of this type were ever acquired by Northern, 6 of the Standerwick vehicles were purchased by Tyne & Wear PTE for use on the Tyne Commission Quay service after they took it over from the NBC subsidiary in 1976 and were all initially operated by Northern on behalf of the PTE.

The service developments during 1975 were mainly confined to the modification of existing routes and the introduction of new work's services to the Tyne Tunnel Trading Estate on North Tyneside and between Stanley and Newcastle. The only new conventional routes inaugurated was one from Stanley to Shield Row operated as a circular, and four in the High Spen area, one of which was a hospital service from Rowlands Gill to Prudhoe Hospital, these being part of a complete revision on 1 November of all the routes in the Ryton, High Spen and Rowlands Gill areas.

December 31 marked the end of Northern's remaining two subsidiaries when at midnight Gateshead & District and Tyneside Omnibus Co. - both of which were still "statutory companies" - ceased trading and were fully absorbed by their parent. This brought to a close an era which had spanned more than sixty years and witnessed the end of the company from which Northern General Transport had been born. Gateshead's 68 buses and the 19 of Tyneside - of which two had

Standing outside Jarrow depot in May 1980 is Northern's NBC-yellow-liveried 4285 (SKO816H). A Marshall-bodied Daimler SRG6, it was new in 1970 to Maidstone & District, passing to Northern in December 1982. Built as a dual-door bus, it was converted to single-door format by Northern in March 1980. (K.A.Jenkinson)

been withdrawn some time earlier - were transferred to Northern along with their operations and depots and thus the restructuring of the company had been completed.

The flow of new buses continued in 1976, and although in slightly higher numbers than in the previous year, it was still found necessary to supplement them with more secondhand acquisitions. Of those delivered new, 33 were single-door Leyland National and 7 were

4582 (9768RH) was one of six dual purpose Willowbrook-bodied Leyland Leopards purchased by Northern from East Yorkshire Motor Services Ltd. in 1976. Painted in corporate NBC red & white local coach livery, it is seen in Newcastle working stage carriage service 725 to Esh Winning in November 1977. (T.W.W.Knowles)

7067 (PPT767P), one of Northern's 1976 vintage Plaxton-bodied Leyland Leopards takes a break in Oxford in May 1982 whilst working a National Holidays tour to Sandown, Isle of Wight. Fitted with draw side curtains, it was painted in NBC's corporate white coaching livery. (F.W.York)

Plaxton-bodied Leyland Leopard coaches, the only double deckers being 11 ECW-bodied Bristol VRTs which had originally been intended to be of dual-door configuration but in the event were 74-seaters with front entrance only. These were joined in July by 10 Marshall-bodied dual-door Daimler SRG6 single deckers obtained from Alder Valley, but which had originally been operated by Maidstone & District, and 6 more Willowbrook-bodied Leyland Leopard semi-coaches from East Yorkshire. Purchased in November were the 5 Marshall bus-bodied Leyland Leopards which had been on loan from Southdown since the early summer, as was, more unusually, a Morris Marina 4-seat car which originated from Venture Transport's taxi fleet. Licensed as a PSV, this car was to be employed on feeder services for tours operated by National Travel North East although in the event it saw little use and was soon re-sold. In an attempt to overcome a temporary vehicle shortage between May and the early autumn, a further 5 Marshall-bodied Leopards were hired from Southdown and in addition, 6 bus-bodied Leopards were borrowed from Yorkshire Traction whilst in August an Alexander coach-bodied Bristol RELH6G was hired from Eastern Scottish. Another temporary member of the fleet, albeit for a different purpose, was an ECW-bodied Bristol LH6L which was borrowed from United for two weeks in November. This was used at Murton, Consett and High Spen depots for driver familiarisation pending the delivery of a batch of 6 buses of this type to Northern in 1977, but in the event these never arrived and were instead diverted to another NBC company. As replacements, Northern placed an order for 6 new Leyland Nationals in March 1977. Meanwhile, surprisingly re-entering service in March 1976 was one of Northern's 1969 Alexander-bodied Leyland Leopard coaches which had eventually been rebuilt after standing out of use since being accident damaged four years earlier! During 1976 the white band below the windows of single deckers was eliminated to leave an unrelieved red livery and at around this same time, NBC's coloured 'double-N' logo on a white background began to be applied to repainted vehicles in place of the previous white logo.

After a period of comparative calm, Northern's service network underwent a deal of change during 1976 and in addition to numerous alterations to existing routes, several new ones were inaugurated throughout the company's territory. Firstly, the workmen's routes serving the Team Valley Trading Estate were revised on 10 January with two new routes being added, whilst during February as a result of the transfer of part of the DHSS from Longbenton to Emerson Industrial Estate at Washington, five new works services were started to this new location. A new conventional circular service was commenced from Newcastle (Marlborough Crescent) to Felling Square and Team Valley in January, replacing some existing services, and was followed in February by two new routes in the Stanley area. Two months later, a further express service was inaugurated, this being the X16 from Washington to Durham whilst in August the X4 from Newcastle to Sunderland was diverted to run via Washington instead of the Boldons, giving it a longer journey time and thus limiting its usefulness to Sunderland passengers. Meanwhile, in June a new route from Sunderland to Peterlee via Seaham was launched as part of a general shake-up of services in the Seaham area which saw the X8 Parkside - Jarrow service lose its Sunderland - Jarrow section. On the property side, the traffic office at Worswick Street, Newcastle was converted to a canteen for the company's employees while some additional land was purchased at Consett to enable the depot to be extended and allow the ultimate closure of that at Blackhill.

The intake of new vehicles in 1977 was entirely single deck, although some double deckers were acquired secondhand but unused. The former comprised 2 Duple coach-bodied Leyland Leopards and 40 Leyland Nationals, 9 of which had been diverted from a Ribble order whilst the latter were 8 ECW-bodied Bristol VRTs (of a lower height than those previously purchased by Northern) acquired in October from Trent Motor Traction to whom they had been delivered new and registered, but never operated. Joining these were 10 NCME-bodied full-fronted Leyland PD3/4s of 1965 vintage purchased from Southdown. None of the latter were used in a normal passenger-carrying role however, having been acquired solely for conversion into driver training vehicles, and all retained their NBC green colour scheme which was then adopted by Northern as its training livery. As had now become customary, two coaches were hired for part of the summer season, on this occasion both being Plaxton-bodied AEC Reliances from National Travel North East. Another hire, which was to become an annual event until 1983, was that of an open-top Alexander-bodied Leyland Atlantean from Tyne & Wear PTE. This was operated on the North Tyneside sea-front service between Whitley Bay and North Shields from Percy Main depot from the end of May to early September. On the debit side, 1977 saw the withdrawal of the first of Northern's former East Yorkshire dual-purpose Leopards together with

Hired from Tyne & Wear PTE for operation on seafront service 327 between Tynemouth and Whitley Bay, open-top Alexander-bodied Leyland Atlantean 627 (SVK627G) was for the 1977 season suitably decorated to commemorate the Queen's Silver Jubilee. (Go-Ahead Northern)

New to Northern in 1976, full-height ECW-bodied Bristol VRT 3337 (TUP337R) which was delivered in NBC-style yellow Tyneside PTE livery was, before entering service, repainted into a special silver livery in December of that year to commemorate the Silver Jubilee of H.M.Queen Elizabeth II. Reverting to yellow livery in January 1978, it received NBC-style corporate poppy red & white colours in October 1980 only to be returned to PTE-style yellow & white in December 1982.

Adorned with NBC corporate poppy red & white livery and carrying a 'please pay on entry' sign in its nearside windscreen, Willowbrook-bodied Bristol VRT 3357 (CUP357S) appears to not know where it is going, according to its destination display.

a variety of other of the company's older vehicles. Amongst these were 16 Routemasters, the first of this type to be taken out of service except for an accident victim in 1976, and whilst some of these were sold to dealers, five were dismantled by Northern to provide additional spares for those still in daily use.

Having built up a large fleet of dual-door single and double deckers, Northern was now beginning to doubt the wisdom of this configuration following the structural weakness attributed to the centre door and additionally from the angle of passenger safety. After deliberating on these matters, it was decided to convert a number of these vehicles to single-door layout and to this end, in the autumn of 1977, a programme was embarked upon which was to continue for around four years. Amongst the first vehicles to be altered in this manner were a number of Marshall-bodied Daimler SRG6s and several Leyland Nationals, the seating capacity of which, as a result, was able to be increased to 49. When the programme was completed in 1981, 85 Leyland Nationals, 15 ECW-bodied Bristol RELLs, 8 Marshall-bodied Leyland PSUR1s, 16 Daimler SRG6s and 33 Park Royal-bodied Leyland Atlanteans had been transformed in this manner and whilst most of this work had been undertaken by Northern in its own workshops, some had been contracted out to other NBC companies such as Crosville and Lincolnshire.

Although the service network underwent less change than in previous years, a further revision of routes was undertaken in the Consett area on 16 July. Additionally, three new express services were inaugurated, the first of which were the X40 Newcastle to Chopwell and X42 Newcastle to High Spen which commenced on 20 June, the third being the X20 from Newcastle to Durham via Newton Hall which began on 10 December. Earlier in the year, the directors of Motor Services; Wakefields; Sunderland District and Venture resolved on 24 March to request the Registrar of Companies to use his powers under Section 353 of the Companies Act 1948 and strike their names off the register. Tynemouth & District followed suit on 14 March 1978 but on 13 June 1979 rescinded this resolution and instead resolved to change their name to The Tyneside Omnibus Co.Ltd. Gateshead & District's directors also resolved to have their name struck off the register on 13 June 1979 whilst the original Tyneside Omnibus Co.Ltd. was struck off on 16 August 1979.

The final two years of the decade witnessed the arrival of no fewer than 170 new buses and coaches of which 78 made their debut in 1978 and the remainder in 1979. In the former year came 11 Leyland Nationals; 6 Plaxton-bodied Leopard coaches; 29 Willowbrook-bodied Leyland-engined Bristol VRTs and 32 ECW-bodied double deckers of this same chassis type, 4 of which had been diverted from a Trent order. Also joining the fleet were a further 3 NCME-bodied Leyland PD3/4s acquired from Southdown for conversion into driver training vehicles. In 1979, another Plaxton coach-bodied Leyland Leopard was delivered together with 38 ECW-bodied Bristol VRTs, 35 ECW-bodied Leyland Atlanteans of which 5 were fitted with 'help'-type front bumpers and 18 Leyland Nationals. 3 each of the latter were diverted from South Wales Transport and East Midland Motor Services whilst 5 of the Atlanteans had originally been intended for Yorkshire Traction. Indeed, the 1979 vehicle programme had originally called for more Atlanteans, but before they were able to be delivered, 19 were substituted by Bristol VRTs. Apart from the summer loan of the Tyne & Wear open-top Atlantean, unusually no other vehicles were hired during 1978, although in the following year several strangers made their appearance. One of these was a Duple-bodied Leopard coach from National Travel East which was hired from August to December and allocated to Stanley depot whilst also in August came a pair of United's Marshall-bodied Bristol LHS6Ls. These were required for use on a service operated by Consett depot which crossed a bridge at Moorside upon which a temporary weight restriction had been placed. In exchange, Northern despatched two of its ECW-bodied Bristol RELLs to United who placed them in service at their Ripon depot. The two LHS6Ls and one of the RELL6Gs returned to their respective homes in

One of a number of NCME-bodied Leyland PD3/4s purchased from Southdown for use as driver training buses, NBC green-liveried T391 (FCD309D) takes a break from its duties at Chester-le-Street depot in May 1980. (K.A.Jenkinson)

New in 1954 to Tyneside, MCCW-bodied Leyland PD2/12 47 (GTY177) was converted to a tree lopper in 1970 and used throughout the Northern group's area. It is seen here at Chester-le-Street depot in 1980, a few months before its withdrawal. (K.A.Jenkinson)

September whilst the other RELL was immediately loaned to West Yorkshire Road Car Co. who was at that time experiencing an acute vehicle shortage. This bus eventually found its way back to its rightful owner in October. A further loan was that of 5 single deckers (3 Leopards, a Bristol RELL and a Daimler SRC6) to United in July to assist them following the disasterous fire at their Durham depot. The crisis over, all of these had returned home by September. In need of some additional vehicles themselves, Northern hired 3 dual-door Leyland Nationals and a Willowbrook-bodied Leyland Leopard from

Former Maidstone & District Marshall-bodied Daimler SRG6 4282 (SKO811M) and Northern's Alexander-bodied Daimler SRG6s 4195 (KCN17J) and 4192 (KCN14J) are seen here after being damaged by fire at South Shields depot in August 1979. As a result, 4282 and 4195 were written-off and scrapped whilst 4192 was repaired to give a further two years service. (K.A.Jenkinson)

Tyne & Wear PTE for varying periods of time between January and July. Meanwhile, in connection with the first stages of the construction of Newcastle's new Metro light railway system in January 1979 Northern found it necessary to hire a number of Alexander-bodied Leyland Atlanteans from Tyne & Wear PTE in order to provide some special rail replacement services it had gained under contract from the PTE. Although 8 different buses were involved, their number fluxuated month by month until July with a maximum of six being hired at any time. As the work on the Metro system progressed, so the need for rail replacement services continued and from September 1979 until November 1980 Northern hired 4 Alexander-bodied Atlanteans from Tyne & Wear PTE, the actual vehicles changing from time to time for maintenance and other reasons. Operated from Percy Main depot, they were employed on services on the north side of the rail loop between Newcastle and Tynemouth (R1 - R3) and Newcastle and Monkseaton (R4). Upon commencement of the final stage of Metro's construction from November 1980 to June 1981, 5 Alexander-bodied Atlanteans hired from Tyne & Wear PTE were allocated to Gateshead depot to bring the total in use by Northern to 9 buses. Perhaps more interestingly however, Northern received a dual-door MCW Metrobus demonstrator from its manufacturer in November using it for driver familiarisation purposes during that and the following month from Gateshead depot prior to the arrival of 15 vehicles of this type which were on order but delayed. Departing from the fleet during this period were the 6 ex.East Yorkshire AEC Renowns which were all removed of service in 1978, 15 more Routemasters and a number of the vehicles taken over from Northern's subsidiary fleets.

Having been on loan to United, Northern ECW-bodied Bristol RELL6G 4217 (LCN244K) was then despatched direct to West Yorkshire Road Car Co. Ltd. who borrowed it to cover a vehicle shortage. Here it is seen in Yeadon operating West Yorkshire's 655 service from Bradford to Leeds on 17 September 1979. (K.A.Jenkinson)

Two of Tyne & Wear PTE's Alexander-bodied dual-door Leyland Atlanteans loaned to Northern for operation on Rail-link service R1 during the construction of the Metro system, 642 and 657 are seen here in the doorway of Northern's Percy Main depot (K.A.Jenkinson)

In retrospect, the 'seventies had proved to be a decade of massive changes as far as Northern was concerned both in its operations and vehicles. Having become part of the National Bus Company, Northern was no longer able to adopt its own policies but had to follow its new master's edicts. Restructuring had caused the demise of all of its subsidiaries and added to this was the co-ordination scheme imposed upon it by the recently-formed Tyneside (and later Tyne & Wear) PTE. The practice of hiring vehicles from other NBC subsidiaries to cover temporary vehicle shortages and additional needs had become commonplace, as had the receipt of new vehicles diverted from other NBC companies, and as well as having to adopt its master's corporate livery and a second colour scheme for vehicles operated on services within the new PTE area (both of which now omitted the white waist band on single deckers), Northern also lost its long distance coach services to National Express and its tours to National Holidays. It still had a responsibility to provide the vehicles used on the latter two operations, however, and thus it was still necessary to maintain a coaching fleet despite it being limited in its use.

INTO THE 'EIGHTIES

Following all the changes of the 'seventies, it was wondered what the new decade would produce and, although not known at that time, the 'eighties were to prove even more eventful. On the vehicle front, 1980 saw the arrival of a massive 103 new vehicles, plus a few acquired secondhand. Of the former, 40 were Roe-bodied Leyland Atlanteans whilst two more of this type with ECW bodywork were diverted from a Yorkshire Traction order. Added to these were 15 Willowbrook '003'-bodied Leyland Leopard coaches which were unusually painted in poppy red & white local coach livery and the first Leyland National 2s to join the fleet, these numbering 31 and including 10 substituted for Bristol VRTs ordered in the 1980 vehicle programme. One of the National 2s was diverted from East Yorkshire Motor Services and was unusual in not being fitted with a roof pod, a feature which made it unique in the Northern fleet for several years. More surprising however was the arrival in September and October of the delayed 15 single-door MCW Metrobuses, a type entirely new to Northern. These, and indeed all the Atlanteans received in 1980 were painted in NBC yellow & white livery for use on Tyne & Wear PTE area routes whilst all the Leyland Nationals wore the standard NBC corporate poppy red livery. Undoubtedly the most unexpected new vehicles to be purchased during 1980, however, were 4 Ford Cortina 1300L taxis which were used by the company in the Consett area on a taxi service started by Venture. The only other permanent additions to the fleet during the year were a trio of Leyland Nationals acquired from the NBC Disposal Pool at Lincoln. These originated from Plymouth Corporation and had been converted from dual to single-door configuration prior to their arrival in the north-east. On a temporary basis, a National Travel East Duple-bodied Leyland Leopard coach was hired from July to November, this being the only 'stranger' to be operated by the company during 1980 except for the PTE Atlanteans and the regular open-top double decker hired from that source. To add a little variety to the fleet, Bristol VRT 3428 and Leyland National 4677 were both painted into Sunderland District Tramways livery in May 1980 to commemorate the Diamond Jubilee of Sunderland District. Additionally, in 1980 as well as being carried in the conventional side positions, the fleet name began to be applied to the front of buses.

Starting life with Sunderland District in 1964 and transferred to Northern in 1975, Marshall-bodied Leyland Leopard AUP341B became a driver training bus in 1977 and four years later was converted to a towing vehicle. (K.A.Jenkinson)

The arrival of such a large number of new vehicles allowed the withdrawal of many of the company's older vehicles and by the summer of 1980 all except 13 members of the fleet had semi-automatic transmission. To enable the training of new drivers on vehicles fitted with this type of gearbox, a start was made in July on the re-equipping of the driver training fleet which until that date had comprised 13 former Southdown Leyland PD3/4s, a solitary Atlantean and a trio of Marshall-bodied Leyland Leopards. Thus, during the remaining part of 1980, 2 Leyland Panthers, a Daimler SRG6, and 3 double deck Fleetlines were converted for permanent driver training use and replaced 2 of the PD3/4s. In 1981, a further 3 Fleetlines were transferred to the training fleet which lost 9 more of its former Southdown PD3/4s. Amongst the other buses withdrawn from normal passenger-carrying duties were all the ex.Alder Valley and some of the former Maidstone & District Daimler SRG6s, the last of the ex.East Yorkshire Leopards and the final 19 Routemasters, the last of which survived until December. Meanwhile, fearing the threat posed by the forthcoming Transport Bill which was to de-regulate long distance services, and determined not to allow new operators the benefits of acquiring cheap secondhand vehicles for use on new competitive services, the NBC adopted a disposal policy in 1980 which decreed that all vehicles sold by its subsidiaries should be suitable only for scrap. To this end, all running units must be removed and the chassis cut through before redundant vehicles were sold. In mid November, a total of 43 buses were withdrawn awaiting disposal and by the start of February 1981 this had risen to 71.

The long-awaited opening of the first stage of the Metro eventually occurred on 11 August when the Haymarket to Tynemouth section became operational. This led to the withdrawal of rail replacement bus

One of five ECW-bodied Leyland Atlanteans fitted with 'help-type' front bumpers, 3544 (MBR444T) seen at Gateshead Interchange in February 1985 was painted in Tyne & Wear PTE yellow & white livery. (K.A.Jenkinson)

Pictured in Newcastle in June 1980 when only a week old is Willowbrook 003-bodied Leyland Leopard 5083 (TUP583V) which, as can be seen, arrived from its builders painted in NBC's poppy red & white local coach livery. (J.Fozard)

services R1-R4 and the transfer of the vehicles which had operated these to the new R5-R8 services between Tynemouth and Newcastle via Wallsend which replaced that section of the railway for conversion to Metro. Later in the year, in November, Tyne & Wear PTE published a consultation document detailing proposed service revisions to accompany the opening of the remainder of the Metro system and from these it was seen that the cross-river local services between Newcastle and Gateshead would all but disappear. Indeed, the service changes were to be extremely wide ranging and to varying degrees affected no fewer than 66 of Northern's existing routes. A revision of Sunderland services in December saw a rationalisation of joint services, most of which became operated either by Northern or Tyne & Wear PTE. Additionally, a new service introduced in December was the X94 (Newcastle - Easington Lane) which, unlike the X6 of 1961, matched its route number with the existing service 194 over the same route.

Despite a general decrease in the number of bus passengers nationally, Northern in 1980 remained one of the most successful of all the NBC's subsidiaries. Despite slimming its fleet by 69 vehicles and suffering a 5% drop in passengers, the company still managed to carry 144,341,000 passengers during the year and recorded an average mileage of 47,619 miles per vehicle, the equivalent of 130 miles per vehicle/day or 183,874 passengers per vehicle/year. With its revenue support of just under 1% of its total revenue, Northern received the third lowest of any of the NBC's subsidiaries and despite costs of 96.5p for every bus mile operated, the company's performance was extremely pleasing and a credit to its management.

Amongst the 55 new vehicles received by the company in 1981 were the first of a new type of double decker, the Leyland Olympian. 28 buses of this type, all with ECW bodywork and licensed as Bristols, were placed in service from August onwards with the first 6 being painted in NBC yellow livery and the remainder in corporate poppy red & white. These had originally been intended as Atlanteans, the order being changed prior to their construction being started! The balance of the year's intake comprised 21 Leyland National 2s, a solitary Duple-bodied and 5 Willowbrook-bodied Leyland Leopard coaches. Of the latter, two were delivered without seats and were fitted with Alexander Y-type seats removed from withdrawn coaches before entering service in December. Also added to the fleet in July/August were 10 coach-seated Alexander-bodied Leyland Atlanteans acquired from Tyne & Wear PTE. Delivered new to the PTE in February 1981, they had never entered service with their original owner and could thus be considered to be new vehicles. They retained their Tyne & Wear PTE yellow & white livery, to which Northern fleet names were added, and after being the subject of a dispute involving the engineering staff, they eventually made their debut on express services in mid-August. Being somewhat slow vehicles, however, they soon became unpopular and were relegated to more leisurely services. During the latter months of the year, three of Northern's 1978 ECW-bodied Bristol VRTs were converted to dual-purpose format by being repainted into a white livery with red lower deck panels and fitted with 70 coach-type seats purchased from United. That company's VRTs from which the seats were removed gained the bus type-seats taken from the three Northern vehicles!

During the year, further service changes were implemented as a result of the construction of the Metro and the subsequent opening of a new large section of the system. The first of these commenced following the closure of the rail service between Newcastle and South Shields on 31 May, these being replacement services numbered R9 and R10. The R9 was a stopping service which operated daily via Jarrow whilst the R10 was a peak hours express route which called only at Gateshead and Tyne Dock. Before the next Metro-related changes were implemented, however, a major revision of services in the Consett area took place on 18 July which affected not only the local routes, but also those to Newcastle and Derwentside. In addition, Northern announced that all its various works services were now available to the general public and also that the Consett and Stanley "Town Tickets" were valid for any 7-day period rather than only on Saturdays and Sundays.

Without doubt, the most sweeping changes to affect Northern were the service revisions brought about by the extension to Gateshead and Heworth of the Metro from Haymarket on 22 November and the implementation of Tyne & Wear PTE's associated transport integration scheme which was designed to encourage (or force ?) travel by Metro rather than by bus wherever this was possible. Under these changes, Northern no longer operated any local services in Newcastle except for the 616/617 from High Spen to Westerhope whilst Tyne & Wear PTE lost all its services in the Gateshead area. Numerous services were

Full-height 1978 ECW-bodied Bristol VRT 3404 (JPT904T) was fitted with coach-type seats in November 1982 and given a new red & white livery as seen here. Its fleet name was placed on its upper deck panels whilst its fleet number was carried above its front nearside wheel arch. (T.Godfrey collection)

Starting life with Plymouth City Transport in 1973 and acquired by Northern from APT, Lincoln in 1980, Leyland National 4690 (UCO47L) passes through the bus wash at Percy Main depot in May 1980. Converted from dual to single door by APT it is seen here painted in NBC-style poppy red & white livery which it cast in favour of NBC-style yellow & white in January 1981. (K.A.Jenkinson)

Delivered new in NBC-style yellow livery in August 1981, ECW-bodied Leyland Olympian 3576 (JTY376X) still wore these colours when photographed in Jarrow bus station in 1985 whilst working service 523 to Heworth. (T.W.W.Knowles)

truncated to terminate at Gateshead or Heworth Metro Interchanges and as a result, a large number of Northern's routes were transferred for operation from different depots. This caused the amalgamation of the allocations of Bensham and Gateshead depots on 1 November (despite both having for many years been garaged at Sunderland Road) and additionally the reallocation of 56 vehicles between other depots. A further consequence of the new integrated transport scheme was an overall reduction in the size of Northern's allocated fleet which was decreased from 756 to 702 vehicles, although in reality no fewer than 114 were taken out of service. Amongst these were the last vehicles acquired with the business of Venture Transport, the last Leyland Panthers, the last of the former Tynemouth Fleetlines and the first of the Bristol RELLs. In addition to these, 46 previously withdrawn buses and coaches were despatched to the NBC Disposal Pool at Lincoln early in November for cannibalisation or resale to other NBC subsidiaries.

For the first few weeks of operation, so enormous were the number of passengers wishing to travel on the new Metro on Saturdays that it was necessary to provide relief buses between the Monument, Gateshead and Heworth, and from Monument/Haymarket to Four Lane Ends. These services were numbered 900 & 901 respectively and although the former was operated solely by Tyne & Wear PTE's vehicles, Northern participated in the 901 service along with the PTE and United. Other significant overloadings led to duplicates having to be run on the 725/6 services to Chester-le-Street as well as on the 721 and X2 routes which carried numerous extra passengers from Worswick Street to Gateshead Interchange who wished to avoid the crush on the Metro before catching their buses there. In order to enable them to be operated on the new integrated Tyne & Wear system on which through bus/Metro ticketing was available, all Northern's vehicles employed on these services were equipped with validators which could accept the new Transfare tickets and, in the case of the Leyland Nationals, this resulted in the seating capacity being reduced from 49 to 48. Also, in December 1981, Northern's NBC version of the Tyne & Wear yellow livery was modified to conform to that applied by the PTE to its vehicles and also to those operated by United in the Tyne & Wear area. This employed white window frames, a white roof and blue beadings and featured Tyne & Wear Transport fleetnames together with the county logo and Double-N symbols on their side panels with the Northern name only appearing on the front and rear. Also receiving a "new" livery was one of the Willowbrook-bodied Leopard coaches which gained a red & blue waistband lettered "Liverpool - Manchester - Leeds - North East Express Service" for use on that service.

Although a total of 74 vehicles entered the fleet during 1982, only 24 of these were brand new, the others being surprisingly purchased from Tyne & Wear PTE. The new arrivals comprised 10 Leyland Leopard coaches of which 6 had Willowbrook bodywork and were painted in local coach livery, the remainder being bodied by ECW and finished in corporate National white. The only new stage carriage

Amongst the MCW-bodied Leyland Atlanteans purchased by Northern from Tyne & Wear PTE in 1982/3 was 3711 (YNL211V) which is pictured here at Jarrow bus station in 1986. Painted in Tyne & Wear PTE yellow & white livery and sporting Northern fleet names, it prepares to leave for Washington on the 526 service. (T.W.W.Knowles)

Passing Jarrow depot in 1985 is Northern 3590, an ECW-bodied Leyland Olympian painted in NBC-style poppy red & white livery. (T.W.W.Knowles)

Mk.2 Leyland National 4675 (UPT675V) is pictured here wearing corporate Tyne & Wear PTE yellow & white livery with Tyne & Wear Transport fleet names on its side panels and a Northern name below its windscreens. Still in service in 1995, it is currently painted in Wear Buses livery.   (Travelscene)

vehicles taken into stock were 14 ECW-bodied Leyland Olympians of which 12 were in NBC poppy red, the remaining pair, which had arrived in NBC yellow being immediately repainted into the new variation of yellow & white before making their debut in service at the end of the year. The 50 secondhand buses were all 86-seat MCW-bodied Leyland Atlanteans of 1979 vintage which were purchased from Tyne & Wear PTE between July 1982 and February 1983. These retained their PTE yellow & white livery and were allocated to several of the company's "yellow" depots. Acquired as a result of the PTA's policy requiring double deckers, the arrival of these buses allowed the departure of a large number of Leyland Nationals, many of which being far from time expired quickly found new owners within the NBC, as well as enabling the last of the hired rail replacement Tyne & Wear Atlanteans to be returned to their rightful owner towards the end of the year. Also withdrawn were the first of the Bristol RELH caoches and, perhaps more surprising, several 1972 Fleetlines. Initially, the 1982 programme had called for 33 Olympians and 10 Leyland Nationals, but in view of the 50 Atlanteans being available from the PTE, this was revised to only 6 Olympians and no single deckers. In order to increase its coaching fleet, Northern refurbished and upgraded some of its Willowbrook-bodied Leyland Leopards which were fitted with Plaxton seats removed from older vehicles and were then painted in NBC corporate white livery. Other of the Willowbrooks, which retained their dual purpose status, were in November painted in a new version of the "local coach" livery, this being white with a black skirt and red waistband upon which the Northern name was applied in white.

In addition to the usual minor service alterations during the spring and summer, Northern found itself involved in the provision of transport for the Pope's visit to York on 31 May when 42 of its vehicles were employed on a park and ride service from Clifton Airfield to Holbeck Road near York Racecourse. Many of these buses had been used to transport pilgrims from the north-east to York prior to their use on the park and ride service, and, except for a solitary Leyland National, all were Bristol VRT or Leyland Atlantean double deckers. Back home, massive service changes were implemented on 16 October in the Washington, Chester-le-Street, Consett and Stanley areas whilst on 15 November, due to fallen wiring in Gateshead, all the Metro services south of Haymarket were suspended for most of the morning. This caused plans to be hastily put into operation to provide replacement bus services until the Metro service could be restored and for this purpose the PTE, United and Northern between them utilised more than 50 buses, 21 of which were from the Northern fleet. Earlier, in March 1982, it was reported that losses in County Durham had now become a matter of considerable concern and the Chairman requested that joint action with United should be taken as a matter of urgency to bring the operations into balance. In October, however, it was noted that the disturbing trends were continuing while in February 1983 it was reported that the operations in County Durham had run at a significant deficit and that possible cost-cutting or revenue support was required.

1983 witnessed more service changes necessitated by the opening on 8 May of a further phase of the Metro, on this occasion on North Tyneside from Tynemouth to Newcastle via Wallsend. As a result, several existing services were revised or withdrawn and a number of new routes were inaugurated in the Wallsend area, with several being diverted to Wallsend Metro station for interchange purposes. A few months later, following the introduction by Low Fell Coaches of a service from Low Fell to Newcastle which avoided having to change to the Metro at Gateshead, Northern in retaliation upgraded its 724 service between Chester-le-Street and Newgate Street, Newcastle, branding it "Cross-Tyne Link". To promote its new image the service was worked by Willowbrook semi-coach bodied Leopards which were fitted with "Cross-Tyne Link" headboards across their front panels. In Sunderland, the town service network was recast on 23 October with almost every route being affected in some way or other. One of the most unusual service alterations during 1983 was, however, imposed by circumstance rather than by design. Due to the bridge at Herrington Colliery becoming unsafe for vehicles of over 2 tons unladen weight in June, Northern's services using this crossing had to operate in the form of two shuttles to either side of the bridge. After around two weeks, a 16-seat Dormobile-bodied Ford Transit was hired from J.P.Charlton of Gateshead to enable the services to once again "work through". and surprisingly, due to it not being fitted with a power door, this little vehicle was crew-operated, a feature not usually associated with minibuses. A second vehicle was also hired from J.P.Charlton to

Leaving Gateshead Metro enroute to Seaham Harbour on the X96 service is ECW-bodied Leyland Leopard 5100 (LFT100X) painted in ExpressLink white livery with red & maroon stripes.   (K.A.Jenkinson)

New in 1980, Northern's Roe-bodied Leyland Atlantean 3447 (AUP347W) was repainted into the old Gateshead & District maroon livery in August 1983 to commemorate the centenary of public transport in that town. (K.A.Jenkinson)

provide cover for the Transit, this being a Deansgate-bodied 19-seat Mercedes L508D coach and both continued in use until 3 March 1984 when, following repairs, the offending bridge was reopened to normal traffic. Further strangers to the north-east were a pair of Bristol VRTs borrowed from Yorkshire Traction to evaluate the benefits of conversion from Leyland to Gardner engines. During their period of operation from Murton depot from 1 to 30 November, one of this duo unfortunately suffered damage in a low bridge accident and as a result had to be repaired before returning to its rightful owner. For the duration of November, Northern loaned 2 of its own Bristol VRTs to Yorkshire Traction in exchange.

The year's intake of new vehicles included 4 more ECW-bodied Leyland Olympians, 7 Leyland National 2s - this time with Gardner 6LXB engines and fully-automatic transmission - and 10 Mk.II MCW Metrobuses, 5 of which were Gardner-engined whilst the remainder had Cummins L10 engines. The most surprising new arrivals, however, were a pair of Roe-bodied Leyland Royal Tiger Doyen coaches which made their debut at the beginning of August. Prior to their somewhat late arrival, Leyland had from June loaned Northern two Leyland Tiger coaches - one Duple, the other Plaxton-bodied - to enable them to meet their summer commitments, these returning home when the new coaches were delivered. In October, the two Doyens were named "Northern Ambassador" and "Northern Diplomat" and it is believed that this was the first occasion that any of the company's vehicles had been "named". Amongst the vehicles leaving the fleet during the year were more Leyland Nationals and, sadly, the last of the Bristol RELLs which operated their final journeys in February. Also disappearing was the white band applied to the NBC poppy red livery on single deckers, the final vehicle painted in this manner appearing in unrelieved red in March. 1983 also witnessed the closure of the Wellington Street bus station at Gateshead and the closure of the ex.Venture depot at Blackhill.

No new single deckers were ordered for 1984 except for 5 Plaxton Paramount-bodied Leyland Tiger coaches and 2 more Royal Tiger Doyens, the remainder of the new vehicle deliveries taking the form of 31 Mk.II MCW Metrobuses which, apart from having curved windscreens were almost identical to the buses of this type received during the previous year. These had originally been ordered as Leyland Olympians in Northern's 1984 vehicle programme! With history repeating itself, due to the late arrival of the 2 Royal Tiger Doyen coaches, Leyland were obliged to once again loan Northern two vehicles on a short term basis. Making their debut at the end of May/early June, they were a Plaxton-bodied Tiger in the livery of Mayne, Manchester and a Duple-bodied Tiger destined for Mercer of Longridge, neither of which reached their intended owners until July when they were returned to Leyland upon receipt of the Doyens. These were, however, not the only strangers to be operated by the company during 1984, as at the start of the year a toilet-equipped Berkhof-bodied DAF SB2300 coach was hired from National Travel London for use on the Rapide service to Torquay. This was joined in March by a National Travel London Bova, and when both were returned to their rightful owner at the beginning of April, a Rapide-specification Plaxton Paramount-bodied Leyland Tiger was hired from National Welsh for the Torquay service. In exchange for the latter, one of Northern's Plaxton-bodied Tigers was despatched to National Welsh and both vehicles returned to their respective homes at the end of May upon receipt by Northern of one of the new Doyen coaches mentioned above. A further temporary departure took place in April when one of Northern's Cummins-engined MCW Metrobuses was loaned to Plymouth City Transport for a couple of weeks for evaluation purposes.

Meanwhile, High Spen depot received its first double deckers during the early summer and, in preparation for their arrival, certain structural alterations had to be made to this depot to enable maintenance work to be carried out on double deck vehicles. High Spen had in fact waited some fourteen years for buses of this configuration following Northern's cancellation of plans made by Venture immediately before its sale to the NBC in 1970 to purchase its first ever double deckers, 6 Alexander-bodied Daimler Fleetlines! At Northern's request, however, this order was changed to 6 Alexander-bodied Leyland Leopards which, upon their arrival in 1971 were numbered 291-6. In addition to the developments at High Spen, approval was given in June for the construction of a new office complex at Northern's headquarters at Bensham.

On the service front, phase six (the final one!) of the Metro saw regular passenger services introduced to South Shields on 24 March. As a consequence, rail replacement services R9 and R10 were withdrawn on the previous day, although somewhat strangely the main bus service changes resulting from the arrival of Metro were not implemented until 8 April! Not long afterwards, several of Northern's cross-river services, and particularly those operating southwards from Newcastle Worswick Street, were diverted from 18 June to operate via the High Level Bridge rather than follow their customary route across Tyne Bridge which was restricted due to major road works. This diversion continued until 29 October when the Tyne Bridge was fully

Seen when brand new in 1984 and before its entry into service is Roe-bodied Leyland Royal Tiger Doyen 7021 (A721ANL) which, although in corporate National Express livery had yet to receive its fleet names etc.

*Picking up its passengers in Harrogate bus station before leaving for Newcastle is Plaxton Paramount-bodied Leyland Tiger 7019 (A719ABB) which wears corporate National Express livery with a large Northern fleet name towards the rear and a National name above its front wheel arch.
(T.Godfrey collection)*

reopened, and during this period the resulting congestion was agrivated further by the closure of West Street, Gateshead and the progressive resurfacing of Durham Road! On 28 October National Travel withdrew its daytime stopping services 201/2 to London as a result of the introduction of its increased Rapide network whilst in November, as a consequence of the Metro now running to South Shields, the X2 service from South Shields to Newcastle was withdrawn.

One of the most important developments of 1984 was, without doubt, the launching by Northern of a new image. The company's management, having for some considerable time felt that public awareness of its operations etc. could be greatly improved, took the decision to adopt a higher profile and to this end evolved a new promotional image under the title "Go-Ahead Northern". This, it was believed, would encourage a sense of belonging, and to highlight this one of the company's Bristol VRTs was painted in a special all-over red livery broken by diagonal white bands and prominently featuring the new "Go-Ahead Northern" name. In addition, a coach-seated Bristol VRT was painted in a new livery of white with red and blue stripes for use on the Tynelink express services and was also adorned with the new-style fleet name. "Tynelink" was the brand name given to the express services running from Teesside and Darlington to Newcastle and for operation on these, United used a similar livery.

Liveries continued to be a subject of interest during 1985 and in January an MCW Metrobus was outshopped in a rainbow colour scheme as an additional promotional tool for Go-Ahead Northern bearing the legend "Don't judge a bus by its colours". At this same time, two of the dual purpose Willowbrook-bodied Leyland Leopards were given Go-Ahead Northern Express Link livery of white with a black skirt and red & black stripes primarily for use on services X11 (Consett to Newcastle via Sunniside) and X30 (Lanchester to Newcastle via Sunniside) and in May these were joined by a further three similarly adorned vehicles of this same type. A month later (in June), two more Metrobuses were given the rainbow promotional livery whilst, more interestingly, one vehicle was painted in each of the former subsidiaries colours. This nostalgic move, which was made for protective reasons to stop anyone else cashing in on the group's old names and liveries, resulted in an Olympian appearing in red & cream with Tynemouth fleet names, a Leyland National in red & cream with Northern names, an Atlantean in green & cream with Tyneside names and a Leyland National in blue & white with Sunderland District logos. In addition to these, 2 Atlanteans wore the old maroon & cream Gateshead colours, these having been thus painted in 1983 to commemorate that undertaking's centenary (i.e. the opening of the steam tramway in 1883).

The year's intake of new vehicles witnessed the arrival of the company's first minis, these being 9 Ford Transits with 16 coach-seated bodywork converted by Alexander. The first of these was finished in a livery of French blue with a white & red waistband whilst the others were painted in a similar fashion to Northern's dual purpose vehicles with black skirt, red lower panels, white upper parts and a red diagonal band and roof stripe. Lettered "Go-Ahead Northern" on their bonnet top and " Mini Link" on their side panels, these were placed in service at Chester-le-Street on a new local route inaugurated on 8 July. Of the other new vehicles delivered in 1985, 6 were Plaxton-bodied Leyland Tiger coaches, of which 2 were equipped to Rapide specification, 28 were bus-seated ECW-bodied Olympians and 4 were coach-seated ECW-bodied Olympians. Of the latter, 2 were finished in Express Link livery of white with red and maroon stripes whilst the other 2 were painted in Tynelink colours with red and blue stripes, the bus-seated examples carrying Tyne & Wear livery. Ironically, following the previous year in which the order for Olympians had been replaced by one for MCW Metrobuses, the 1985 vehicle programme had originally called for 43 Metrobuses which were later cancelled in favour of 45 Olympians!

Although the majority of the vehicles displaced by the new arrivals were offered for sale, a small number were retained by the company for further use in a variety of roles. At the start of the year, 4 of the 1976 ECW-bodied Atlanteans were taken into Northern's Bensham workshops for conversion to make them suitable for operation on the Tyne Commission Quay ferry service from Newcastle Central Station and after having their lower deck seating reduced to 15 to allow ample luggage space, they took up their new duties at the start of June, replacing vehicles hired from Tyne & Wear PTE. June also saw 2 Atlanteans converted into permanent driver trainers whilst 2 other

Wearing an experimental red livery relieved only by a diagonal white band and carrying the then-new Go-Ahead Northern name is ECW-bodied Bristol VRT 3411 (JPT911T), seen here passing through Chester-le-Street on its way to Seaham Harbour in July 1985. (K.A.Jenkinson)

buses of this same type were modified by the fitting of tables to their upper decks for use as mobile survey vehicles.

Before the summer's coaching season began, all Gateshead's coach allocation was transferred to Philadelphia, although of much greater importance were the changes made to the structure of the company on 1 September. In order to enable Northern to respond more quickly to customer demand at local level, the company was split for operational purposes into five units, each under the control of a District Manager. Unlike other NBC "splits" this change did not result in complete autonomy for the new units and neither did it result in any operational changes, separate fleet names or individual liveries. Indeed, the only visible indication of the new units was the small stickers which began to appear immediately behind the entrance door on most vehicles which stated "Go-Ahead Northern ----- District". The new districts were : Gateshead (which controlled the depots at Gateshead,

Standing in South Shields on a muddy winter's day, full-height ECW-bodied Leyland Atlantean 3550 (MBR450T) carries Go-Ahead Northern fleet names on its red & white livery. (K.A.Jenkinson)

MCW Metrobus 3618 (A618BCN) was one of seven buses repainted into a livery of diagonal multicoloured stripes to promote the new Go-Ahead Northern fleet name which was carried below the lower deck side windows and along the base of the advertising posters. It is seen here at Gateshead Metro in 1985. (K.A.Jenkinson)

Winlaton and High Spen); Tyne (Percy Main, Wallsend, Jarrow & South Shields); Sunderland (Philadelphia, Sunderland & Washington); Derwentside (Consett & Stanley) and East Durham (Chester-le-Street & Murton plus responsibility for all coaching activities). In addition to all the above changes, the Northern National Omnibus Co. Ltd., which had been formed from the C & E Bus Co. Ltd. by the NBC during the 1970s as a subsidiary of Trent Motor Traction but had never been operational, suddenly sprang to life on 1 September when, following the transfer of its registered office to Queen Street, Gateshead, it was granted licences for 25 vehicles. All these were transferred from Northern and comprised the 9 coach-seated Ford Transit minis, 9 Plaxton-bodied Tiger coaches, 4 Leyland Royal Tiger Doyen coaches and the 3 rainbow-liveried MCW Metrobuses. These all remained under the ownership of Northern General, however, with whose fleet name they continued to be adorned.

During the final months of the year, Northern purchased 3 ECW-bodied Bristol LH6L buses from United (at their written down value of £nil) for operation on the 322 service from Wallsend to Holy Cross Estate which temporarily replaced the nine services which had been diverted away from a bridge in St.Peter's Road over which they had previously passed and upon which a weight restriction had now been placed. Entering service from "yellow" Percy Main depot on 21 October, these buses retained their former owner's NBC poppy red livery, however, to which Northern fleet names were added. A further 2 buses acquired secondhand were both Leyland Nationals which were returned to the company by the National Coal Board to whom they had been sold a year earlier. Neither saw further service after "returning home" and instead they were dismantled for spares.

Liveries once again came to the forefront in November when a Leyland National and 2 Bristol VRTs were painted in an experimental scheme of red and white. On the single decker a broad white band upon which continuous "Go-Ahead Northern" fleet names were added was positioned below the windows whilst on the VRTs a similar band was applied together with white upper deck panels. Although no other buses were treated in this same manner, this trio heralded a new permanent livery which was to make its debut in February 1986. This turned out to be red (of a shade slightly lighter than the pre-nationalisation colour) with white window frames and roof, and, with its Go-Ahead Northern fleet names below the windows in its traditional place, how attractive it looked. Its introduction, together with the implications of the new 1985 Transport Act, sounded the death knell for the Tyne & Wear PTE corporate livery applied to Northern vehicles and the last repaints in yellow & white were completed towards the end of February with a Bristol VRT and a Leyland National being the last recipients. Indeed, during March the PTE-liveried members of the fleet began to lose their Tyne & Wear Transport fleet names and NBC logos, having these replaced by black 'Northern' fleet names, further signifying the impending ceasation of the close co-ordination which had existed for more than a decade. Meanwhile, to cause some confusion, the Gateshead & District Omnibus Co.Ltd. was struck off the Register of Companies with effect from 22 November 1985 after which, in

One of the first minis to be operated by the Northern group, coach-seated Ford Transit 208 (B208GNL) shows its MiniLink name as it works a Chester-le-Street local service in July 1985. (K.A.Jenkinson)

Awaiting its passengers at Park Lane, Sunderland, Leyland National 4651 (NGR951T) wears its owner's new red & white livery with Go-Ahead fleet names. The position of its front registration plate typifies Northern's buses of this type. (T.S.Blackman)

Passing through Stockton-on-Tees whilst working a duty on the X10 service in 1990 is coach-seated MCW Metrobus 3785 (C785OCN) painted in ExpressLink colours. (T.W.W.Knowles)

January 1986, the Company Secretary was instructed to register a new subsidiary company in the same name! This, however, no doubt had different Articles of Association etc. and was registered on 26 March 1986 as a wholly-owned subsidiary.

No fewer than 80 new buses and coaches were added to the fleet during 1986 comprising 41 MCW Metrobuses (of which 30 were painted yellow), 5 Plaxton-bodied Leyland Tigers and 32 Alexander and 2 Reeve Burgess-bodied Mercedes L608D minis (although originally 50 minibuses had been ordered!). 11 of the Metrobuses were coach-seated and painted in Express Link livery as were the 5 Tigers while all the Mercedes minis were fitted with 19 coach seats to give them a dual-purpose role. Perhaps the most unusual purchase of 1986 was that in July of an East Lancs-bodied Leyland PD2/37 from Calvary Coaches of Washington. After modification and painting in NBC green & white livery, it took up its duties in the driver training fleet in September. In addition to all the above, Northern found it necessary to hire 2 Bova Europa coaches from United for use on additional National Express Rapide services introduced with the summer timetable on 27 April and in exchange for these, 2 of Northern National Omnibus Co's Leyland Tigers were loaned to United (who gave them United fleetnames and numbers). Meanwhile, during February and March, 12 of Northern's withdrawn Park Royal-bodied Atlanteans were taken into the company's workshops at Bensham where their roofs were removed and they were painted all-over cream for sale to an overseas buyer. In addition, 3 more vehicles of this same batch, complete with roofs, were similarly painted as part of this same contract. Unfortunately, the deal was never completed, however, and all except 2 of these buses were ultimately sold to British buyers. One of the open-top escapees was repainted light blue and lettered "Go-Ahead Northern" whilst in August the other, still in cream livery, was made available for use as a mobile grandstand.

As far as its operations were concerned, Northern revised the route of its original Mini Link service in Chester-le-Street on 8 March, adding hail and ride facilities on certain roads at this same time, and on 26 July launched a second Mini Link route in this town. Following the delicencing of the 9 Ford Transits, both the Chester-le-Street Mini Link services were maintained by some of the new Mercedes vehicles. Another new service was the X2 (the second to carry this number!) which began on 30 August. This was operated jointly with United between Broomside and Dunston Metro, although it ran on Saturdays only with four journeys in each direction.

By now, the much publicised D-day was looming forth, the day on which the full effects of the 1985 Transport Act would be felt throughout the country as bus services were deregulated to allow any operator to run anywhere, provided that the service had been registered 42 days in advance. Northern, like most other operators, had spent most of the winter of 1985/6 deciding on which services it would register commercially and for which of those put out to tender by local authorities it would submit bids. This was no easy task and it took many long hours by the traffic department before its plans for the future were laid in February 1986, and even then there was no certainty that all the decisions taken would prove correct in the long term. The registration of its commercial network covered approximately 55% of the present total of operations and ranged from a minimum of 47% to a maximum of 68% according to location. The last new service to be introduced before D-day was the 66 which commenced on 14 October to coincide with the opening of phase two of the new Metro Centre shopping complex at Dunston and ran non-stop from Gateshead Metro Interchange on a 10-minute frequency during shopping hours.

Prior to this upheaval taking place within the bus industry, however, Northern, following its registration of Gateshead & District Omnibus Co.Ltd., decided to register three more wholly-owned subsidiaries - The Tynemouth & District Omnibus Co.Ltd. which was incorporated on 9 May 1986, and The Sunderland & District Omnibus Co.Ltd. and The Venture Transport Co.Ltd. both of which were incorporated on 14 May.

One of the first MCW Metrobuses to be purchased by Northern, 1980 Mk.I 3496 (DVK496W) was originally operated in NBC-style yellow livery. Having been repainted into red & white and adorned with Go-Ahead Northern fleet names, it is seen here leaving Gateshead Metro on the 51 service. (K.A.Jenkinson)

PRIVATISATION AND DEREGULATION

D-day, the 26th October 1986, finally arrived and as had been expected brought with it a massive reorganisation of services. As far as Northern was concerned, whilst several existing routes continued unchanged, equally as many were altered in some way or other and added to these were numerous new routes. D-day also witnessed the introduction of the company's first minibus services outside Chester-le-Street with the conversion of existing routes or the opening of new ones in several other areas within the company's territory. From this date, a total of 26 services were placed under the Mini Link banner and, in addition to licencing some of the new Mercedes for the first time, the Ford Transits were also returned to service. Thus, Northern's little buses could now be seen in such places as Sunderland, Stanley, Seaham Harbour, Murton, Blaydon, Chester-le-Street, Durham and Consett in addition to being used on three new local routes in Washington which were identified by coloured destination blinds rather than by service numbers. Northern buses were, however, no longer to be seen in Bishop Auckland following the splitting of the Sunderland - Durham - Service at Durham between Northern and United. As a further result of this reorganisation of its services, 19 of the "X" routes were now operated under the 'Go-Ahead Northern Express Link' banner of which five were new including the X47 Newcastle to Crook and X95 Newcastle to Parkside via Washington and Sunderland. Additionally, 5 services (2 of which were X-routes) running from Newcastle to Whickham, Marsden, Cleadon Village and Hadrian Park were marketed as "City Link" and operated by the former Tyne & Wear PTE coach-seated Alexander-bodied Atlanteans to which appropriate vinyls were affixed.

The reorganisation of so many services led to a massive reallocation of vehicles between depots and also left Northern with a number of buses surplus to its immediate requirements. This resulted in the delicencing of all but 10 of its 59 Leyland National 2s which were then placed in store for reinstatement if and when required. This, to a certain degree, turned out to be sooner rather than later and by the start of 1987 several of these buses had been returned to service. Although no further new vehicles were placed in service before the year ended, 2 Plaxton-bodied Leyland Royal Tiger coaches equipped to Rapide specification were hired from Yorkshire Traction in December 1986, both of which were given Northern fleet names and numbers. Their arrival allowed the Bovas hired from United to be returned and, in turn, the 2 Plaxton-bodied Tigers to come home from that company, one of them having by that time gained Northumbria fleet names! More unusually, however, Northern borrowed a 61-seat MAN bendi-bus from Midland Red North for a short period in December for evaluation purposes, although this was not used in service during its stay. Equally as interesting was the appearance of two of Northern's Willowbrook dual purpose-bodied Leyland Leopards in a white livery relieved only by a maroon band and skirt. Carrying no fleet names, these were used in direct competition to similar-liveried coaches of Watson's of Annfield Plain on services operated in the Consett area but lasted only a for a short time after which they were repainted with a standard red band and black skirt.

Following the three month 'freeze' placed on all bus services under conditions laid down in the Transport Act, what can best be described as "full deregulation" took place on 25 January 1987 when operators were allowed to withdraw or modify their existing routes or start new ones. Having gained experience of their "new" network in the period since 26 October 1986, Northern made alterations to 65 of its services, introduced 10 new routes and completely withdrew 2. At this time, Northern's fleet totalled 734 vehicles comprising 57 minis, 447 double deckers, 162 single deckers and 68 dual-purpose vehicles and coaches.

With the exception of a solitary Plaxton-bodied Leyland Tiger coach of Rapide specification, the only other new vehicles to be taken into stock during 1987 were 38 Alexander-bodied Dodge/Renault S56 minis fitted with 19 coach-type seats. Pending the arrival of some of these however, 5 Freight Rover Sherpa 16-seaters were hired from Northumbria Motor Services for a period until the beginning of July, whilst in the final month of the year an Alexander-bodied 25-seat Renault S50 was borrowed for evaluation from its bodybuilder. Another bus gained on long term loan was a Roe-bodied Leyland PD2A/37 in the livery of the erstwhile Teesside Railless Traction Board. Owned by the North East Bus Preservation Group, this was for driver training purposes only and not for use in a normal passenger-carrying role. Also transferred to Northern's driver training fleet were 2 of the Tyne Commission Quay Atlanteans and the 3 ex.United Bristol LH6Ls which had been withdrawn from service at the end of March. In the opposite direction, Northern loaned one of its Dodge S56 minibuses to Luton & District in April for driver training duties and a Cummins-engined Leyland Olympian to Grampian Regional Transport in August whilst later in the year 6 Dodge minis were despatch on loan to London Country North East for operation on some new services in the Hatfield and Hertford areas.

By the early months of the year, the repainting programme had reduced the number of vehicles still wearing Tyne & Wear PTE livery to a mere handful and by July the yellow & white colours had been eliminated completely, thus marking the end of yet another era. Prior to this, however, one of the Ford Transit minis was, in January, repainted into blue & white and given Sunderland District's old-style "garter" logo to promote the new high frequency hail and ride Minilink services in the Houghton-le-Spring area on which the Transits were to be used, whilst during the following month 9 Leyland National 2s were repainted in all-over fluorescent orange with blue wheels. Initially adorned with neither fleet names nor fleet numbers, several of these buses were placed in service on two new routes commenced on 23 March from Felling Square to the Metro Centre at Dunston to compete with services started by Easyway Bus Services and the North East Bus Company, a partnership formed by some ex.Northern drivers. Coincidentally, the drivers of the orange Nationals were kitted out with white shirts and flourescent orange bow ties, and ultimately a sticker bearing the legend 'Dipton Orange' was placed inside the windscreens of the buses concerned which were then used on a service in the Stanley area. A further non-standard repaint concerned one of the company's Plaxton-bodied Leopards which in February was given a white livery with broad yellow band and was lettered "Savabus". This was used together with the two unlettered white & maroon-liveried Leopards on the services in the Consett area competing against Watsons of Annfield Plain. These were later replaced by a pair of the orange Leyland Nationals and, to further promote the services upon which these buses were used, free oranges were distributed at Stanley bus station on 30 April! A further new service to be operated in that area was one from Stanley bus station to Quaking Houses which was started on 25 March following the collapse of its former operator, Mowbray Coaches (Diamond) of Stanley.

Hurrying towards Houghton-le-Spring whilst on driver training duties is red & white liveried former Teesside Roe-bodied Leyland PD2 JVN40E which was purchased specially for this purpose. (K.A.Jenkinson)

Painted in all-over orange livery and displaying 'Dipton Orange' fleet names at the top of its windscreens, Go-Ahead Northern Leyland National 4676 (UPT676V) leaves Stanley bus station on the Flint Hill circular 700 service in 1987. (T.W.W.Knowles)

One of the most significant milestones in Northern's history was reached in 1987, some seventy-five years after the company's foundations had been laid. This brought the company into independent ownership for the very first time, it having previously always been part of a large group - first British Electric Traction, then the Transport Holding Company and finally the National Bus Company. Following the advent of the 1985 Transport Act in which it was stated that the giant National Bus Company had to be sold-off to the private sector, moves towards this goal were started in 1986 and, one by one, its subsidiaries were offered for sale. In the case of Northern General Transport Co. Ltd., this was placed on the market during the early part of 1987 and attracted interest from a number of prospective buyers who, along with the company's own management team, submitted bids. After waiting with some trepidation, the announcement was eventually made that the company's management had been the successful bidder and thus, on 7 May 1987, Northern became the 32nd of the NBC's subsidiaries to be privatised by sale to a new company, Go-Ahead Northern Ltd. formed for the purpose by the management team.

One of the first tasks to be addressed by the company's new owners was that of greater passenger awareness of its services and to this end Northern formed Rider Panels in each of its operating areas. These consisted of a small number of regular passengers who met on a regular voluntary basis to discuss bus travel in their particular area with members of Northern's local management. This enabled the company to forge a closer relationship with its customers and, in addition, to be able to provide and modify its services wherever a need was found, provided of course that such moves were viable.

With the summer just beginning, a large revision of Northern's local bus services took place on 13 June and on 11 July a new route was begun from Houghton-le-Spring to Stockton-on-Tees to compete directly with that operated by Trimdon Motor Services, although in the event this proved to be comparatively short-lived and was withdrawn on 27 October. Further changes to the network of routes in Gateshead, Seaham, Chester-le-Street, Washington and to the MetroCentre at Dunston were implemented during August, September and October, and on the 24th of the latter month the Birtley town services were withdrawn and taken over on contract by local operator, A-Line. Prior to this, in September, 2 of Northern's orange-liveried Leyland Nationals were despatched to Sunderland District for use on a new free service started in competition to OK Travel in retaliation for that operator gaining the contract for three services previously operated by Northern. Still bearing no fleet name, these two buses merely had the slogan 'Ride the Big Orange' affixed to their rear engine panel. Finally, on 31 October, Sunderland's Houghton-le-Spring Minilink network was completely revised with several new services being introduced and a number of existing routes withdrawn. It should perhaps be pointed out that Northern was not unusual in its frequent service changes as similar actions were being regularly taken by operators throughout the whole of Britain, this being one of the consequences of the early period of deregulation. On the vehicle front, the rear-end advert craze which had become increasingly familiar with other operators eventually spread to Northern during the early summer with an MCW Metrobus being the first - but certainly not the last - to be adorned in this manner.

The only new buses to be taken into stock during 1988 were 19 Alexander-bodied 25-seat Renault S56s of which 6 were painted in Sunderland District blue and white livery and most of the remainder were all-over white. Also added to the fleet on a permanent basis was

---

Page 106, left column, top to bottom :

Painted in Go-Ahead Northern red & white livery with Go-Ahead Gateshead fleet names, MCW Metrobus 3645 (A645BCN) is pictured leaving Gateshead Metro in September 1993. (K.A.Jenkinson)

Awaiting its departure to Washington at Park Lane, Sunderland in September 1989 is Go-Ahead Northern all-red liveried MiniLink Iveco minibus 318 (E292VOM). (S.A.Staddon)

Given B & C fleet names for operation on competitive services, Go-Ahead Northern's ex.Hills of Tredegar Plaxton Paramount-bodied Leyland Tiger 7048 (JSK328, originally F597BTG) is seen at the MetroCentre in January 1993 working service B to Blackhall Mill. (S.A.Staddon)

Low Fell Coaches Duple-bodied Leyland Tiger 4766 (F902JBB) stands at the Newcastle terminus of the Cross-Tyne service in March 1994. (K.A.Jenkinson)

Page 106. left column, top to bottom :

Wearing a promotional livery for Voyager minibreaks is Coastline ECW-bodied Leyland Olympian 3748 (B748GCN) seen here at Blackpool. (T.W.W.Knowles)

Passing through the bus station at Wallsend Metro in March 1994 whilst working Coastline service 321 is Alexander-bodied Dodge S56 245 (D245VNL) painted in Go-Ahead Northern MiniLink livery. (K.A.Jenkinson)

Resting in Stanley bus station in March 1994 is Shaws Coaches Talbot minibus C27LTN. (K.A.Jenkinson)

Painted in Northern's now-discontinued Express Link livery and adorned with Wear Buses vinyls, coach-seated ECW-bodied Leyland Olympian 3668 (C668LJR) leaves Gateshead Metro on an X5 journey to Hartlepool in September 1993. (K.A.Jenkinson)

A rather dirty Supershuttle-liveried Leyland National 4712 (FTN712W) arrives at Gateshead Metro on a journey from the MetroCentre in 1988. (K.A.Jenkinson)

TERMINATES HERE
57 HEWORTH Q.E. Hospital
GO-AHEAD GATESHEAD

minibreaks
THEATRE
Private Charter
Day Excursions
B748 GCN

186 Washington
MINI LINK
318
IVECO
E292 VOM

MINI LINK

BLACKHALL MILL
SERVICES B&C
SERVICES B&C
JSK 328

GET HAPPY WITH AIRTOURS VALUE FOR CHILDREN TO FLORIDA.
35
C27 LTN

LOW FELL COACHES
CROSS TYNE SERVICE
LOW FELL COACHES
SERVICE
F902 JBB

EXPRESS LINK
HARTLEPOOL

9 9 Newcastle
Metro BUSES
MBR 454T

221 CHESTER LE STREET
Shaws Coaches
8112
M812 HCU
PLAXTON
POINTER

308
NEWCASTLE Eldon Square
Jesmond
Sandyford
COAST ROAD
WHITLEY BAY
COASTLINE
Leyland
C670 LJR

Metro TAXIS

JUMPER FROM CUPBOARD
N22
COASTLINE
OPTARE
L389 AVK

BUS STATION
WOODHOUSE ESTATE
OK TRAVEL
OJD 62R

NORTHERN

53 DURHAM
GYPSY QUEEN
GYPSY QUEEN
H802 OPT

X5 NEWCASTLE
FAST-FREQUENT
DIRECT-COMFORTABLE
Wear EXPRESS
C787 OCN

The only Leyland Lynx buses to join Go-Ahead Northern were twelve examples purchased in 1989 as part of the company's vehicle evaluation programme. Used on the 194 service from Heworth to Easington Lane for which a route diagram was placed externally above the windows on each side, all were transferred to Sunderland District in 1991 upon completion of their trials. Here, 4725 (F725LRG) collects its passengers at Houghton-le-Spring Parish Church in March 1989. (M.Duffy)

the Alexander-bodied Renault fitted with electronic destination equipment which had been on loan from its manufacturer during the previous year and which now also wore Sunderland District colours. Perhaps more surprising was the acquisition of three secondhand vehicles for use solely in the driver training fleet following a decision to revert to manual gearbox training, these being an East Lancs-bodied Leyland PD2/37 purchased from Lancaster City Transport, an Alexander bus-bodied Ford A-series 27-seater from Stringfellow of Fleetwood and a Caetano-bodied Ford A-series 27-seat coach gained from Bandwagon Coaches, Edinburgh. For evaluation purposes a tri-axle 27-seat Talbot Express Pullman was used in service from Winlaton depot for a few days in January and, after visiting Northumbria it returned to Northern early in February for a week's operation at Chester-le-Street whilst an NCME-bodied Renault S56 demonstrator was used from Winlaton depot for a few days in May. An even greater surprise, however, was the appearance in service for two weeks during March of two Routemasters for the purpose of the reappraisal of crew operation following positive feedback from a number of Scottish Bus Group companies. One of this duo was hired from Strathtay Scottish and was employed mainly on the 66 service from Heworth to the MetroCentre whilst the other, hired from Pegg of

Rotherham (Rotherham & District) and still in London red livery, was placed on the 53/4 Saltwell Park/Bensham circular routes. Although popular with passengers and crews alike, it was decided because of limited life expectancy of this type of bus that more effective ways of service improvements could be achieved by the continuation of one-person-operation and thus, sadly, the Routemaster was not to reappear on a permanent basis in the Northern fleet until 1992 when one made a welcome return, albeit only for special usage.

Furthering attempts to introduce a more local image to its operations, on February 13 Northern relaunched Venture as the trading name for all its operations from its High Spen depot, several of which were revised at this same time. To this end, a Leyland National was in November 1987 repainted into an attractive yellow, cream and maroon livery which resembled that of the erstwhile Venture company and in February all High Spen's vehicles began to appear adorned with window stickers bearing the legend "Venture - with Go-Ahead Northern". So successful did this experiment prove, that on 24 April a similar exercise was carried out on North Tyneside where window stickers depicting a coastal scene and carrying the lettering "The Coast Line" were applied to all the company's buses. This scheme was further projected on 7 May in Gateshead where the local fleet was given window stickers depicting a flaming torch and the legend "Go-Ahead Northern Gateshead - In Pursuit Of Excellence". These were soon removed, however, due to them obscuring passengers views from the windows. Although all the buses carrying these various local identity labels remained in the standard red & white fleet colours to capitalise on the Group-wide advertising support, the company's coaching fleet underwent change following the introduction of the Voyager name. A new deep red livery with gold lining was introduced, to which the Voyager fleet name was added in gold lettering, giving the

---

Page 107, left column, top to bottom :

Sporting new Metro Buses fleet names as it stands outside Percy Main depot in April 1995 is 3554 (MBR454T), an ECW-bodied Leyland Atlantean which began life with Northern. (K.A.Jenkinson)

Coastline's coach-seated ECW-bodied Leyland Olympian 3670 (C670LJR) is one of several vehicles of this type which carry a diagramatic map for service 308 (Newcastle - Blyth) on their side panels. It is seen taking a Sunday rest at Percy Main depot in April 1995. (K.A.Jenkinson)

Disgorging its passengers at Bishop Auckland bus station in October 1989 is OK Motor Services ex.London Buses ECW-bodied Bristol LH6L OJD62R. (T.G.Walker)

Gypsy Queen's Carlyle-bodied Dennis Dart 4755 (H802HPT) hurries through Witton Gilbert on its way to Durham in March 1994. (K.A.Jenkinson)

Page 107, right column, top to bottom :

Shaws Coaches Plaxton Pointer-bodied Dennis Darts were all given a new livery of white with a single blue band as illustrated by 8112 (M812HCU) at Chester-le-Street depot in April 1995. (K.A.Jenkinson)

Pictured inside Wallsend depot in March 1994 is one of Metro Taxis Austin black cabs.

Approaching Wallsend Metro in March 1994 is Coastline's Optare Metrorider 389 (L389AVK) which at that time was only a few weeks old. (K.A.Jenkinson)

Wearing corporate NBC unrelieved poppy red livery, Leyland National 4450 (MCN849L) carries its registration number plate immediately below its windscreens in typical Northern fashion at that time. (T.Godfrey collection)

Looking immaculate in its Wear Express livery is freshly repainted Wear Buses coach-seated MCW Metrobus 3787 (C787OCN) at Gateshead MetroCentre. (L.Simpson)

Collecting its passengers in Washington bus station in 1989 is Go-Ahead Northern's Minilink-liveried Reeve Burgess-bodied Iveco 49.10 minibus 316 (F316MTN). (M.Duffy)

As part of Go-Ahead Northern's vehicle evaluation programme, a number of DAF Optare Deltas were placed in service during August 1989 and used mainly on the Consett - Stanley - Chester-le-Street - Sunderland corridor. Operating one of these services, 4743 (F743RTY) collects its passengers at a busy Chester-le-Street Market Place. (M.Duffy)

Strathtay Scottish Routemaster WLT943 collects its passengers at Gateshead Metro on 19 March 1988 whilst being evaluated by Go-Ahead Northern on the 66 service to the MetroCentre standing alongside it is Go-Ahead Northern Leyland Atlantean 3454 (AUP354W). (E.Waugh)

vehicles to which it applied a most attractive appearance. The coaches used on National Express Rapide duties were not, however, affected by this change and continued to wear its familiar corporate white livery with red & blue stripes etc. Meanwhile, the old NBC poppy red bus livery was finally eliminated in May except for the two Bristol LH6Ls used solely for driver training purposes, and thus the last remains of nationalisation had now been laid to rest.

The first fares increase since deregulation was implemented on 3 April 1988 when around 6% was added to all the company's fares and during the year the fleet was gradually equipped with new Almex Magnet ticket machines which provided greater information relating to passenger journeys etc. During the following month, Northern ceased running on behalf of National Holidays, but more importantly was restructured with Northern General Transport Co. Ltd., Northern National Omnibus Co. Ltd. and Go-Ahead Northern Engineering

Never easy to photograph were the Alexander-bodied Renault S56 minibuses painted in the navy blue & white Minilink livery. Adorned with a Sunderland District garter on its sides and Go-Ahead Northern fleet names on its bonnet is 295 (E295ETY) at Sunderland. (S.A.Staddon)

Services Ltd. all becoming wholly-owned subsidiaries of Go-Ahead Northern. This, of course, was for administrative purposes and did not affect the travelling public or indeed the outward appearance of the company. On the service front, the 66 from Gateshead Metro Interchange to the MetroCentre at Dunston was on 7 May rebranded "Super Shuttle" and for its operation 5 Leyland National 2s were painted into a special livery of red & white with a blue skirt and yellow window surrounds and were adorned with appropriate lettering along the length of their side panels.

The first stage of a diversification plan was achieved on 1 July 1988 when Go-Ahead Northern won a Regional Health Authority contract to carry non-emergency out-patients to and from hospitals in the Newcastle area, replacing a similar service previously provided by the Northumbria Ambulance Service. For this new operation, for which wheelchair accessible taxis were required, Northern purchased 24 new Austin FX4 London-style 'black cabs', placing these in service at the beginning of August. To supplement these, 6 of its Ford Transit minibuses (which were given an attractive yellow, white and black livery) were transferred to the new Caring Cars hospital contract duties and in November the fleet was further expanded with the purchase of

---

Page 110, left column, top to bottom :

Kneeling and with its ramp extended is Coastline's low-floor Wright-bodied Dennis Lance SLF 4771 (M471FJR) at Percy Main depot in March 1995. (K.A.Jenkinson)

Looking immaculate in Voyager livery, Duple-bodied Leyland Leopard 7011 (HCU11W) awaits its passengers at Beamish Open Air Museum whilst working a private hire duty in 1989. (K.A.Jenkinson)

Carrying branding for the 53 & 54 services on its standard livery, Go-Ahead Gateshead Wright-bodied Dennis Dart 8017 (J617KCU) leaves Gateshead Metro in September 1993. (K.A.Jenkinson)

Parked outside Saltmeadows Road depot, Gateshead in the evening shadows of a November 1995 day is Plaxton-bodied Volvo B10M 6831 (CAZ6831, originally D855FRF) still painted in the livery of its former owner, Armstrongs of Ebchester. (K.A.Jenkinson)

Page 110, right column, top to bottom :

Passing through Darlington in November 1994 whilst on loan to Northern is Brighton & Hove Plaxton-bodied Dennis Javelin 504 (F504LAP). (K.A.Jenkinson)

One of several Go-Ahead Gateshead Optare Metroriders painted in a special livery for operation on services to the MetroCentre, 336 (J936JJR) leaves the complex's bus station for Sunniside in September 1993 (K.A.Jenkinson)

With its windscreens rebuilt, Wear Buses Leyland Lynx 4722 (F722LRG) leaves Gateshead Metro on the 194 service to Easington Lane in November 1995. (K.A.Jenkinson)

Seen in Sunderland in 1994 wearing Wear Buses 'Mini Link' fleet names on its side panels is Alexander-bodied Mercedes Benz L608D 237 (D237URG). (B.Newsome)

Low Fell Coaches Reeve Burgess-bodied Mercedes Benz 709D 370 (G703NGR) leaves Gateshead Metro to return to its depot in September 1993. (K.A.Jenkinson)

325 Verne Road
COASTLINE
Whitley Bay · Rake Lane Hospital · New York · Meadowell
Easy Access
COASTLINE
M471 FJR

Brighton & Hove
504
F504 LAP

Private Charter
Voyager
7011
HCU 11W

SUNNISIDE
GO AHEAD GATESHEAD
METROCENTREMINI
J936 JJR

194
WEAR BUSES
F722 LRG

54 SALTWELL PARK NEWCASTLE
53
54
GO-AHEAD GATESHEAD

WEAR BUSES
D237 URG

ARMSTRONGS
ARMSTRONGS

LOW FELL COACHES
ENGLISH ESTATES
LOW FELL COACHES

111

In addition to operating a fleet of black cabs, Metro Taxis also acts as an agent and dealer for Austin FX4s. Awaiting sale outside Metro's sales office in March 1994, which coincidentally is also Coastline's Wallsend depot despite the Go-Ahead Northern name board, are a pair of black cabs - E727EFT and C342CUU.   (K.A.Jenkinson)

12 new MCW Metrocab taxis. Following the success of this new venture, Go-Ahead Northern began to seek further expansion and in December 1988 set up a company under the title of Visitauto Ltd. for the purpose of purchasing the old-established business of Metro Taxis of Newcastle, a thriving taxi and private hire company. The newly-acquired fleet which was made up of private-style cars was mainly used for contract-hire work and, after being quickly merged with Northern's Caring Cars operation, the black cabs when not in use on the hospitals contract were employed as normal taxis. A further vehicle converted for the transportation of the disabled was a Leyland National which, after being fitted with a centre door with wheelchair ramp and 23 coach-type seats, was repainted into Voyager livery for use throughout Northern's operating area.

Meanwhile, on 9 September a new service (X96) from Parkside to Newcastle via Sunderland and the Boldons began, restoring the direct express connection between Sunderland and Newcastle lost when the X4 was diverted via Washington in 1976. Running in conjunction with the X95, it gave Seaham two express services to Newcastle per hour and to Sunderland. In order to compete with a service running a few minutes in front of Northern's 745 introduced by Law Travel of Stanley, additional journeys were added on 27 September, upon which "Big Orange" Leyland Nationals were introduced offering special promotional fares. On 19 November, a new service from Stanley to Burnhope (extended to Durham on Saturdays) was started to further compete with Law Travel whilst at around this same time the use of "Big Orange" vehicles on the 64/65 services in Gateshead ceased and were replaced by conventional double deck operation. Finally, on the run-up to Christmas, a new park and ride service was started on Saturdays linking the various coach parks at the MetroCentre with the main areas of the shopping complex. This was devised and operated by Northern who employed 10 Leyland Nationals and a number of minibuses on this internal service which carried over 17,000 passengers on each day of its operation. A further innovation was the reintroduction on 26 November of through fare ticketing arrangements in Tyne & Wear which were lost at the time of deregulation. Publicised as Metrolink Transfare Tickets, they were available for through journeys involving changes between bus and Metro at 26 designated interchange points as well as a limited number of changes from one bus to another, again at specified points and British Rail's Newcastle to Sunderland service.

According to figures produced during 1989, Northern General was the most profitable of any of the former NBC companies in the period ending 30 June 1988, recording pre-tax profits of £3.3 million on a turnover of £58 million. This was, of course, most pleasing for its new owners who obviously felt that they had made a sound investment. As will be seen later, however, this situation was to change for a variety of reasons over which the company had little or no control.

1989 proved to be another year of expansion, restructuring and change, and one in which buses of two new types entered service. These were 12 Leyland Lynx (11 with Gardner 6LXCT engines and 1 with a Cummins L10 engine) and 14 Optare Delta-bodied DAFs which were joined by 6 Reeve Burgess-bodied 25-seat Iveco 49.10s, 5 Alexander-bodied Leyland Olympians, 2 Rapide specification Plaxton-bodied Leyland Tigers and 2 Austin FX4 black cabs. Of the two new models, the Lynx was the first to enter service, doing so on 18 March on the 194 (Heworth - Easington Lane) and 294 (Heworth - Fatfield) services (for which they carried dedicated route lettering above their side windows) and it was not until 5 August that the first of the DAF Optares made its appearance. These were employed mainly on the 775/8 (Consett - Sunderland) and 745 (Consett - Newcastle) routes and all were painted in standard Go-Ahead Northern livery. During April, a programme was started on the re-engining of a number of Leyland National 2s which were given Leyland TL11 engines in place of their original 0.680 power units and at this same time several were fitted with fully-automatic transmission. This work continued for fourteen months during which time 24 buses were thus treated.

In addition to purchasing a number of secondhand vehicles in 1989, several were hired for short periods for a variety of reasons and amongst these were a DAF Optare Delta which was evaluated in service for a week in February, a CVE Omni minibus which was tested at Gateshead for a couple of weeks at the end of April/early May and a Robin Hood-bodied Mercedes mini which was used by Winlaton depot

---

Page 111, left column, top to bottom :

Having just arrived in Newcastle on the 708 service from Lanchester in March 1994, the destination screen on Northern's Wright-bodied Dennis Dart 8038 (J638KCU) has already been set for its return journey.   (K.A.Jenkinson)

Freshly repainted into the new simplified Wear Buses livery, MCW Metrobus 3776 (C776OCN) leaves Gateshead Metro during November 1995 enroute to Sunderland.   (K.A.Jenkinson)

Arriving back at OK's Bishop Auckland depot early in November 1995 after working a morning school's journey is MCW Metrobus 3491 (DVK491W) which still retained its Tyne Rider livery and fleet names.   (K.A.Jenkinson)

Seen at Stanley bus station on the X36 service to Newcastle in March 1994 is Northern's Superliner-liveried coach-seated ECW-bodied Leyland Olympian 3522 (C522LJR).   (K.A.Jenkinson)

Page 111, right column, top to bottom :

Still wearing its Shaws Coaches white & blue livery but now fitted with Northern fleet names, Plaxton Pointer-bodied Dennis Dart 8115 leaves Gateshead Metro bound for Chester-le-Street in October 1995.   (K.A.Jenkinson)

Painted in the new simplified Go-Ahead Gateshead livery, Wright-bodied Dennis Dart 8068 (K368RTY) passes through Gateshead Metro on the 54 service in October 1995.   (K.A.Jenkinson)

Seen in Washington bus station in August 1991, Go-Ahead Northen Leyland National 4720 (TJR720Y) wore a blue, maroon & white livery.   (S.A.Staddon)

Despite having its Shaws Coaches fleet names removed, Plaxton-bodied Leyland Leopard 5122 (DBB32V) still wore that operator's unrelieved blue coach livery as it worked Stanley local service 711 to Quaking Houses in October 1995.   (K.A.Jenkinson)

New to OK Motor Services in 1994, Alexander-bodied Volvo B10B L212KEF was repainted into Low Fell Coaches livery in 1995 and is seen here leaving Gateshead Metro on the Cross-Tyne service in October 1995.   (K.A.Jenkinson)

Roe-bodied Leyland Royal Tiger Doyen coach 7013 (A213XJR) is seen here after receiving all-red Voyager livery.

for two weeks towards the end of June. A longer-term hire was that of 2 Dormobile-bodied Freight Rover Sherpas from late June until October. Both owned by Carlyle Bus Centre, these had been new to Badgerline and London Country North West. Permanent acquisitions were 2 Duple 340-bodied, toilet equipped DAF MB230 coaches purchased from a dealer to allow the return of the 2 Plaxton-bodied Leyland Royal Tigers to Yorkshire Traction and 16 minibuses. The latter comprised 4 Carlyle-bodied 25-seat Iveco 49.10s originally operated by London Buses, 2 PMT-bodied and 2 Robin Hood-bodied Ford Transits new to PMT, 5 Carlyle-bodied Transits which began life with Bristol Omnibus Co., a Mellor-bodied Ford Transit from Allen of Coventry and 2 coach-seated Mercedes L508Ds. The Transits were all added to the Metro Taxis fleet and were painted into that company's white, yellow & black livery whilst the 2 Mercedes which were originally purchased for use as driver trainers were found to be in such good

Painted in Voyager livery, Northern's 1978 Leyland National 4634 (KBR634T) which has been converted for the carriage of disabled passengers by the addition of a wheelchair ramp immediately forward of the rear nearside wheel arch, is seen here at Sunderland in March 1989 promoting Go-Ahead Northern holiday tours. (M.Duffy)

condition that both were placed in a fleet livery to permit use as private hire vehicles. A further vehicle to join the fleet was a Leyland National acquired from West Riding. Ironically this bus had started life with Northern General before being sold to West Riding in 1982 for conversion for the carriage of disabled passengers. Upon its return to the north-east, it was repainted into Care Bus orange livery with a brown skirt and yellow window surrounds and roof. Meanwhile, on the subject of liveries, in February a number of Winlaton depot's Renault

Used for a time on a free internal shuttle service at the Metro Centre at Dunston were several Alexander-bodied Renault S56 minibuses painted in a special livery for this purpose. One of the buses concerned was 278 (E278BRG) seen here taking a brief rest in the MetroCentre's bus station. (M.Duffy)

minis which had originally entered service in all-over white were repainted into a white livery with grey skirt and four stripes of red, blue, yellow and green for use on routes serving the MetroCentre and were given "MetroCentre Minis" fleet names to which was added in smaller lettering "owned and operated by Go-Ahead Northern". Later, in July, one of Northern's MCW Metrobuses was given a predominantly white promotional livery to which various Norwegian adverts were added for its use on a tour of Norway which lasted for six weeks whilst in October a Metrobus and 2 Olympians were painted white to promote the 1990 National Gardens Festival which was to be located at Gateshead. On the debit side, in March the solitary Venture-liveried Leyland National was repainted into standard Go-Ahead Northern colours, much to the regret of a great many people, although to the relief of Busways managers who regarded the colours as far too close to their own!

Furthering its aims towards continued expansion, in May Go-Ahead Northern purchased the business of the Langley Park Motor Company who traded under the title of Gypsy Queen. An old-established company started in 1921 by the Simpson family and later passing to one of their relatives, Gerald Cox, Gypsy Queen maintained a half-hourly service from Langley Park to Durham in addition to undertaking private hire and contract work. Its fleet, comprising 4 Bedford coaches and 2 Volvo B10Ms (1 with Plaxton coach bodywork, the other with Duple 55-seat bus bodywork), was retained by its new owner who took the decision to operate it as a separate subsidiary under its existing title from its present depot at Front Street, Langley Park. Fleet numbers were allocated but were not carried on the vehicles. Not included in the deal, however, was Gypsy Queen's preserved 1931 Robson-bodied Bedford WLB which was retained by Gerald Cox.

Following much speculation, the company was further restructured, with Go-Ahead Northern Ltd. being the holding company controlling four subsidiaries, viz: The Northern General Transport Co.Ltd which was registered as "trading as Go-Ahead Northern" and had operating

Gypsy Queen Duple-bodied Bedford YMT B693JBB approaches Durham on the service from its home base at Langley Park. Note the destination board above its radiator grille. (T.W.W.Knowles)

One of a pair of ECW-bodied Bristol LH6Ls purchased from United, 4872 (AHN603M) still wears its former owner's NBC poppy red livery but has received Northern fleet names and numbers. (S.A.Staddon)

discs for 623 vehicles; The Northern National Omnibus Co. Ltd. which also traded as Go-Ahead Northern and had operating discs for 156 vehicles (i.e. all the minibuses except for the Ford Transits, plus some coaches); Visitauto Ltd. which traded as Metro Taxis and held licences for 20 vehicles in addition to operating 38 taxis and The Langley Park Motor Co. Ltd. which traded as Gypsy Queen and held 6 vehicle discs. In addition, the company had applied for a further operators licence and 90 vehicle discs under the name Coolfirm Ltd. of which more later.

Prior to the above changes, Northern further demonstrated its dedication to customer care by putting selected staff through a ten-week course in basic sign language in order to equip them with the means to "talk" to deaf and hard of hearing passengers. This extended the company's endeavours towards the disabled as already it provided talking timetables on cassette tapes for the blind and additionally had a scheme to assist them in familiarisation with various types of vehicle. Another instance of co-operation following the close links it had already established with the MetroCentre was implemented on 1 April when two new minibus services under the title of "Hyperlink" were started from Wallsend and North Shields to the North Eastern Co-op's Benton Hypermarket. These supplemented the "big bus" service already operated to the hypermarket and linked in with the Metro services, thus enabling Transfare tickets to be used. More work was also obtained at the start of September when Go-Ahead Northern was successful in gaining a large number of additional schools contracts. During that same month, Northern opened a new depot in Toward Road, Sunderland which was to house the overflow from its Park Lane premises. Originally opened by Durham District Services, it had latterly been used by United as its Sunderland base.

Further expansion was achieved on 16 September when the stage carriage part of the business of Law Travel of South Moor, Stanley was purchased. Law, as has been related earlier, had run services in competition with Northern in the Stanley and Consett areas and although 5 of its vehicles (3 coach-bodied Bedfords and 2 Alexander bus-bodied Leyland Leopards) were taken over by Northern as part of the deal, being found to be in poor condition none were used by their new owner and instead they were quickly offered for disposal. Law Travel retained the coaching side of its business and still continues this today. This was, however, by no means the last acquisition to be made by Go-Ahead Northern in 1989 for on 18 November its new subsidiary, Coolfirm Ltd. purchased the assets of Tyne & Wear Omnibus Co. from a Jersey-based company which also owned Trimdon Motor Services, and was itself then sold on the same day to Busways Travel Services Ltd. of Newcastle (formerly Tyne & Wear PTE). Tyne & Wear Omnibus Co. had, since its formation in 1987, been a thorn in the side of Busways and it was with much relief that this particular predator had now been eliminated. Although not in direct competition with Go-Ahead Northern, Tyne & Wear Omnibus Co. had destabalised the network generally and its aged fleet of high-floor Bristol LHs were thought to create a poor image for the industry. At the time of its demise, Tyne & Wear Omnibus Co. was operating a fleet of 88 Bristol LH-type buses on fifteen routes in and around Newcastle and Sunderland. The company's depot at Saltmeadows Road, Gateshead was not, however, sold with Coolfirm Ltd. but retained by Go-Ahead Northern after it had been vacated by Busways early in 1990. In complete contrast, a further acquisition completed by Go-Ahead Northern during the final weeks of 1989 was the purchase of twenty public houses from Scottish & Newcastle Breweries !

As 1989 drew to a close, it could be reflected that the 'eighties had been perhaps the most eventful years since the company was founded. With deregulation followed closely by the transfer of Northern from the state to the private sector, the opening of the Tyne & Wear Metro and the massive MetroCentre shopping complex, and the purchase of three bus and coach operators, a taxi firm and a string of licenced hostelries, what could the next decade hold in store?

Within days of the start of 1990, Go-Ahead Northern gained victory in one of its battles with a competitor only to become locked in combat with another. On 6 January, following the withdrawal by Smiths of Sacriston of their services from Langley Park to Chester-le-Street and Durham, Go-Ahead Northern ceased its 'Big Orange' operated journeys on the 725. On the same day (6 January) a new Minilink service was introduced between Newcastle and Whickham which was designed to shadow a service over the same route operated by Derwent Coaches of Swalwell. Meanwhile, as a result of falling receipts, a drop in the number of passengers being carried and a dramatic downturn in the company's financial position, it was found necessary to take some drastic measures for reasons of economy. Amongst these were several service revisions on 1 April brought about mainly due to a massive retendering exercise by Durham County Council, a depot closure and the almost non-appearance of new vehicles. The depot involved in the cuts was Murton which closed on 17 February when its services and vehicle allocation were transferred to Philadelphia and Sunderland depots while the only new vehicles to be added to the fleet were 5 DAF Optare Deltas and, for Metro Taxis, 4 Austin FX4 black cabs. The Deltas, which entered service on the X66 service from Gateshead Metro Interchange to the MetroCentre at Dunston on 14 April, were all painted in Supershuttle livery as replacements for a similar number of the Shuttle-liveried Leyland National 2s which were then modified by the repainting of the upward rear stripe in green for use on the new Garden Festival Shuttle services operated jointly with Northumbria and Busways which were introduced on 18 May from Gateshead Metro and Eldon Square, Newcastle. The only other vehicle to join the fleet during 1990 on a permanent basis was a Plaxton Paramount-bodied Leyland Tiger coach which was purchased secondhand from Fishwick of Leyland whose two-tone green livery it at first retained when it entered service in the late autumn. A further two vehicles operated from Winlaton depot for a few days in October for evaluation purposes were a Reeve Burgess-bodied 33-seat Leyland Swift and an Optare Metrorider. Somewhat

Loading its South Shields-bound passengers at Park Lane bus station, Sunderland in February 1990 is ECW-bodied Leyland Olympian 3659 (C659LJR) which was painted in a special promotional livery for the National Garden Festival at Gateshead. (T.G.Walker)

surprisingly, 2 of the Leyland National 2s which had been in store, unlicenced, since deregulation in October 1986 were repainted and returned to service in March and May, leaving only 3 buses of this type still mothballed. A further indication of the economies being made by the company was the withdrawal of far more vehicles than those taken into stock during the year. Amongst these were the last of the dual-door Atlanteans, the final examples of the Willowbrook-bodied Bristol VRTs, the first mass withdrawal of the dual-purpose Willowbrook 003-bodied Leyland Leopards and one of the Leyland Royal Tiger Doyen coaches.

Go-Ahead Northern's position was not eased when, in June, the Northern Area Health Authority prematurely terminated the company's Caring Cars contract operated under the Metro Taxis banner. This resulted in a revised bid having to be submitted when this work was retendered, in the knowledge that if this was not accepted the majority of the minibus work would have to cease, with a question mark over the size of the black cab fleet. In the event, although some of the Caring Cars work was lost, the majority was fortunately retained and the resulting measures which had to be taken were far less drastic than had originally been anticipated. Further jobs were threatened when, in June, staffing levels on Tyneside and Wearside were reviewed as the company negotiated a cost-cutting package with the trade unions. The depots targetted were Sunderland, Philadelphia, Washington, Wallsend, Jarrow, Percy Main and South Shields where, it was stated, unless substantial savings could be made, around 350 jobs would have to be axed. After protracted discussions between the parties concerned, and the failure to reach any satisfactory agreement, over 200 redundancy notices were issued early in August. These affected 50 engineering staff at the company's central workshops, all 80 staff at Jarrow depot which as a result seemed set for closure, and 100 at Sunderland, Philadelphia and Washington whilst South Shields depot was only reprieved by its staff agreeing to accept a cut in pay in return for a lump-sum consideration. Sadly, Jarrow depot closed early in September, although the adjacent bus station, also owned by Go-Ahead Northern, remained in use despite the whole of the site being placed on the market. Although an offer was quickly received from the food chain, Kwik Save, South Tyneside Council refused to support plans to redevelop the depot and bus station with a superstore and car park and thus the bus station continued in use. The depot and the undercover bus station were eventually demolished in February 1994. A further depot to close was that at High Spen which had been gained with the Venture Transport business in 1970. No sooner was its allocation and services transferred to Gateshead and Winlaton depots on 22 September than this property too was put up for sale.

Meanwhile, one of Voyager's Plaxton-bodied Leyland Tiger coaches was transferred to the Gypsy Queen fleet in May and on 16 June the extension to East Hedley Hope of that subsidiary's service between Langley Park and Durham was withdrawn only ten weeks after it had been added. Following this, Go-Ahead Northern began a shoppers shuttle service from the Tyne Commission Quay to the Eldon Centre in Newcastle for Norwegians arriving on the Fred Olsen Lines ferry from Kristiansand each Saturday. Despite the loss of some of its work and the sale of 6 of its Ford Transit minibuses, Visit Auto Ltd. (Metro Taxis) applied to increase its operators licence from 20 to 50 vehicles in September and registered its first commercial bus service. This was the M10 (Ryton to Newcastle), a minibus route which had been started by Go-Ahead Northern on 26 May and was transferred to Metro Taxis on 27 October. Two days later, Metro Taxis took over three PTE contracted off-peak minibus routes radiating from Felling Square which had previously been maintained by Northumbria Motor Services subsidiary Moordale Coaches. As a result of some new contract work being gained for the night bus service amongst others, Metro Taxis now found that it had a need for larger capacity vehicles and to this end 4 Plaxton and 2 Willowbrook-bodied dual purpose Leyland Leopards were transferred from Go-Ahead Northern. Whilst some of these retained the livery in which they were received, others had their red band repainted yellow to make them more campatible with Metro's colour scheme. Also transferred to the Metro Taxis fleet were the 2 Care Bus Leyland Nationals which had been converted for the carriage of the disabled. Although not connected with any of the above events, it should perhaps be noted that the last Leyland Nationals to retain "Big Orange" livery were repainted into standard fleet colours during December, thus bringing to an end the use of special-liveried vehicles for competitive operational purposes.

PROUD OF OUR ROUTES

Due to the continuing downturn in its financial situation, the company announced in September that it was to be reorganised into five new autonomous companies in an attempt to make its services more cost-effective, give more local responsibility and bring operations closer to the communities which they serve. The three existing subsidiaries : Metro Taxis, Gypsy Queen and Voyager were, however, to continue their present roles and remain largely unchanged as was the existing central engineering operation, with head office support being given for such areas as finance, marketing and training. The five new subsidiaries, which were to become operational in January 1991, were to be The Northern General Transport Co. Ltd. (trading from Chester-le-Street, Consett and Stanley depots); The Tyneside Omnibus Co. Ltd. (trading as South Tyne Buses from South Shields depot); The Tynemouth & District Omnibus Co. (trading as Coastline Buses from Percy Main and Wallsend depots); The Sunderland & District Omnibus Co. (trading as Wear Buses from Sunderland, Philadelphia and Washington depots) and The Gateshead & District Omnibus Co. (trading as Go-Ahead Gateshead from Gateshead and Winlaton depots). All had their registered offices based at 117 Queen Street, Gateshead which of course was also that of their parent, Go-Ahead Northern). Despite none of the new subsidiaries becoming operative until the start of 1991, almost all the buses operated by South Shields depot had gained "South Tyne Buses" fleet names on their existing Go-Ahead Northern red & white livery by mid-September. Whilst 'Durham Country' and 'Greater Gateshead' fleet names had been proposed by an agency, both were rejected and their adoption was not considered.

Before 1990 ended, however, one of Go-Ahead Northern's Mercedes minis was permanently transferred to subsidiary Gypsy Queen into whose livery it was repainted whilst two new minibus services were introduced between Washington and Chester-le-Street to compete directly with St.George Travel of Washington following that operator's service extension. Perhaps more surprisingly, Go-Ahead

Leaving Gateshead Metro is Go-Ahead Northern red & white-liveried Leyland National 4667 (UPT667V) which had details of services 607/8/9/12 painted on its cove panels and a faded advert for the MetroCentre between its wheel arches. (K.A.Jenkinson)

Northern loaned one of its Plaxton-bodied Leyland Leopards to General Omnibus Services for operation on its two Chester-le-Street circular services which served Grange Villa, Pelton Fell and Newfield. Appearing to be helping a competitor rather than challenging it, this aid was given as a result of Aidobourne having given notice to de-register its two routes (which passed to Go-Ahead Northern on 2 January 1991 on which date General Omnibus Services ceased trading) but being required to run them for the 42-day statutory deregistration period. The "General" name has more recently been revived, however, on coaches of the company's successor.

1991 began with a flourish as the new subsidiaries became operational and their vehicles began to appear carrying their new identities. In each case, this was initially applied in the form of a rather small white transfer incorporating the new trading name and a drawing of a local landmark, this being in conjunction with a prominent Go-Ahead Northern fleet name. The drawing used for Durham was its Cathedral whilst for Wearside it was Penshaw Monument, South Shields was Marsden Rock, Coastline featured Tynemouth Castle and Gateshead retained its flaming torch. Also in January, Go-Ahead Northern applied for planning permission to change the use of the former Tyne & Wear Omnibus Co. depot at Saltmeadows Road, Gateshead partially to a commercial garage and partly into warehouse and storage facilities.

Following the revision of the Chester-le-Street Minilink services on 2 February, Wear Buses suddenly found itself under threat with the introduction of a new service from Sunderland to Silksworth by G.Bell who now runs George Bell Travel. In retaliation, the Go-Ahead Northern subsidiary introduced an identical service on 23 February which it hoped would cause the independent operator to withdraw from the scene, although in the event the plan did not succeed. A wider-reaching change to Go-Ahead Northern's services took place on 4 March when Scotswood Bridge across the river Tyne was closed to enable major repair work to be carried out, a task which took until 28 March 1992 to complete. As a result, all the bus services using this river crossing had to be diverted including several opertated by Go-Ahead Northern and its Metro Taxis subsidiary.

Disaster struck towards the end of April when, due to a dispute ostensibly over pay but in practice as much due to the restructuring of bargaining to a subsidiary level, strike action was implemented at Chester-le-Street, Consett and Stanley depots. This quickly spread to Sunderland, Washington, Philadelphia and South Shields depots and ultimately, on 5 May to Gateshead depot. Although Winlaton depot

Calling at Wallsend Metro on its way to Killingworth in March 1994 is Go-Ahead Northern Wright-bodied Dennis Dart 8014 (J614KCU). (K.A.Jenkinson)

continued to work, its staff operated an overtime ban and the only depots not taking any form of action were those on North Tyneside and the company's Metro Taxis, Voyager and Gypsy Queen subsidiaries. Despite numerous meetings taking place between the parties involved, no form of settlement could be reached and as the strike continued,

Go-Ahead Northern group ECW-bodied Bristol VRT driver trainer T507 (RCN167N) leaves Gateshead Metro in 1993 sporting a white & black livery adorned with red lettering. (K.A.Jenkinson)

Leaving the DHSS offices at Longbenton, Newcastle on a workers service is Metro Taxis former Northern Plaxton-bodied Leyland Leopard 5070 (EGR570S) followed by Metro Taxis Willowbrook-bodied Leopard 5096 (LFT96X). (K.A.Jenkinson)

Painted in a special red & white livery for operation on the Tyne Commission Quay service is Go-Ahead Northern 3700 (VFT200T), an MCW-bodied Leyland Atlantean acquired from Tyne & Wear PTE in 1982. (T.W.W.Knowles)

several other operators stepped in to take over a number of Northern's services. These included United, Busways and several independents including Hylton Castle Motors of East Boldon (who trade as Catch-a-Bus) and OK Travel, all of whom gained some short term benefit from Northern's troubles, but whose main concern was for the travelling public. Eventually, after taking the dispute to arbitration, a 7% pay increase - which was slightly higher than that which the company had originally offered - was awarded to driving staff and a return to work was made on 28 May. In an attempt to recapture its passengers, and as a good will gesture, Go-Ahead Northern offered a special 10p fare for any journey south of the Tyne for the next two days and whilst most of the operators who had provided replacement services during the dispute quickly withdrew these, a small handful continued for several more weeks. It was estimated that the strike cost Go-Ahead Northern around £850,000 and that the long term losses the company had to face could amount to between 5% and 8% of its income. There being no winners in such situations, it was also estimated that some drivers had lost up to £800 in earnings!

The first new vehicles to be taken into stock during 1991 were 4 Plaxton Expressliner-bodied Volvo B10M coaches which made their debut at the beginning of the year and were noteworthy in being the first of this type to be owned by any operator, rather than leased from National Expressliners Ltd. Although these were fitted with onboard toilets, they were not, however, equipped to National Express Rapide specification. During late April/early May, a Reeve Burgess-bodied Dennis Dart in London Buses livery was evaluated in service from Winlaton depot whilst soon afterwards a new Carlyle-bodied Dennis Dart was purchased for use in the Gypsy Queen fleet. May also witnessed the application of cove panel lettering to 2 Leyland Nationals to promote the 607-9/12 services between western Gateshead, the MetroCentre and Newcastle and the conversion of 2 of the former Tyne & Wear PTE MCW-bodied Atlanteans for use on the Tyne Commission Quay ferry service for which they were given a new livery of all-white relieved only by red lower deck panels. During June, 2 Plaxton Expressliner-bodied Volvo B10Ms less than a year old were acquired from Yorkshire Voyager while a month later a Plaxton-bodied Leyland Tiger coach was purchased from Plymouth City Transport. Also in June, an Optare Metrorider minibus was evaluated for a couple of days and 2 of South Tyne's Leyland Nationals were given an experimental livery which featured blue lower panels, red waistband and white upper parts.

From July, part of Tyne & Wear PTE's Care Call contract was gained by Metro Taxis from Busways and for use on this, 7 new Atlas-converted 11-seat Renault Masters and 2 older Mercedes were hired from the PTE, all of which were painted in the standard Care Call livery of brown, orange & yellow. In addition to these, 2 all-white liveried Carlyle-bodied Freight Rover Sherpa minibuses were hired from Carlyle Bus Centre for use on two new local services in Spennymoor which were started on 27 July in competition with local operator, Gardiners who had continued to operate between Sunderland and Durham following the ending of the Northern strike. These two buses remained on loan until October when they were returned to Carlyle following the liquidation of that company. Extra journeys were also registered from 20 July between South Shields and Fellgate Estate/Boldon ASDA due to Catch-a-Bus also continuing to run post-strike services to these destinations. A new service was also registered from South Shields to Sunderland to shadow Catch-a-Bus route 6 but this was then cancelled without having ever operated, the extra journeys to Fellgate Estate and Boldon ASDA also being deregistered from 3 August. To further challenge some new competitors, additional journeys were introduced on 10 August on service 154 to combat continued competition from Bleanch, Hetton-le-Hole, whilst on 9 September a half hourly service was introduced on the 535 between Houghton-le-Spring and South Hetton to compete with Safari Coaches and five days later the X5 had its frequency increased to half-hourly between Newcastle and South Hetton in retaliation for JHM Travel of Peterlee having commenced a competitive service from Peterlee to Newcastle. During this period, however, the greatest rivalry was on the Durham to Sunderland corridor where there were now nine buses per hour compared to three per hour before the strike when Go-Ahead Northern was the sole operator. Of these, Gardiners of Spennymoor, Scarlet Band of West Cornforth and Bell Brothers of Sunderland operated three while Go-Ahead Northern's subsidiary Wear Buses operated the remaining six.

Returning to the vehicle front, in September Go-Ahead Northern ordered no fewer than 40 Dennis Darts which were to be fitted with Wrights Handybus bodies and in November received 14 new 26-seat Optare Metroriders which were allocated to Winlaton depot and painted in MetroCentre Minis livery which incorporated Go-Ahead Gateshead fleet names. Prior to their arrival, an Optare Metrorider demonstrator was loaned to the company from 1 November in lieu of the late delivery of the new vehicles while during the previous month 2 Bristol LH6Ls had been borrowed from Northumbria for driver training purposes. Within the existing fleet, 3 Leyland Olympians were upgraded by the fitting of coach-type seats and were repainted into a special promotional livery for the 308 service (Newcastle to Blyth via Whitley Bay), this being red and white in different proportions to the standard application with the addition of between-decks promotional lettering. At around this same time, most of North Tyneside's Alexander-bodied Renault minis had their coach-type seating replaced by standard bus seats removed from withdrawn Bristol VRTs whilst a Gateshead MCW Metrobus was repainted into standard red and white with a blue skirt and diagonal stripe which was swept upwards towards the front. Given Go-Ahead Gateshead fleet names, this served as the prototype for a new livery introduced to the Gateshead fleet during the following year.

In October, a further additional operators licence was issued to Go-Ahead Northern under the name of The Venture Transport Co. Ltd. This was for 30 vehicles and although its registered office was shown as 117 Queen Street, Gateshead, its operating centres were listed as

Illustrating the then new Go-Ahead Gateshead livery as it leaves Gateshead Metro for Leam Lane Estate is MCW Metrobus 3644 (A644BCN). (K.A.Jenkinson)

Coach-seated ECW-bodied Leyland Olympian 3671 (C671LJR) was one of three given a special dedicated livery for the Newcastle - Blyth 308 service. In this view at Park Lane, Sunderland on 20 August 1992, however, it was operating a Voyager excursion to Lightwater Valley in North Yorkshire. (S.A.Staddon)

Having just left South Shields depot to take up its duties on the 526 service, VFM Buses Leyland National 4687 (BGR687W) shows off its then-new two-tone blue livery in November 1992. (K.A.Jenkinson)

the Go-Ahead Northern depots at Chester-le-Street, Consett and Stanley. Despite gaining this new licence, it was not used until August 1992, of which more later. Meanwhile, following a change in regulations Go-Ahead Northern's driver training fleet was updated with the purchase from Western Scottish of 4 Alexander-bodied Seddon Pennine VII single deckers. These retained their former owner's livery of white with black relief which it was decided was to be to adopted as standard for all the company's driver trainers. The arrival of these buses enabled the 3 Leyland PD2s and the solitary remaining former Southdown Leyland PD3 - which were the last front-engined double deckers in the fleet - to be withdrawn, although one of the PD2s was retained by VFM for preservation by a group of staff.

The start of 1992 saw Tyneside Omnibus Co. introduce a new identity and livery to its South Shields-based fleet from 13 January. The first buses to be adorned with the new VFM (meaning Value For Money) fleet name and painted in pale blue with dark blue relief were the 13 new Dennis Darts, a Leyland National 2 and an ECW-bodied Leyland Atlantean, although it was not long before several more vehicles began to appear in this manner. Concurrent with the launch of its new identity, VFM Buses introduced a new customer's charter which promised comfort, cleanliness, safety, facilities for the disabled and customer care as well as a comprehensive service network. A further promise was made by the company to invest the money raised by the eventual closure and sale of Jarrow bus station into new facilities for the town. All of this was aimed at rebuilding the status of the company which, to an extent, was still struggling to overcome the effects of the 1991 strike.

Following the rebranding of its operations on South Tyneside, Go-Ahead Northern undertook a similar exercise in North West Durham in March when the gradual rebranding of its Gateshead & District subsidiary as Go-Ahead Gateshead was speeded up and its old-established "Northern" identity was relaunched at Chester-le-Street, Consett and Stanley depots. In a similar fashion to VFM Buses at South Shields, Northern also introduced a customers' charter and adopted the legend "Proud Of Our Routes" which in addition to appearing on the company's publicity material was, along with a stylised drawing of a DAF Optare Delta, also applied to its buses as part of its fleet name. In addition to bringing its operations closer to its passengers, Go-Ahead Northern's Marketing and Training Services subsidiary which already provided considerable training and further education facilities for its own staff began to offer its services to other bus operators in close collaboration with Bus & Coach Training. Being the only company within the bus industry to participate in the pilot "Investors in People" training scheme, it was soon called upon to provide training advice to several bus operators around the country.

As far as its services were concerned, several new ones were introduced whilst others were modified to meet passenger requirements. On 26 January Metro Taxis won the contract to operate Tyne & Wear PTE's five night services, all of which ran on a circular basis from Newcastle Central Station, while six days earlier Safari Coaches restarted its service between Houghton-le-Spring and South Hetton much to the annoyance of Go-Ahead Northern. Other competition had disappeared, however, following the demise of Bleanch, Hetton-le-Hole and JHM Travel of Peterlee, both of whom had ceased trading. Following the reopening of Scotswood Bridge on 28 March, Go-Ahead Northern's services in that area were able to return to their original routes and in May, comparative newcomer Welcome Passenger Services of Gateshead withdrew its two routes which served the MetroCentre in order to give more concentration to its other services which thankfully did not compete with Go-Ahead Northern. Meanwhile, a new service launched on 9 May by VFM Buses was the X23 running every 20 minutes between Sunderland (which had just been granted 'City' status) and Blackett Street, Newcastle via Fellgate Estate. Marketed as the "Two Cities Express", this was operated by 4 dual-purpose Plaxton-bodied Leyland Tigers suitably adorned with promotional lettering.

During the early part of 1992, Go-Ahead Northern announced plans for the development of a Guided Transport Expressway (GTE) which would link Sunderland with Newcastle and would also serve both Gateshead, Washington and the constantly expanding Nissan car plant and would provide a park-and-ride station between Washington and Springwell. At an estimated cost of £2.5 million, it was stated that this would be quicker and cheaper to build than an extension to the Metro and would also serve additional communities such as Springwell and Wrekenton which could not be effectively served by rail solutions. The new GTE would, if plans came to fruition, be served by adapted DAF-Optare articulated buses which could be built and operational within eighteen months. In order to evaluate this type of bus, a Dutch DAF articulated single decker was demonstrated later in the year between Gateshead and the MetroCentre. Despite these proposals,

Wearing the attractive red & white Northern proud of our routes livery, ECW-bodied Leyland Atlantean 3559 (MBR459T) still looks immaculate despite it being almost fifteen years old. It is seen here resting between duties in Stanley bus station in March 1994. (K.A.Jenkinson)

Evaluated by Go-Ahead Northern and operated on a free service to the MetroCentre, left hand drive DAF bendibus VP-18-HK seen here collecting its passengers at Gateshead Metro on 14 July 1992 carried Go-Ahead Northern fleet names in its windscreen and side windows and was numbered 7771. (S.A.Staddon)

Picking up its passengers at the Newcastle terminus of the Cross-Tyne service is Low Fell Coaches Plaxton-bodied Bedford YMT 4764 (D913URG) which in August 1995 was transferred to OK at Bishop Auckland for driver training duties, although it is still available for normal service when the necessity arises. (K.A.Jenkinson)

Tyne & Wear PTE continued to investigate the possibility of the more expensive extension its Metro system to Sunderland via existing British Rail alignments and later adopted this scheme at a cost exceeding £50 million although also proposing to re-examine 'Busway' opportunities.

Fleet-wise, 1992 had opened with a great deal of activity including the entry into service of the new Dennis Darts (2 of which had arrived before the end of the previous year but had not yet seen service) and for Metro Taxis some new black cabs. Of the new additions, the new Wright-bodied Dennis Darts continued to arrive throughout January and were ultimately allocated to Tyneside Omnibus Co. (13), Tynemouth & District (2), Gateshead (10) and Northern General (15). Those for Tyneside were painted in the new VFM Buses two-tone blue livery, Tynemouth's duo (which sported Go-Ahead Northern fleet names) and Gateshead's 10 were red and white with the latter additionally having a blue skirt and forward-sloping diagonal band together with Go-Ahead Gateshead fleet names and promotional lettering for services 53 and 54 while the 25 for Northern were in standard red and white and carried the company's new "Northern - proud of our routes" fleet names. The arrival of these new single deckers allowed the withdrawal to take place of a large number of Mk.I Leyland Nationals as well as several older double deckers. The new black cabs for Metro Taxis were Austin FX4s of which 2 arrived in January to be followed by a further 2 in April. More surprising, however, was the return home of one of Northern's Routemasters which, since its departure from the fleet in 1980 had seen service with Stevensons of Spath, Uttoxeter, Stagecoach in Perth and Magicbus in Glasgow. Under the care of the company employees' enthusiast group GANBEA, it was to be repainted back into Northern's 'Tynemouth-style' livery which had been carried by some of its Routemasters during the late 'sixties and was ultimately to be used on a new circular service from Tynemouth via Whitley Bay, the Stephenson Railway Museum and North Shields Ferry at Spring and August bank holidays and on the first Sunday of May, June, July and August in addition to being available for private hire. To further enhance the coach fleet, a secondhand Plaxton Paramount 3500-bodied Volvo B10M was purchased in March from Hills, Tredegar in whose livery it entered service adorned with Voyager fleet names. This was joined in April by a similarly-bodied Leyland Tiger acquired from Fishwick of Leyland and in May and July by 2 Plaxton-bodied Tigers from Anslow of Pontypool. Also acquired secondhand for the Metro Taxis fleet were a pair of Austin FX4 black cabs, one of which replaced an accident-damaged FX4, the other allowing the withdrawal of one of the MCW Metrocabs. Also making their debut were the first of 25 more Wright-bodied Dennis Darts, 15 of which were placed in the Northern fleet. The remaining 10 which did not enter service until September were for Sunderland & District.

Continuing to seek further expansion and consolidation, Go-Ahead Northern in June purchased the capital and assets of Robert Tindall Coaches (Tyneside) Ltd. of Lowreys Lane, Low Fell in a deal which included that operator's depot at Quarryfield Road, Gateshead, its services and 13 vehicles. Having started in business in the late 'fifties as a taxi operator under the title of Low Fell Taxis, Robert Tindall in partnership with Leslie Pickering purchased a minibus in 1963,

Repurchased from Stagecoach and returned to Northern's Tynemouth-style livery is much-travelled Routemaster 2099 (EDS508B) which began life registered RCN699. Now officially preserved, it is, however, regularly used on special duties during the summer months of each year. (B.Newsome)

Arriving at Stanley bus station in March 1994 is Leyland National 2 4667 (UPT667V) wearing the cream & blue livery of Shaws Coaches. Like all Shaws buses of this type, 4667 was transferred to the company from Northern with whom it began its life. (K.A.Jenkinson)

operating this between Newcastle and Woolsington Airport (now Newcastle Airport), renaming the business Low Fell Taxis & Minicoaches in 1968. Developing further and acquiring a full-sized coach, the title Low Fell Coaches was adopted and a limited company was formed, and in 1983 a licence was granted for the operation of a cross-Tyne stage carriage service from Low Fell to Newcastle. This, together with an irregular service from Newcastle to Queen Elizabeth Hospital and a handful of tendered off-peak routes passed to Go-Ahead Northern upon its acquisition of the Low Fell Coaches business as did 5 Merecedes minis, 5 Bedfords, 1 Leyland Leopard, 1 bus-bodied Leyland Tiger and 2 Dennis Javelins, one of which was fitted with a 55-seat bus body by Duple. In a similar fashion to Gypsy Queen, Low Fell Coaches was retained as a separate subsidiary keeping its white & blue livery and current fleet name and was to be managed on behalf of its new owner by the Tindall family.

No sooner had the dust settled on the above deal than Go-Ahead Northern made a further acquisition, this being the business of Shaws Coaches of Craghead which was taken over by the Go-Ahead Group and licensed under Venture Transport Co. Ltd. on 1 August. A comparatively new company founded in the early 'eighties, it operated a mixed fleet of 6 Leyland coaches and 5 minicoaches (1 Fiat, 1 Talbot Express, 1 Toyota and 2 Mercedes) and in addition owned 2 Peugeot 405 cars, a Rolls Royce Silver Shadow limousine and a Seddon-Atkinson recovery truck. Although Shaws main activity was in the private hire field, it also maintained a number of schools contracts and operated a stage carriage service from Stanley to Chester-le-Street. Of the vehicles acquired by Venture, 2 of the Leyland Leopards and a 12-seat Mercedes L207D were already withdrawn and these were quickly sold by their new owner. To replace them, 2 Leopards - 1 Willowbrook and 1 Plaxton-bodied - were immediately transferred to Shaws from Go-Ahead Northern, both having been repainted into their 'new owner's' livery of white with a broad blue waistband. As with Low Fell Coaches, Venture, trading as Shaws Coaches, was to be operated as an "arms-length" subsidiary from Shaws' depot at Shafto Bank, Craghead.

Having added two more companies to its growing portfolio and introduced new local identities in South Shields, Gateshead and North West Durham during 1992, Go-Ahead Northern now turned its attention to its Sunderland & District subsidiary which, on 1 September, was relaunched trading as "Wear Buses" from its depots at Sunderland, Philadelphia and Washington. Adopting a new livery of pale green & grey with a bright green skirt and broad diagonal band, its fleet was updated by the entry into service of the 10 new Wright-bodied Dennis Darts which were joined by 4 Leyland National 2s transferred from Go-Ahead Gateshead and, two months later, following the lead set by other Go-Ahead Northern subsidiaries, Wear Buses introduced a Customers' Charter. In addition, 5 Leyland Olympians had also been repainted into the new livery in time for the launch whilst the last of Sunderland's Bristol VRTs had been replaced by Leyland Atlanteans. Later in the month, on 27 September, 2 Reeve Burgess-bodied Mercedes minibuses were transferred from Go-Ahead Northern to Shaws Coaches for operation on the Spennymoor town services which had been placed under Shaws control ten days earlier.

Meanwhile, Friends of the Earth won support from Go-Ahead Northern for its Charter for Cleaner Buses. The Charter asked for financial incentives from the Government for the purchase of new engines that meet the 1995/6 emission standards and in return, signatory companies undertook to ensure that their fleets would be maintained and inspected according to manufacturers specifications and that complaints from the public relating to smoke emissions from specific vehicles would be followed up immediately. In December, Go-Ahead Northern further confirmed its commitment to environmental improvement by launching a specially designed 'Breathe North' booklet and designating an environmental hotline at North Shields-based subsidiary Coastline Buses for reporting smoky buses. To further support the cleaner air campaign, Coastline Buses was already using low sulphur diesel fuel within its fleet and was looking at further ways of meeting the environmental challenge.

Only 2 new vehicles joined the fleet during the latter part of the year, these being a pair of new Plaxton Paramount 3500-bodied, all-white liveried, Volvo B10Ms purchased from dealer stock. Destined for allocation to National Express contracts, both were placed in store until the spring of 1993 when they made their operational debut. During the final month of the year, one of Go-Ahead Northern's time-expired Leyland National Is was converted into a mobile library and classroom and transferred to Low Fell Coaches. Painted in a predominantly white livery and decorated with various pro-reading slogans, it was used to tour schools in the Gateshead area to promote a greater interest amongst young people in books and other reading material. Operationally, two additional services lettered 'B' and 'C' were started

Freshly repainted in Superliner livery is Northern's coach-seated MCW Metrobus 3779 (C779OCN) seen outside Chester-le-Street depot in April 1995. (K.A.Jenkinson)

Despite being lettered for the Two Cities Express service from Sunderland to Newcastle, VFM Buses Plaxton Paramount 3200-bodied Leyland Tiger 5119 (A719ABB) hurries past South Shields market in November 1995 on its way to Boldon Asda on the 530 service. (K.A.Jenkinson)

on 2 December between the MetroCentre at Dunston and Blackhall Mill to compete with services operated by Classic Coaches of Annfield Plain which duplicated existing services. These were operated by Go-Ahead Gateshead using two Plaxton Paramount-bodied Leyland Tigers which, although retaining Voyager livery, had their customary fleet names replaced by a new "Services B & C" title, this representing "Bright & Cheerful" and at the same time lost their fleet numbers. A further new title - and livery - to appear at this same time was the "Superliner", this being applied to one of Northern's coach-seated MCW Metrobuses. Of all-over red with two-tone grey bands above the wheel arches and at upper deck floor level, it carried bold "Superliner" lettering on its upper deck side panels and in smaller graphics below its windscreens and featured the Northern name below its side windows. Soon after its introduction, this livery which was ultimately to replace the Express Link colour scheme and identity within the Northern fleet, was applied to further coach-seated Metrobuses and a Leyland Olympian whilst Wear Buses replaced the old Express Link livery with its own two-tone green & light grey Wear Express colour scheme to which was added promotional lettering for the X4, X5, X95 and X96 services. December also witnessed the completion of the repainting of the Tyneside Omnibus Co. fleet into VFM Buses colours and, following the withdrawal earlier in the year of more Leyland National Is, only 3 buses of this type now remained licenced. For the fast service between Sunderland and Newcastle, VFM Buses added 'Two Cities Express' lettering to some of its Plaxton Paramount-bodied Leyland Tiger coaches. Meanwhile, looking towards the future, Go-Ahead Northern during the run-up to British Rail privatisation expressed a firm interest in that undertaking's Carlisle, Newcastle and Middlesbrough line, providing that it was offered as a separate franchise, believing that this could be operated profitably and interlinked with the company's network of bus services. This was not to be, however, as British Rail ultimately announced that this particular line would be included in the large package embracing all the Regional Railways lines between Humberside and the Scottish border.

1993 opened with the entry into service of the first of 24 new Wright-bodied Dennis Darts, of which 18 were allocated to the Go-Ahead Gateshead fleet with the remaining 6 joining Tynemouth & District. Upon their arrival, some Gateshead examples had their diagonal blue band continued upwards across the front of the roof and around the destination screen, although these were quickly modified with the additional blue being replaced with white. At the same time, the earlier batch lost their promotional lettering for the 53 and 54 services. Also acquired was a secondhand Austin FX4 black cab for use in the Metro Taxis fleet and, more surprisingly, for Low Fell Coaches came a 50-seat Alexander PS-bodied Dennis Lance previously used as a demonstrator by Hestair Dennis. In addition, a new image was also introduced in January for Tynemouth & District, although this was less radical than those applied to other members of the Go-Ahead Northern group. Using a new livery of red & cream which was similar to that applied to the Tynemouth fleet in pre-NBC days, it incorporated on the side panels and below the windscreens Coastline fleet names below which was the legend "The Driving Force of North Tyneside". Consideration had been given to using either Tynemouth or Tyneside fleet names, but it was felt that neither would have been acceptable to older staff who might still feel some loyalty to the other company. Sunderland District had been ruled out on the same grounds. Inter-fleet transfers saw a Duple-bodied Bedford coach move from Gypsy Queen to Low Fell Coaches, its replacement being Voyager's sole remaining Leyland Royal Tiger Doyen, and a Willowbrook-bodied Leyland Leopard transferred from Low Fell Coaches to Shaws Coaches who also received an Alexander-bodied Mercedes minibus from Northern and 2 Leyland National 2s from Go-Ahead Gateshead. All except the pair of Leyland Nationals were repainted into their respective new owner's liveries and were appropriately lettered before entering service.

The start of 1993 also witnessed changes to a number of services, particularly south of the Tyne, with modifications to existing routes in the Gateshead area being implemented on 9 January and around Low Fell on 13 February. Amongst these was the withdrawal of Go-Ahead Gateshead's 24 service (Newcastle - Allerdene) which on the latter date was replaced by a new hourly service (also numbered 24) operated by Low Fell Coaches between Gateshead Metro and Team Valley (Retail World) and the diversion of several routes in Newcastle city centre to operate via a loop after entering the city from the south via Tyne Bridge or the west via High Level Bridge. Further competition was encountered from Classic Coaches who, on 8 February, extended their two Blackhall Mill services into Newcastle from their previous terminus at the MetroCentre with Go-Ahead Gateshead subsequently extending its B and C services into Newcastle via the same route on 20 February, thus continuing the "war" between these two operators. In the meantime, Classic Coaches (who lettered some of its vehicles "Classicliner" in a very similar style to Northern's 'Superliners') had started a service from Chester-le-Street to Newcastle (Worswick Street) on 11 January, running via Birtley and Low Fell and as was to be expected, it was not long before Go-Ahead Northern took retaliatory action. On this occasion it was Shaws Coaches who challenged Classic, starting on 30 January with an identical route timed 3 minutes before its competitor. Also on this same date, Shaws introduced two new circular services in the Stanley area, one of which served Annfield Plain, the other Flint Hill in response to similar services started by Hunters of Tantobie and Star Travel of Dipton. In addition to the above, Shaws Coaches had also, on 4 January, gained the Durham County Council-contracted service from Consett to Newcastle which had previously been operated by Northumbria Motor Services. For these additional services, 6 Leyland National Is were reinstated and, together with a National 2, were transferred to the Shaws Coaches fleet to which others followed. On the brighter side, Wear Buses found competition reduced on the Durham - Sunderland corridor following the withdrawal by Scarlet Band of West Cornforth and Gardiners of Spennymoor of their competitive services.

Early in February Coastline successfully beat off seventeen other challengers to be selected by the Government to stage the first low-floor bus experiment outside London. The company had chosen its 325/326 routes for this experiment, these operating on a circular basis between North Shields and Whitley Bay and serving part of the sea front and four Metro stations as well as Rake Lane General Hospital. In connection with this experiment, a grant was available through Tyne & Wear PTE to enable Coastline to purchase five low floor buses and, after examining various types, an order was placed for Dennis Lances fitted with Wright Pathfinder bodies. In preparation for this new operation which was scheduled to start in April 1994, conversion work on stops along the 325/6 services began in August 1993. In the event, however, the start of the new operation was delayed by late delivery of the buses from Wrights.

Meanwhile, in March 1993 Go-Ahead Gateshead updated its fleet with the addition of 17 new 26-seat Optare Metroriders and 6 DAF Optare Deltas, five of which were painted in Supershuttle livery for operation on the service from Gateshead Metro to the MetroCentre upon which they displaced the 1990 batch. The arrival of these new vehicles allowed all Go-Ahead Gateshead's remaining Leyland Atlanteans to be withdrawn along with a few Leyland National 2s. Although a number of the former were transferred to Northern as replacements for Bristol VRTs, others were placed in store at the former Tyne & Wear Omnibus Co. depot at Saltmeadows Road, Gateshead whilst the deposed National 2s found a new lease of life with Wear Buses. Also moving between companies in March was 3536,

ECW-bodied Leyland Atlantean 3536 (MBR436T) was the first double decker to join the Metro Taxis fleet in whose yellow, white & black livery it is seen here behind Percy Main depot in April 1995.   (K.A.Jenkinson)

Acquired by Northern from Tyne & Wear PTE in August 1982, MCW-bodied Leyland Atlantean 3708 (YNL208V) was transferred to Shaws Coaches in 1994 and given that company's cream & blue livery and fleet names. Here it enters Gateshead Metro in June 1994 on its way to Durham on the 221 service. (M.Duffy)

an ECW-bodied Atlantean which was transferred from Tynemouth to Metro Taxis to become the latter's first double decker. As well as adding new vehicles to their combined fleet, the Go-Ahead Northern Group also turned their attention towards the secondhand market and in March purchased 4 previously-used Austin FX4 taxicabs for the Metro Taxis operation and replaced one of Low Fell Coaches Duple-bodied Bedfords with a vehicle from Gypsy Queen. At around this same time, all the Low Fell Coaches and Shaws Coaches vehicles were allocated fleet numbers within the Go-Ahead Northern series, but in a similar fashion to the Gypsy Queen fleet, these were not carried on the vehicles and were "on paper only" for administrative purposes.

At the start of May MCW Metrobus 3509 was repainted into a special silver livery to commemorate Northern's 80th Anniversary whilst during April a stranger in the Sunderland area appeared in the form of a Wright-bodied Mercedes Benz 709D minibus which was evaluated by Wear Buses. Meanwhile, 5 more Leyland National 2s were transferred to Shaws Coaches at the start of May for additional responsibilities (mainly in the battle with Classic Coaches) while during the following month another Leyland National was repainted into a two-tone blue and white promotional livery for Go-Ahead Northern Engineering Services Ltd. to whom it was then transferred. In its new role it was available for hire to other operators - including those outside the Go-Ahead Northern Group - as and when required. It has since been repainted into an all-over white scheme onto which panels carrying the fleet name of the subsidiary for whom it is working can be attached.

Amongst the service changes implemented during 1993 was a reorganisation on 6 March of some of the routes in the Whickham and Winlaton areas and, on that same date, the replacement of conventional routes 607-9/12 between High Spen, Chopwell and Gateshead by seven new minibus services, two of which were extended through to Eldon Square, Newcastle in the evenings and on Sundays. Some nine days later, Classic Coaches increased its attack on the Go-Ahead Northern Group when it began operating hourly on Shaw's original 729 service between Chester-le-Street and Stanley. To exasperate matters further, on this same date Gardiners of Spennymoor also began an hourly service between these two points, and thus a week later Shaws Coaches introduced additional journeys on the 729 service. After launching its new onslaught, Classic Coaches withdrew its original 736 and 738 services between the Metro Centre and Chopwell on 17 April, with Go-Ahead Gateshead following suit a week later when it ceased operating its competing services B & C. The battle between these two companies was, however, far from over, for on 19 April Classic began operations on Northern's 709 service from Stanley to Newcastle via Beamish in addition to threatening further expansion in other parts of the company's territory. This new encroachment by Classic immediately led to Shaws Coaches introducing journeys on the 709 using its recently-acquired additional Leyland Nationals!

As had become customary, the seasonal services were again restarted at the beginning of May, although this year some of them were allocated to different operating companies within the Go-Ahead Northern Group. The 333 (Tynemouth to Whitley Bay Holiday Park open top service), 375 (Whitley Bay to Beamish) and 377 (No Place to Whitley Bay) were registered by Metro Taxis instead of Tynemouth whilst the 555 (Souter Lighthouse to Jarrow Monastery Museum) was registered by VFM Buses in place of Go-Ahead Northern while the 400 service (North Tyneside Heritage Circle) was retained by Coastline for operation by preserved Routemaster 2099. In order to maintain its new services, Metro Taxis received a further two ECW-bodied Atlanteans, both of which were repainted into their new owner's yellow and white livery, and open-top Park Royal-bodied Atlantean which retained its predominantly blue livery and Go-Ahead Northern fleet names. Later in May, on the 22nd, Consett bus station was closed for redevelopment and as a result all its services were transferred to unprotected stands in Consett Front Street. This was far from popular with passengers and Go-Ahead Northern was quick to emphasise the fact that this move was not of their making!

Perhaps one of the most unusual operations launched during 1993 was that by Metro Taxis under the 'Taxibus' banner. Commencing on 5 June and running between Benwell and Newcastle (Newgate Street) and serving Dolphin Street Community Centre, Newcastle College and the Royal Victoria Infirmary enroute, it was operated by a solitary Metro Taxis Ford Transit minibus. Being withdrawn on 9 July, the publicity material issued in connection with this service unbelievably carried the date of its withdrawal from the start, following (it is understood) Busways having raised strong objections to the registration! Meanwhile, Low Fell Coaches service 24 was extended across the Tyne Bridge from Gateshead Metro to Worswick Street, Newcastle from 5 July.

At the start of August, Wear Buses received 4 new Optare Metroriders for use in the Washington area where all the minibus services were revised in addition to being numbered rather than colour coded. These were the forerunners of more buses of this make and model which were to join the Wear Buses fleet early in 1994 and although the first 3 of the expected 13 arrived in November, they were placed in store until being used to compete with Wearside Buses (Redby Travel) service 13 between Houghton and Newcastle, running as duplicates on the 194 service as far as Heworth. Also making their debut were 4 new and 2 secondhand Austin FX4 black cabs which joined the Metro Taxis fleet during the autumn. Although the above were the only additional vehicles to be received during the second half of 1993, a Wright-bodied Volvo B10B was inspected at Bensham during the early autumn but was not used in service whilst an Alexander Dash-bodied Volvo B6 was tried by VFM Buses at South Shields. A

Wearing a white & black livery and owned by Northern subsidiary Quality Bus Engineering, Leyland National 4652 (752TNU, originally MGR952T) is used by all the Go-Ahead Group companies as well as being hired to other operators to cover for vehicles undergoing repair. It is seen here fitted with temporary Northern fleet names as it undertakes a duty on service 20 at Gateshead Metro in June 1994. (M.Duffy)

DAF Optare Delta demonstrator was used by Northern at Stanley and Consett depots for a few weeks during September and October, this following an Alexander Strider-bodied Dennis Lance which in September was used by Go-Ahead Gateshead for comparison with the company's DAF Optare Deltas. On the reverse side of the coin, leaving the company temporarily was one of Go-Ahead Gateshead's Wright-bodied Dennis Darts (8080) which was used by Dennis for demonstration to several companies including Keighley & District and Harrogate & District during September. Adding a further touch of variety to the north-east, one of the company's MCW Metrobus double deckers was, during the late summer, repainted into a white livery to which illustrations of various Group vehicles were added in order to promote the Go-Ahead Northern Transport & Leisure Group. A similar poster was also affixed at this time to numerous hoardings throughout the region.

As they had threatened earlier, Classic Coaches expanded further on 8 August when they extended their Newcastle to Chester-le-Street 21 service through to Durham via the Arnison Centre, Pity Me with Shaws Coaches introducing an identical extension to their 221 service a week later. Classic gained a further foothold in the area on 30 October when it launched a new service (121) from Sacriston to Newcastle via Chester-le-Street and Wrekenton, following this on 6 November with a new route (007) from Chester-le-Street to Dipton via Pelton, Stanley, Annfield Plain and Catchgate. As had now become customary in view of the extent to which Classic continued to replicate existing routes, with journeys timed a few minutes in front of Northern's buses, on 13 November Shaws Coaches began a service numbered 721 from Sacriston to Newcastle, supplementing this from 20 November with Go-Ahead Northern's 55 service between Newcastle (Worswick Street) and Barley Mow Estate via Wrekenton. In order to challenge Classic's other new operation, Shaws Coaches began an identical service (006) between Chester-le-Street and Dipton on 29 November. Partly as a result of these new services, Shaws Coaches gained their first ever double deckers, a trio of MCW-bodied Leyland Atlanteans transferred from elsewhere within the Go-Ahead Northern Group which were quickly repainted into their new owner's cream and blue livery. Before the month ended, further competition was experienced when Redby Coaches of Sunderland, who cheekily continued to use its Wearside Buses fleet name, began a service from Houghton-le-Spring to Newcastle via Washington on 29 November. In response to this, Wear buses on 18 December extended its 194 service through to Newgate Street, Newcastle from its former terminus at Heworth.

EXPANSION OUTSIDE THE NORTH-EAST

Undoubtedly, the most unexpected news of the year was that of Go-Ahead Northern's purchase in the latter part of November of Brighton & Hove Bus and Coach Co.Ltd., this being the Group's first expansion outside its established area. In addition to giving the Group a foothold in the south of England upon which it might be possible to build in the future, this deal added a further 154 vehicles to its combined fleet. The origins of Brighton & Hove Bus & Coach Co.Ltd. date back more than a hundred years to September 1884 when the Brighton, Hove & Preston United Omnibus Co. Ltd. was formed by the amalgamation of most of the local independent horse bus operators. Setting up its headquarters at Conway Street, Hove, the company was purchased by Thomas Tilling Ltd. on 28 November 1916 and on 26 November 1935 its name was changed to Brighton, Hove & District Omnibus Co. Ltd. Adding trolleybuses to its fleet in 1939, although these were stored throughout the war and did not make their debut in service until January 1945, the company passed to the BTC in 1948 along with all Tilling's other road passenger transport interests and ultimately to the NBC upon its formation in 1969. Placed under the control of Southdown Motor Services, it continued thus until 21 April 1986 when it became completely autonomous under the title of Brighton & Hove Bus & Coach Co. Ltd. in preparation for its sale by the NBC to the private sector and adopted a striking new livery of cream with red relief and a black skirt. Purchased by its management in May 1987 on the day after Go-Ahead Northern's own management buy-out, it soon developed its own vehicle policy and purchased Scania double deckers and Dennis Javelin coaches. At the time of its purchase by Go-Ahead Northern, Brighton & Hove operated a fleet of 149 buses, coaches and minibuses from depots at Conway Street, Hove and Whitehawk Road, Brighton in addition to maintaining small outstations at Newhaven, Shoreham and Steyning. Under its new ownership, the company is to be operated as a completely separate subsidiary, retaining its existing livery and fleet name. Following its success in gaining Brighton & Hove, Go-Ahead Northern made a bid for London Buses subsidiary Westlink which was initially successful but, following reversal of the government's proposals to deregulate London, Go-Ahead Northern withdrew.

Back on the home front, following the problems experienced by United Bus who controlled DAF Bus, Go-Ahead Northern were reluctant to confirm orders for further DAF SB220 chassis in its 1994 programme, not knowing whether or not these would be delivered. Being satisfied with those already in service, however, and having no complaints with Optare's Delta bodywork, the company decided to once

The most recent additions to the Brighton & Hove fleet are Marshall-bodied Dennis Darts, one of which (7 - N507KCD) picks up its passengers outside Brighton's Imperial Arcade in October 1995. (T.S.Blackman)

Seen at Preston bus station in November 1992 whilst on its way to Blackpool is Northern's National Express Rapide-liveried Duple 340-bodied DAF 7035 (340GUP) which prior to its sale in 1994 donated its registration number to former Gypsy Queen Volvo B10M 7037. (K.A.Jenkinson)

again specify the latter but to have these mounted on Dennis Lance chassis. An order was thus placed for 14 vehicles of this new combination, all of which were to be placed in the Go-Ahead Gateshead fleet upon their arrival in mid-1994, although the DAF option was kept open for the remaining five vehicles from that year's orders.

Having celebrated its 80th Anniversary in 1993, Go-Ahead Northern entered 1994 full of confidence and began the year by changing its official title to the Go-Ahead Group, reflecting the extension of its holdings with the purchase of Brighton & Hove. This move was also designed to dispose of the confusion between the subsidiaries Go-Ahead Gateshead, Northern General and the parent group and at this same time, the Group's engineering company, Go-Ahead Engineering Ltd. changed its trading title to Quality Bus Engineering (QBE). In addition to being responsible for its six free-standing bus and coach operations and Brighton & Hove Bus & Coach Co. Ltd., the Go-Ahead Group also controlled Go-Ahead Leisure which owned 22 public houses, QBE which undertook major repairs and overhauls for both the Group and outside operators, and Metro Taxis which ran 35 black cabs, rented out a radio circuit and acted as a main agent for sales and repair for Austin FX4s.

The first month of the year saw the remainder of the 13 Optare Metroriders enter service with Wear Buses when on 15 January Sunderland services 149, 222 & 254 were converted to minibus operation. This removed most of the surviving Leyland Atlantean's from the Wear Buses fleet, although a tiny handful were reinstated at a later date. Of greater importance, however, was the arrival in February of the first of the 5 Wright-bodied Dennis Lance SLF low floor buses. Painted in Coastline livery and sporting that company's fleet name, it was to be some time before it was to enter revenue-earning service, however, and was at first only used for demonstration purposes. Also new was a Plaxton bus-bodied Dennis Javelin which entered service in the Low Fell Coaches fleet in February whilst at the end of that month Gypsy Queen withdrew the Group's solitary Leyland Royal Tiger Doyen which had started life in the Northern fleet in 1985. During the early part of the year, work was progressing on the rebuilding of Wear Buses Leyland National 2 4701 which had entered QBE's workshops in January. Amongst the many modifications undertaken to this bus was the fitting of a Volvo engine in place of its original Leyland power unit, equipping it with fully-automatic Voith transmission and the fitting of a Permo heating system which allowed its 'roof pod' to be removed. It was some time before this project was completed and early May before it returned to service. In addition to several more vehicles being repainted into Superliner livery during the early part of the year, a number of Go-Ahead Gateshead's Metrobuses were given dedicated vinyls for routes 58 and 59 (Newcastle to Felling).

Seeking further expansion following its acquisition of Brighton & Hove Bus and Coach Co.Ltd., the Go-Ahead Group on 13 March 1994 purchased Grandforce Ltd. the holding company of City of Oxford Motor Services Ltd., The Wycombe Bus Company Ltd., Exeter City Nipper Ltd. and Carfax Travel Ltd. of which only the first two were active bus and coach operators. Registered on 6 December 1906, City of Oxford Motor Services Ltd., formed to take over tramway operations in that city which had commenced in December 1881, ultimately became part of the BET group and in 1969 passed to the NBC. During

Adorned with Cityline fleet names, Oxford Bus Company 955 (KYV452X) is one of a number of Leyland Titans acquired from London Buses. (T.W.W.Knowles)

Displaying Wycombe Coach Company fleet names, Plaxton Paramount-bodied Leyland Tiger 1763 (A213DPB) is seen at Brighton whilst undertaking a private hire duty. (T.S.Blackman)

Leaving Gateshead Metro enroute to Wardley, Go-Ahead Gateshead 3749 (C749OCN) is one of several of that company's MCW Metrobuses to be given route diagrams on its upper deck panels for the 58 and 59 services. (K.A.Jenkinson)

the following year the 34-vehicle South Midland Motor Services fleet was transferred to the company from Thames Valley. In May 1984 under NBC's reorganisation plans, the country bus operations were formed into a separate company under the title of South Midland Ltd. and upon privatisation the latter was purchased by its management, later being sold to Transit Holdings Ltd. whilst in 1986 City of Oxford was bought by Grandforce Ltd., a company formed by its management. In response to Transit's increased competition in Oxford, Grandforce registered a new company on 27 October 1989 under the title of Exeter City Nipper Ltd. in order to begin operations in Exeter in Transit Holdings' heartland, although a series of difficulties prevented these from starting. Later, City of Oxford purchased The Wycombe Bus Company Ltd. which had been incorporated on 7 November 1990 as a subsidiary of the Berks Bucks Bus Co. Ltd. to operate the former Alder Valley services in High Wycombe. When purchased by the Go-Ahead Group, City of Oxford and The Wycombe Bus Company operated a fleet of 204 buses, coaches and minibuses from depots at Newlands, High Wycombe and Cowley Road, Oxford. As with Brighton & Hove Bus and Coach Company, the Go-Ahead Group's new acquisitions were to retain their autonomy and keep their existing liveries and fleet names.

Following the examples set by National Express, Stagecoach Holdings and Badgerline, the Go-Ahead Group announced in March that it was to seek full listing on the London Stock Exchange by the summer, the flotation being in the form of a placing. This was achieved on 9 May when trading in the company's shares commenced, the Go-Ahead Group being valued at £40.1 million and having an annual turnover of approximately £75 million.

Meanwhile, in March the Go-Ahead Group in partnership with the Tyne & Wear PTE planned to install real-time information systems in central Gateshead as part of its continuing drive to increase passenger numbers through upgrading the quality of service available. This involved Go-Ahead Gateshead installing Bus Tracker on some of its high frequency services which were often affected by traffic congestion such as those operating from Newcastle city centre to Saltwell Park, Lobley Hill and Whickham via Gateshead Metro where there would be information displays. The Tru-Time visual information system, as it was named, was finally installed at nine bus stops in Gateshead and Bensham and became operational in the summer of 1995. Further indicating the Go-Ahead Group's commitment to quality, VFM Buses in April achieved BS5750 accreditation for its quality system which controlled its operations.

During the early part of the year the Group's north-east service network had seen little change except for minor modifications to some of its routes and it was not until June that any major developments took place. These were implemented mainly as a result of increased competition from independent operators within its area starting on the 6th of that month following changes made by Classic Buses on 10 May to some of its services. On that date, Classic withdrew its 007 and 121 services and in their place began four new routes - the 21A from Chester-le-Street to Newcastle, a circular service from Stanley to Flint

Leyland National 1s from the reserve fleet including 4639 (FPT109S). Minus fleet names and numbers, it is seen at Gateshead Metro in June 1994 operating a works service on which, according to its destination display, all passengers were welcome. (M.Duffy)

125

Go-Ahead Gateshead Optare Sigma-bodied Dennis Lance 4776 (L476CFT) is seen here in Gateshead in June 1994 operating service 124 from Newcastle to West Auckland introduced in retaliation to OK Travel's increased competition in the Gateshead area. In addition to carrying dedicated route lettering along its side panels, it also carries the legend 'The Way Ahead' on its sides and windscreen. (M.Duffy)

Hill via Dipton (numbered 70) which competed not only with Shaws Coaches and Northern but also with local operators Hunter and Star Travel, the 78 from Stanley to Newcastle via Craghead, Grange Villa and Pelton and the MC1 from Stanley to the MetroCentre via Pelton, Birtley and the Team Valley Retail Park. In response, Go-Ahead Gateshead ceased operation of its 55 service whilst Shaws Coaches withdrew its 006 and 721 routes and began new services 728 and 809 which mirrored Classic's 78 and MC1 as well as introducing extra journeys on the 221 Durham - Newcastle service, some of which were operated by Northern. In addition, Northern added some extra journeys to its 700 service in response to Classic's 70. Further competition was faced from OK Travel of Bishop Auckland who suddenly increased its presence on Tyneside on 1 May by starting a new service (87) from Wardley (Ellen Wilkinson Estate) to the MetroCentre via Gateshead. This brought a quick response from Go-Ahead Gateshead who began a service on 28 May from Wardley to Gateshead (M76) upon which through ticketing was available to the MetroCentre via services M20-M23. Prior to this, on 21 May OK Travel launched a further new service, the 182 from Chester-le-Street to the MetroCentre via Birtley and Team Valley Retail Park and at the same time extended its Birtley town service (22) to run from Rickleton to Newcastle via Birtley, Low Fell and Gateshead. The expected retaliation from the Go-Ahead Group came on 25 June when Northern began a service (20) which shadowed OK's revised 22 and Go-Ahead Gateshead inaugurated two new services which instead of competing directly with OK's new routes, struck at OK in its traditional operating area. One of these, numbered 124, ran from Newcastle (Newgate Street) to Bishop Auckland competing directly with OK's 724 whilst the other (182) went from Bishop Auckland bus station to West Auckland and was operated by minibuses from a new outstation at Bishop Auckland. The Go-Ahead Gateshead vehicles used on the new 124 and 182 services (new Dennis Lances and Optare Metroriders respectively) were given the fleet name 'Way Ahead' whilst the associated promotional leaflets carried the slogan 'We're not just OK - we're really Way Ahead'. On 21 May, OK Travel also increased its activities in the Sunderland area, an action which led Wear Buses to take responsive measures with the introduction on 9 July of a service (61) from Hetton-le-Hole to Sunderland via Houghton-le-Spring, Herrington Burn and East Herrington and the diversion of service 164 (Easington Lane - Seaburn) over roads served by OK service 156. With both sides blaming the other for this latest bus war, recruitment and other operational problems led both operators to de-register their new competitive services in August and return to status quo. Meanwhile, Wearside Buses (Redby Travel) had withdrawn its Sunderland to East Herrington services (41 and 42) on 24 May and, its competition having now been eliminated, Wear Buses likewise withdrew its 241 and 242 services on 4 June.

As far as the fleet was concerned, May saw the arrival of 2 Plaxton Paramount 3500-bodied Leyland Tigers acquired from Go-Ahead Group subsidiary Brighton & Hove, both of which were placed in the Voyager fleet at Chester-le-Street depot whilst transferred from Gypsy Queen to Northern was a Plaxton-bodied Leyland Tiger which was then repainted into Superliner livery. Although the remaining 4 Wright-bodied Dennis Lance SLF's had still not been delivered, the solitary bus of this type which had arrived earlier in the year was by no means idle and was in July loaned to Brighton & Hove for trials. In the opposite direction, Go-Ahead Gateshead evaluated a 42-seat MAN 11.190-Optare Vecta demonstrator for four weeks in June/July, using it mainly on the 53 and 54 services from Newcastle to Saltwell Park. Meanwhile the 14 new Optare Sigma-bodied Dennis Lances for Go-Ahead Gateshed had begun to arrive at the start of June with the first two entering service on the 3rd. of that month. Whilst all were adorned with standard Go-Ahead Gateshead livery, 3 as mentioned above carried promotional lettering for the 124 Newcastle to West Auckland service and 'The Way Ahead' fleet names whilst 4 had standard 'Go-Ahead Gateshead' fleet names and lettering for services 25-28 (Newcastle to the Low Fell area). More unusual, however, was the purchase in July from the Ministry of Defence of 2 Wadham Stringer-bodied Leyland Leopards which were to be adapted for driver training work and would replace 2 of the three remaining former Western Scottish Seddon Pennines used for this purpose. Also converted for driver training duties in June was 3452, a Roe-bodied Leyland Atlantean which had its staircase and several of its seats removed. Toward the end of the summer, a further flow of new vehicles began to arrive, this continuing for the remainder of the year by which time 19 Optare Metroriders had been added to the fleet (4 for Go-Ahead Gateshead, 10 for Wear Buses, 4 for Coastline and 1 for Gypsy Queen) together with 9 Plaxton Pointer-bodied Dennis Darts (3 for VFM Buses and 6 for Shaws Coaches), 17 Marshall-bodied Dennis Darts for Wear Buses and the remaining 4 of Coastline's low-floor Wright-bodied Dennis Lance SLFs. Of these, the Shaws Coaches Dennis Darts were painted in an all-white livery relieved only by a single blue band at roof level and

Northern's Superliner-liveried Plaxton Paramount-bodied Leyland Tiger 5126 (B513JVK) approaches the MetroCentre in October 1995 on its way to Stanley on the X36 service. (K.A.Jenkinson)

Operating the 54 service at Gateshead Metro in June 1994 whilst on loan to Go-Ahead Gateshead is all-white liveried Optare Vecta-bodied MAN demonstrator L822XMR. (M.Duffy)

Painted in National Express Rapide livery, Northern National Plaxton-bodied Leyland Tiger 7032 (CU6860) was originally registered F32LCU. It is seen here at Manchester Airport in May 1995 operating National Express 780 service. (J.A.Godwin)

OK Travel's Alexander Dash-bodied Volvo B6 L415KEF operating one of the company's new Gateshead area services which competed with Go-Ahead Gateshaed passes one of the latter operator's MCW Metrobuses, Sunderland-bound 3760 (C760OCN) at Gateshead Metro in June 1994. (M.Duffy)

prominent blue fleet names. Not to be left out, Metro Taxis gained 2 new Reliant Metrocabs. Additionally, an order was placed by the Go-Ahead Group for no fewer than 120 Marshall-bodied Dennis Darts for delivery between 1995 and 1997, although it was understood that a sizeable number of these would be allocated to the Brighton & Hove and Oxford Bus Company fleets. As was customary, the new 1994 arrivals had enabled a number of older vehicles to be withdrawn and sold whilst others were transferred amongst the Group's northern subsidiaries.

Operationally, except for the competitive services mentioned above, and a few revisions necessary as a result of the closure of Northern's Consett garage on 14 May, it was not until 31 July that any other major changes took place within the Go-Ahead Group's territory. On this date, as a consequence of retendering in County Durham, several services were lost, although except for the X7 (Consett - Washington) and Shaws Coaches 771 (Consett - Newcastle) which both passed to OK Travel, all were weekday evenings and Sunday operations. A total of 18 routes were involved of which 8 were gained by OK Travel, 4 by Classic Buses and 3 by Stanley Taxis, the remaining 3 being withdrawn without replacement. Prior to the above changes, Metro Buses on 9 July introduced a new service (M42) which operated on a circular basis in both directions serving Whitley Bay, Preston Hospital, North Shields and Tynemouth whilst Coastline on 24 July started the 374 service from New York to Cullercoats Sea Life Centre for the duration of the school holidays.

Other than the competitive battle with OK Travel referred to above, the Go-Ahead Group's network remained constant during the next couple of months and it was October before any alterations of note took place. On the third of that month, Wear Buses took over the Tyne & Wear PTE contract for the Sunday journeys on the 297 service between Heworth Metro and Brady Square which had been operated by Calvary Coaches of Washington and also gained the tendered 775 (Sunderland - Fencehouses) operation from OK Travel. A month later, on 19 November, Classic Buses once more invited attention by introducing new services from Stanley to South Stanley and from Gateshead Metro to Saltwell Park (circulars) and Lobley Hill, again duplicating existing routes.. The Go-Ahead Group responded quickly and on 3 December began an identical service from Stanley to South Stanley (804) operated by Shaws Coaches, following this on 10 December with new Go-Ahead Gateshead services 73/4 (Gateshead to Saltwell Park) and seven days later with the 75/6 services from Gateshead Metro to Lobley Hill. Prior to starting its new competitive routes, Classic Buses had, on 16 November, withdrawn its service from Stanley to the MetroCentre on which Shaws Coaches shadowing service (809) was surprisingly continued. Go-Ahead Gateshead repainted five of its MCW Metrobuses into a new blue, green and white livery and gave them 'Tyne Rider' fleet names for use on new services 73/4 which were actually operated by Low Fell Coaches despite being registered to Go-Ahead Gateshead. Meanwhile, Northern had taken over the operation of Star Travel of Dipton's journeys on the 700 (Stanley - Flint Hill) and 711 (Stanley - Quaking Houses) services from 19 November and after at first operating these with buses displaying 'on hire to Star Travel' window stickers, they were taken over properly on 12 December upon which date Gypsy Queen took over the operation of the 711. A new bus station on the site of the previous one was opened at Consett on 18 December to which all the services operating in the town were then transferred.

Classic Buses of Annfield Plain has introduced several services in competition with those operated by the Go-Ahead Group and operates these with a variety of vehicles painted in a red livery not unlike that used by Northern on its Superliner vehicles. Plaxton-bodied Leyland Leopard AJO311R tries hard to imitate Northern's livery and identity with the fleet name Classicliner to which has been added 'not part of the Northern group' and 'proud of our quality'. It is seen here at Gateshead Metro in June 1994 operating the 21 service to the City of Durham. (M.Duffy)

Still seeking expansion, the Go-Ahead Group after abandoning its bid to acquire London Buses subsidiary Westlink at the start of the year expressed an interest in other of the London Buses companies which were to be sold to the private sector during the latter part of 1994 and to this end, a bid was submitted for London Central Bus Company Limited who operated from four depots at Bexleyheath, New Cross, Peckham and Camberwell. This proved successful and that company was added to the Go-Ahead Group's growing portfolio in October adding around 530 more buses to the Group's combined fleet (including a large number of Routemasters and Leyland Titans) as well as giving it an important foothold in the capital upon which it could perhaps build in the future. Additionally, upon learning in July that Darlington Borough Transport was being offered for sale, the Go-Ahead Group submitted a bid for this too, although this proved not to be accepted and in the event the company was closed rather than sold following the registration of all its services by Stagecoach. During the early autumn the Group's Oxford subsidiary was relaunched as The Oxford Bus Company and at the same time its red and white livery was modified by the changing of its black skirt to blue, making it similar to that used by Go-Ahead Gateshead. During the autumn Metro Buses (Newcastle) Limited was formed to take over the bus operations of Visitauto Ltd. who traded as Metro Taxis.

The final acquisition in 1994 took place on 30 December when the old-established business of Hammel's of Stanley was purchased following its proprietor's decision to retire. This company which was the sole survivor of the original nine who operated under the Diamond fleet name was immediately placed under the control of Venture Transport, its 6 buses (1 Bedford YNT, 1 Bedford YMT, 3 Dennis Javelins and 1 Dennis Dart) being transferred to Northern's Stanley depot. Despite being given Venture legal lettering, the 6 buses concerned were to retain their two-tone grey and red livery and Diamond fleet names in order to maintain the goodwill built up by their original owner. Hammel's garage at Front Street, Stanley was not included in the deal. Meanwhile, Shaws Coaches had vacated its original depot at Callington Place, Craghead in September, its fleet moving to Northern's Chester-le-Street premises which already housed the Group's Voyager coaches as well as a large number of Northern's buses.

During the first month of 1995 further service changes were implemented when on the 28th the 221 from Newcastle to Chester-Street and Durham once again became jointly operated by Northern and Shaws Coaches in retalliation to changes made by Classic Buses to its services on 14 January. Shaws Coaches also ceased operating the 709 (Stanley - Beamish - Ouston - Newcastle) service on 29 January, instead doubling its frequency on the 728 which ran from Stanley to Newcastle via Craghead and Ouston, again in response to Classic Buses whilst Northern retained its hourly journeys on each of these routes. Shaws Coaches on this same date additionally withdrew its 817/8 Stanley - Frost Hill circulars but began a new 710 service from Kip Hill to Aylward Place via Stanley in order to compete with a similar service operated by Stanley Taxis. The latter, together with the 715 service was withdrawn on 1 April, however, following complaints by Stanley Taxis to the Monopolies and Mergers Commission and agreement by Stanley Taxis to some reallocation of stands in Stanley bus station.

Before any other major service changes were made, the Go-Ahead Group further expanded its empire by purchasing the old-established and important independent operator OK Motor Services Ltd. of Bishop Auckland in March 1995. Founded in 1912 by Wade Emmerson who started a twice-weekly service between Bishop Auckland and Evenwood using a 14-seat Gladiator, the fleet had grown to 36 vehicles by the outbreak of World War II whilst its services included one from Bishop Auckland to Newcastle. After the first double deckers were purchased in 1946, steady expansion was achieved with the purchase of other Bishop Auckland area independent operators and in 1976 a base was also established in Newcastle in order to extend the company's coaching activities as well as to undertake a number of contracts. Upon deregulation in 1986, the company extended its area of operation to such places as Peterlee, Sunderland and Stockton-on-Tees by gaining a number of tendered services and soon afterwards commercially registered several new routes in those areas. The death of Wade Emmerson in 1994 undoubtedly left the company vulnerable to a takeover bid and after the Darlington Transport-Stagecoach fiasco towards the end of that year it was feared that the same could happen to OK, thus prompting its sale to the Go-Ahead Group. By this time the company boasted a fleet totalling 225 vehicles (26 mini/midibuses, 56 double deckers and 142 single deckers and coaches) and operated

Tucked away in Chester-le-Street depot in April 1995 is driver training bus T517 (HTY257W), a Wadham Stringer-bodied Leyland Leopard acquired from the Ministry of Defence. (K.A.Jenkinson)

Acquired with the business of Hammell of Stanley, Plaxton-bodied Dennis Javelin 4798 (H447EVK) still wearing two-tone grey & red Diamond livery leaves Stanley bus station on the 718 service to Durham in September 1995. (Travelscene)

although this was partly replaced by an OK Travel route using the same number. Both Classic and Shaws also registered services from Stanley to Quaking Houses and Burnhope, although neither of these actually operated and were ultimately de-registered. At around this time, Go-Ahead Gateshead introduced new magnetic card readers and began to fit its buses with Wayfarer III ticket machines, being followed soon afterwards by Wear Buses and VFM Buses.

During May 1995, the Go-Ahead Group underwent a degree of management restructuring and at the same time moved its head office from Queen Street, Bensham to Cale Cross House, Pilgrim Street, Newcastle. Under this restructuring Paul Matthews, previously a Director of Go-Ahead Gateshead was promoted to the new post of Managing Director for the north-east, Kevin Carr, formerly Manager of VFM Buses and Coastline also took on the responsibility for Go-Ahead Gateshead, Low Fell Coaches, Metro Taxis and Metrobuses and Ian Banwell, previously Manager of Wear Buses had Northern General, Shaws Coaches, Gypsy Queen and Diamond added to his portfolio while Charles Marshall who was Managing Director of OK Motor Services also took on the responsibility for the non-National Express coaching operations. Almost before the ink had dried on these changes, Low Fell Coaches was moved to become part of OK Motor Services, this being witnessed by the repainting of two of OK's Volvo B10Bs into a new style of Low Fell livery for the Cross-Tyne service, while Shaws Coaches contracted with the transfer of some of its work to both Northern and OK. Additionally, the Voyager coach operation also became part of OK Motor Services and was incorporated with OK's Tyneside coaching business as well as with the coach work of Low Fell Coaches. As a result of these alterations, the former OK depot at Team Valley now confined itself to OK bus work together the remaining bus work of Low Fell Coaches thus placing more of the 'low-cost' and competitive operations with OK. At this same time, Metro Buses ceased its operations, its vehicles and services passing to Coastline whilst the Go-Ahead Group's depot at Saltmeadows Road, Gateshead became the new home for Low Fell's coaches.

June 1995 also witnessed further expansion when the Go-Ahead Group purchased the old-established business of Ebchester-based

from depots at Bishop Auckland, Peterlee, Team Valley, Evenwood and Butterknowle. Under its new masters it was to be maintained as a separate subsidiary, retaining its existing fleet name and distinctive cream, red and maroon livery.

Throughout the early part of 1995, the battle with Classic Buses continued unabated and in April, following its withdrawal from local services in Gateshead, Classic began new routes between Chester-le-Street and Ouston, Consett and Delves Lane and Consett and Castleside. In response, Northern augmented its 733, 734, 745 and 747 services from 13 May whilst later that month Classic Buses introduced a new route from Stanley to Shotley Bridge, withdrawing its Stanley - Dipton/Flint Hill circular in the process. This time it was Shaws Coaches who retaliated with a new shadowing service numbered 719 commencing on 10 June. On this same date, Shaws Coaches, however, withdrew its 809 service (Stanley - MetroCentre),

Adorned with route lettering on its roof edge and below its windows, Go-Ahead Gateshead Optare Sigma-bodied Dennis Lance 4784 (L484CFT) leaves Gateshead Metro for Barley Mow Estate in November 1995. (K.A.Jenkinson)

London Central's Optare Spectra-bodied DAF SP8 (K308FYG) is seen here enroute to Crystal Palace a few weeks prior to the company being acquired by the Go-Ahead Group. (T.W.W.Knowles)

Armstrongs Coaches together with its 14 buses and coaches (3 coach-bodied and 1 bus bodied Leyland Leopards, 1 Volvo B10M coach, 4 Scania coaches, 1 Scania bus, 3 Mercedes Benz minibuses/coaches and 1 Ford Transit minibus). As Armstrong's depot was not included in the deal, the acquired fleet was moved to the Go-Ahead Group's premises at Saltmeadows Road, Gateshead which is also home to OK, Voyager and Low Fell's coaches. Whilst the buses acquired from Armstrongs were quickly given OK Travel fleet names (the Scania/Plaxton also receiving OK livery), the coaches retained the title of their previous operator. Three of the acquired Leopards were, however, immediately withdrawn before being allocated 'paper' fleet numbers while the former Armstrong operations were integrated into those of OK.

New vehicles arriving during 1995 comprised 2 National Express-liveried Volvo B10Ms with Plaxton Premiere 320 C49Ft bodywork for Voyager, 5 Optare Delta-bodied DAF SB220 single deckers for Go-Ahead Gateshead which made their debut in June, 10 Optare Metroriders for Coastline and 4 Plaxton Verde-bodied Volvo B10Bs for Go-Ahead Gateshead, these being the first of an order for 30. Transfers between the Group's various north-east subsidiaries continued as in previous years and in addition 2 of Voyager's Leyland

Hurrying towards Washington bus station in November 1995 is Wear Buses Leyland Lynx 4723 which carries a diagramatic route map for the 194 and 294 services above its side windows. (K.A.Jenkinson)

Painted in Wear Express livery, Wear Buses coach-seated Volvo-engined Leyland National 2 4720 (TJR720Y) leaves Gateshead Metro in early evening shadows on 4 November 1995 bound for Peterlee. (K.A.Jenkinson)

Tiger coaches were despatched to Brighton & Hove with a similar coach going to London Central while 2 of Shaws Leyland Tiger coaches were transferred to The Oxford Bus Company. On the reverse side of the coin, 2 of Northern's Mercedes Benz minibuses which had earlier been sent southwards to High Wycombe returned to their native north-east in April to join the Metro Buses fleet whereas 6 of the one-time Northern Alexander-bodied Mercedes 609D minibuses which had been transferred to Wycombe Bus moved onwards to Brighton & Hove for use on a contract connected with H.M.Prison at Lewes. Other changes saw the transfer of the 5 Tyne Rider-liveried MCW Metrobuses to Low Fell Coaches and the numbering 'on paper' of the OK fleet to facilitate entry to the Go-Ahead Group computer system,

Carrying Transfare information below its destination screen, Coastline 3480 (AUP380W) is seen at Wallsend Metro in November 1995 whilst working the 305 service to Newcastle. (K.A.Jenkinson)

Painted in an all-over advertising livery for Blaydon Shopping Centre, Go-Ahead Gateshead Optare Metrorider 342 (J942JJR) arrives at the MetroCentre in October 1995 on the M12 service. (K.A.Jenkinson)

Standing outside the Eldon Centre, Newcastle before taking up its next duty on the 771 service to Consett is Shaws Coaches ex.Northern Leyland National 2 4664 (UPT664V). (K.A.Jenkinson)

Painted in an all-over advertising livery to publicise its owner's Go'n'Save Travel Card is Go-Ahead Gateshead MCW Metrobus 3750 (C750OCN) seen leaving Gateshead Metro in November 1995 enroute to Leam Lane Estate on the 649 service. (K.A.Jenkinson)

One of a large number of Leyland Leopards operated by OK Travel, Duple-bodied NWO450R seen here in the yard at Team Valley depot in April 1995 was acquired from National Welsh in 1989. Note irs route number box inside the top of its nearside windscreen. (K.A.Jenkinson)

although the numbers were not displayed on the vehicles themselves. The 'Tyne Rider' Metrobuses did not remain long with their new owner, however, and following their withdrawal on 30 June one was sent to Oxford for evaluation by the Wycombe Bus Company. Returning to the north-east after a few weeks, it then joined two of its sisters still in their blue, white & green livery had been reinstated for use on schools services by OK Travel at its Bishop Auckland depot along with a pair of ECW-bodied Atlanteans transferred from VFM Buses and two double deckers of this combination from Metro Buses, all of which at first retained their existing liveries and fleet names.

Starting in June, several vehicles were repainted in simplified liveries with Northern applying a darker shade of red as used on its Superliner vehicles, Go-Ahead Gateshead employing red lower deck and blue upper deck panels and white window frames and roof for its transformed double deckers and red above a blue skirt with white roof for its single deckers. Wear Buses omitted adopted a bright green colour scheme with grey lower deck window surrounds and white upper deck windows surrounds and roof for its double deckers and two-tone green with white window frames and roof for its minis whilst VFM Buses added a dark blue skirt to its existing scheme on its Olympians. Larger fleet names were applied at this same time to the buses of Northern and Go-Ahead Gateshead and in the case of the new-liveried

Still in the all-white livery in which it was acquired by the Go-Ahead Group from Armstrongs of Ebchester, Plaxton Paramount-bodied Scania K113CRB CAZ6833 (originally F30UHN) stands on the forecourt of Saltmeadows Road depot, Gateshead in November 1995. (K.A.Jenkinson)

Resting in the yard of Saltmeadows Road, Gateshead depot in November 1995 is Low Fell Coaches Mercedes Benz 811D M65HTY. (K.A.Jenkinson)

Northern buses, the company's 'Proud of our Routes' slogan was omitted. Coastline's livery remained unchanged as did OK Travel, Shaws Coaches, Gypsy Queen, Low Fell and Diamond. Other changes involved Shaws Coaches Plaxton Pointer-bodied Dennis Darts which, although retaining their all-white livery with blue roof band had their fleet names replaced with red Northern lettering while a couple of OK-liveried coaches were given Gypsy Queen fleet names.

Following the withdrawal from most of its local services by Calvary Coaches of Washington on 10 June, Wear Buses started a new service (W9) between Concord bus station, Washington and Barmston Ferry while OK took over the Tyne & Wear PTE contract for service 297 (Heworth Metro - Brady Square) which operated evenings and Sundays only. On 1 July, however, numerous changes were implemented when all the previous Low Fell Coaches service registrations were cancelled and replaced by new OK Motor Services registrations. Additionally, Go-Ahead Gateshead introduced two new routes - 24 (Newcastle - Wrekenton) which replaced Low Fell's 24 (Newcastle - Team Valley), and M46 (Newcastle - Sunniside) which replaced most of the former OK 646. In County Durham, OK took over Shaws Coaches share of services 221, 709 and 728 and Northern's share of the 709 and 728 while the 725 reverted to wholly Northern operation and gained OK's journeys on the 765. OK further lost the 44 (Durham - East Hedley) service to Gypsy Queen to compensate for its loss of the 711 (Stanley - Quaking Houses) to Diamond. During July, Coastline's 301 service from Whitley Bay to the MetroCentre was truncated to terminate at Gateshead Metro but, after gaining a subsidy from Tyne & Wear PTE was reinstated during shopping hours to its full length on 30 September while from 10 September the 307 between Wallsend and Newcastle was withdrawn. With effect from 9 September, Northern introduced a new service numbered 747 from Newcastle to Castleside to compete with a new route commenced by Classic Buses while on 16 September Wear Buses began three new services in order to combat competition from Redby Coaches, these being the X91 Newcastle - Silksworth and the 242/243 which operated

White-liveried ex.Armstrong of Ebchester Wadham Stringer-bodied Mercedes Benz 709D 9821 (F821PBP) had already gained OK Travel fleet names when photographed in the gloom of Saltmeadows Road depot, Gateshead in November 1995. (K.A.Jenkinson)

Former VFM Buses ECW-bodied Leyland Atlantean 3548 (MBR448T) repainted in OK Travel livery leaves Gateshead Metro for Leam Lane on the 88 service in November 1995, its driver having forgotten to change its destination display. (K.A.Jenkinson)

Engineless and with some of its windows removed, Go-Ahead Northern MCW-bodied Leyland Atlantean 3446 (AUP346W) awaits its fate in the yard of North East Bus Breakers at Annfield Plain in April 1995. (K.A.Jenkinson)

Resting at York's Minster coach park whilst undertaking a private hire duty from Gateshead are Low Fell Coaches Plaxton Paramount-bodied Dennis Javelin E151AGG and Reeve Burgess-bodied Mercedes Benz 609D F901JBB. (K.A.Jenkinson)

Still sporting Coastline's red & cream livery and Transfare legends but adorned with Northern Proud of our Routes fleet names, ECW-bodied Leyland Atlantean 3553 (MBR453T) leaves Stanley bus station in October 1995 whilst working local service 804 to South Stanley. (K.A.Jenkinson)

Leaving Coastline's Percy Main depot is orange, yellow & black-liveried Tyne & Wear PTE Renault Master Carebus H252MRD. (Travelscene)

via different routes between Sunderland and Washington. By this time, the commercial services of the whole Go-Ahead Group (North East) were being marketed as 'Network North East' with a new leaflet being produced which contained summary timetables and a synoptic colour-coded map.

Meanwhile, as part of its restructuring plans, the Go-Ahead Group surrendered its Low Fell Coaches and Gypsy Queen licences, transferring all their vehicles to OK Motor Services Ltd. and similarly surrendered its Venture Transport Co. licence with its Shaws Coaches and Diamond vehicles being transferred to Northern General Transport Co. ownership. All the previous fleet names were retained, however, as trading identities as had been the Metro Buses fleet name after its transfer to Tynemouth & District (Coastline). Under this reorganisation, the Northern National Omnibus Co. now became responsible only for the Group's National Express contracts for which it retained 13 coaches and these will be transferred to the Wear Buses Philadelphia depot upon the completion of rebuilding work, its Voyager operation having already been transferred to OK Motor Services Ltd. Additionally, Tynemouth & District (Coastline) took over responsibility for the orange and cream liveried Renault Master Carebuses owned by Tyne & Wear PTE which were equipped to carry wheelchairs as well as seated passengers and had previously been operated on the PTE's behalf by

Standing in the yard of OK Travel's West Auckland workshops in October 1995 are ex.Tyne & Wear PTE MCW-bodied Leyland Atlantean VFT185T and former VFT Buses ECW-bodied Atlantean 3558 (MBR458T), the latter having been recently transferred to OK for school bus duties. (K.A.Jenkinson)

Low Fell Coaches and Metro Taxis. Also at around this same time it was learned that the Office of Fair Trading had referred the Group's takeover of OK Motor Services Ltd. to the Monopolies and Mergers Commission who had been asked to report back by the end of the year.

In addition to maintaining a wide range of local bus services throughout County Durham, Tyneside and Wearside, the various operating companies within the Go-Ahead Group also provide numerous schools and works services with financial support from Durham County Council and Tyne & Wear PTE, these all being

Painted in Go-Ahead Gateshead's new double deck livery with red lower and dark blue upper deck panels, white window frames and roof, MCW Metrobus 3644 (A644BCN) leaves Gateshead Metro in November 1995 enroute to Springwell Estate. (K.A.Jenkinson)

Freshly repainted in Masons red & cream livery and sporting new-style Northern fleet names, former Shaws Coaches MCW-bodied Leyland Atlantean 3707 (YNL207V) stands in Stanley bus station in October 1995. (K.A.Jenkinson)

With that rare commodity, rain, threatening, VFM Buses ECW-bodied Leyland Olympian 3590 (JTY390X) collects its passengers in South Shields in September 1995, thus preventing them from a soaking. Its livery had been modified by the addition of a bright blue skirt. (Travelscene)

preventing the further use of buses which could not offer the environmental performance of modern vehicles would greatly assist the ongoing protection of the planet. Due to their disposal at an earlier age, coaches were, however, not included in this embargo and were to continue to be sold for further use where appropriate. Meanwhile, Northern and Wear Buses continued to refurbish a number of their Leyland National 2s, fitting them with Volvo engines and Purmo heating and in addition Wear Buses fitted one of its buses of this type with a Cummins engine, Voith transmission and Purmo heating. Following the experimentation with new simplified liveries, these began to be more widely applied during the final months of the year with Wear Buses minis and Northern's Optare Delta-bodied DAF SB220s in particular being amongst the first to be thus treated. Similarly, a repainting programme was put into motion to rid OK of its multitude of different colour schemes brought about by the transfer of several vehicles from other operators within the group, all of which were to be given standard OK colours, whilst the three former Low Fell Coaches Bedfords transferred to OK were used primarily as driver trainers, although all were still available for normal passenger carrying duties whenever this was necessary.

As the Go-Ahead Group heads towards 1996, it does so with increasing confidence having grown considerably since its humble

Wearing Northern's revised livery and new large fleet names, Optare Delta-bodied DAF SB220 4746 (G746RTY) arrives at the MetroCentre in October 1995 on its way to Delves Lane on the 745 service. (K.A.Jenkinson)

available to the general public - a fact often publicised on destination blinds - whilst OK Travel also run a daily express service between Peterlee and Blackpool, a journey which takes 4 hours 55 minutes.

During the early autumn of 1995, the Go-Ahead Group took the decision to sell all its subsequent redundant buses for scrap, believeing that such action would not only prevent competitive operators from gaining cheap, secondhand vehicles but would also assist the industry in general to portray a better image. Additionally, it was thought that

beginnings over 80 years ago. Now the fifth largest bus and coach operating Group in Britain, it has indeed come from No Place to success and no doubt its expansion will continue throughout the remaining years of the present decade so that by the millennium it will cover even more parts of the country than it does today. It is still in the north-east that the company will always be best remembered, however, an area in which, under the Northern banner, it has been proud of its routes since 1914.

Looking immaculate in its attractive promotional livery, the legends on Go-Ahead Gateshead MCW Metrobus 3618 (A618BCN) seen at Gateshead Metro in November 1995 state that the company operate a network of 52 routes of which 99% are run without subsidy. (K.A.Jenkinson)

OPERATORS ACQUIRED BY THE NORTHERN GROUP

Date	Operator
1 January 1914	Gateshead & District Tramways Co. Ltd., Gateshead *Note A*
1 January 1914	Jarrow & District Electric Traction Co. Ltd., Jarrow *Note A*
1 January 1914	Tynemouth & District Electric Traction Co. Ltd., North Shields *Note A*
1 January 1924	Isaac E.Walton (Crescent Bus Co.), Gateshead
1 April 1925	Hall Brothers (Invincible Bus Co.), Seaham Harbour
28 October 1928	Hallett's Bus Service, Pelton Lane Ends
25 February 1929	G.R.Hunter, Hebburn-on-Tyne
1930	General County Omnibus Co., Chester-le-Street *Note A*
14 January 1930	Wakefields Motors Ltd., North Shields
15 March 1930	Stobie & Curry (Castle Motor Services), Forest Hall
11 April 1930	Eastern Express Motors Ltd., West Hartlepool
1 June 1930	Atkinson & Browell (ABC), Consett
1 January 1931	Sunderland District Omnibus Co. Ltd., Sunderland
17 September 1931	G.W.Hetherington & Co. Ltd. (A1 Service), Coundon *Note B*
March 1932	G.Flynn, Jarrow
21 March 1933	Fawdon Bus Co. Ltd., Newcastle-on-Tyne *Note C*
24 June 1933	Tyne & Mersey Motor Services Ltd., Newcastle-on-Tyne *Note C*
27 June 1933	G.Maugham (Diamond), Craghead
22 November 1933	Leeds & Newcastle Omnibus Co. Ltd., Northallerton *Note C*
28 January 1934	Ennis & Reed, Crook
23 March 1934	T.Harrison (Diamond), South Moor
23 March 1934	J.Long (Diamond), South Moor
23 March 1934	J.G.Robinson (Diamond), West Stanley
4 October 1934	R.M.Prinn (Direct), Sunniside
December 1934	White & Nxon, Langley Park *Note D*
14 March 1935	Cowley & Bracegirdle, Birtley
1936	Tyneside Omnibus Co. Ltd., Wallsend
17 June 1937	Charlton's Blue Safety Coaches, Hebburn-on-Tyne
14 July 1939	T.Cook, Consett
January 1949	Dixon Brothers (The Witbank), Lanchester
24 May 1950	Hollings Garage & Engineering Co. Ltd., Wallsend *Note E*
15 November 1950	Marshall & Co. Ltd., Newcastle-on-Tyne
15 November 1950	Crown Coaches, Washington
August 1951	J.W.Hurst & Son, Winlaton
7 March 1953	Hunters Bus Co. Ltd., Great Lumley
March 1954	Bee Line Continental Tours Ltd., Newcastle-on-Tyne *Note A*
July 1954	Dales Coaches, Swalwell
21 January 1963	Hunters, Washington
1 May 1970	Venture Transport Co. (Newcastle) Ltd., Consett *Note A*
December 1988	Metro Taxis, Newcastle-on-Tyne *Note A*
May 1989	Gypsy Queen, Langley Park *Note A*
16 October 1989	Law Travel, South Moor *Note F*
June 1992	Low Fell Coaches, Low Fell *Note A*
1 August 1992	Shaws Coaches, Craghead *Note A*
November 1993	Brighton & Hove Bus & Coach Co. Ltd., Brighton *Note A*
13 March 1994	City of Oxford Motor Services Ltd., Oxford *Note A*
13 March 1994	The Wycombe Bus Co. Ltd., Oxford *Note A*
13 March 1994	Exeter City Nipper Ltd., Oxford *Note G*
October 1994	London Central Buses Ltd., London *Note A*
30 December 1994	J.H.Hammell (Diamond), Stanley *Note A*
March 1995	OK Motor Services Ltd., Bishop Auckland *Note A*
May 1995	Armstrongs, Ebchester

NOTES

A Maintained as a subsidiary / trading name
B Acquired jointly with Sunderland District Omnibus Co. Ltd. and United Automobile Services Ltd.
C Acquired jointly with several other BET and Tilling Group companies.
D White & Nixon was a consortium of T.D.Laing, Langley Park; J.White, Chester-le-Street & T.Hutchinson, Sacriston
E Acquired by Tynemouth & District Omnibus Co. Ltd.
F Only the local bus operations were acquired
G Non-operational company